OFF THE BEATEN PATH®
TENNESSEE →

Help Us Keep This Guide Up to Date

We would love to hear from you concerning your experiences with this guide and how you feel it could be improved and kept up to date. Please send your comments and suggestions to:

editorial@GlobePequot.com

Thanks for your input, and happy travels!

OFF THE BEATEN PATH® SERIES

NINTH EDITION

OFF THE BEATEN PATH®
TENNESSEE →

A GUIDE TO UNIQUE PLACES

JACKIE SHECKLER FINCH

travel

Guilford, Connecticut

All the information in this guidebook is subject to change. We recommend that you call ahead to obtain current information before traveling.

To buy books in quantity for corporate use
or incentives, call **(800) 962-0973**
or e-mail **premiums@GlobePequot.com.**

Text design: Linda R. Loiewski
Maps: Equator Graphics © Morris Book Publishing, LLC

ISSN 1539-8102
ISBN 978-0-7627-5057-3

Printed in the United States of America
10 9 8 7 6 5 4 3 2 1

To my parents, Jack and Margaret Poynter, for instilling in me the desire to travel. And to my first traveling buddies—my sisters, Elaine Emmich, Jennifer Boyer, Juliette Maples, and Jeanine Clifford; and my brothers, Jim and Joe Poynter.

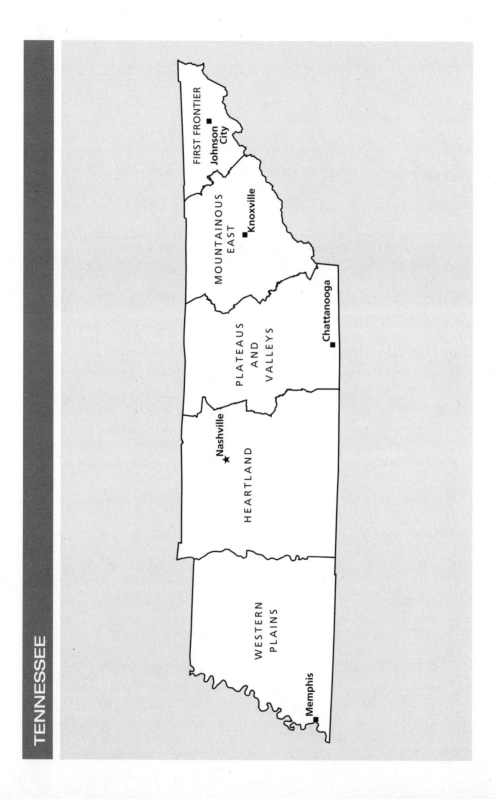

TENNESSEE

FIRST FRONTIER

Johnson City ■

MOUNTAINOUS EAST

Knoxville ■

PLATEAUS AND VALLEYS

Chattanooga ■

HEARTLAND

Nashville ★

WESTERN PLAINS

Memphis ■

Contents

Acknowledgments

Many thanks to Tennessee residents, public relations officials, and business owners who took the time to help me update this book. Thanks especially to Cindy Dupree of Tennessee Tourism who shared little nooks and crannies in this wonderfully diverse state. I'm grateful to Amy Lyons and the friendly and professional staff at The Globe Pequot Press. My gratitude to my daughter, Kelly Rose, for helping carry the load and to my grandson, Logan Peters, for his computer expertise. My appreciation to my granddaughter, Stefanie Rose, and grandson, Sean Rose, for their encouragement. And a special remembrance to my husband, Bill Finch, who taught me how to value every day on this earth.

—Jackie Sheckler Finch

Introduction

The word "Tennessee" conjures up many different images. To the lover of country music, Nashville comes to mind when Tennessee is mentioned. To the blues aficionado or the Elvis fan, it's Memphis. To white-water buffs, it's more than likely the Ocoee River. To conservationists and outdoors lovers, it's probably the Great Smoky Mountains or West Tennessee's Reelfoot Lake. To football fans, it's definitely the University of Tennessee's Volunteers.

As with any state, Tennessee is many things to many people. It's a fun and funky state to explore. From the mountainous east to the delta plains of the Mississippi River in the west, the variety of natural and man-made wonders and attractions the state has to offer is awesome.

Once you drive across the back roads of this long and narrow state, you'll never again think of it in the same way. I'm here to help you do just that. In reality it would take volumes to detail all that can be done and seen in Tennessee. However, in the book you now hold in your hands, I have narrowed your choices considerably by taking you off the interstates and onto the side roads, where the unique character of the state truly shines through.

My philosophy is important to understand here because I stayed true to it while writing this book. First of all, to me off the beaten path is more of an attitude than a place. I can enjoy something that's offbeat, funky, and unusual and consider it off the beaten path—even if it's on a major highway or in the middle of the city. Even though I may view it as off the beaten path, you may not. Don't worry; I'm sure we'll agree on something else.

Second, there are two types of people who will use this book: tourists and explorers. The tourists will bring home souvenirs; the explorers will bring home *experiences*. I'm an explorer, so don't expect too many stops at gift shops.

The state has a great highway system that is easy to follow, and while I won't be taking you down too many of the major highways, it is reassuring to know that they are usually nearby—in case you need to make a quick escape back to civilization.

As you drive along, look for signs that sport the image of the mockingbird, the state's official bird. They are mounted directly above the state highway designation numbers and signify that you are on a stretch of the 2,300 miles of the Tennessee Scenic Parkway System. Consisting primarily of two-lane roads, it connects the state's parks, major lakes, and historical sites, as well as this book's lesser-known attractions.

Along the way you'll meet whittlers and collectors, and you might meet Dolly Parton. You'll meet ladies with hair higher than a church steeple and a hip guy who gives tours from a pink Cadillac. By the time you finish your journey, I'll have you floating on a lake 300 feet below the Earth's surface, playing miniature golf on the side of a mountain, cruising on a lake created by the strongest earthquake on record, and eating the world's sweetest-tasting, vilest-smelling vegetable.

Don't overlook some of the state's better-known tourist traps. Sometimes our trip down the less-traveled paths of the state will intersect with the well-worn trails in order to highlight an event, an attraction, or a person worth visiting. I have found that sometimes it's worth fighting a crowd to see or do something that you'll probably never get a chance to see or do again.

Music is a big attraction as well as a big industry in Tennessee. From the birthplace of the blues in Memphis to the birthplace of the Grand Ole Opry in Nashville to the songs of the Appalachian Mountain folk in East Tennessee, music is an important part of the heritage of our state.

Our tour of the state will touch on much of that heritage and the people who have contributed to it. We'll visit the commercial monuments that honor Elvis Presley, Carl Perkins, Dolly Parton, and Loretta Lynn, among others. We'll also take a hike back into the woods to see the monument erected where Patsy Cline lost her life in a plane crash. We'll visit a museum honoring the best soul singers of the 1950s and 1960s, and we'll sit back and enjoy Sunday services at a Cowboy Church that passes a Stetson hat instead of the plate.

Southern hospitality is more than a myth in Tennessee, and our people may well be the state's friendliest attraction. There is one thing you'll never have to worry about as you travel through the state: You'll never truly be lost. Knock on any door or stop by any store, and chances are you'll get the directions you need, plus a whole lot more. Just when you think you've met the world's most colorful person, you'll meet one just a bit more fun. That's the way it is in Tennessee.

The state is full of crossroad communities with colorful and descriptive names. Usually the community has little more to offer than a gas station–general store combination, but here's where you'll usually find the most intriguing characters of the area.

In the summer these folks will be sitting on the porch of that store solving the world's problems. In the winter you'll find them sitting around the potbellied stove. There are more than 100 such communities with colorful names around the state, including Fly, New Flys Village, Defeated Creek, Ugly Creek, Pretty Creek, Dull, Soddy-Daisy, Bell Buckle, Gilt Edge, Finger, Frogjump, Nutbush, Bucksnort, Only, Who'd A Thought It, and Skullbone.

This book has been broken down into five major areas:

The First Frontier. More than 200 years ago this part of the state was America's new frontier. Explorers, including Daniel Boone, blazed paths across the Appalachian Mountains, establishing some of the first settlements outside the original 13 colonies.

Much of the area is heavily forested, with the extreme east and southeast parts quite mountainous. Davy Crockett was born here, and the state of Franklin, which never quite made it to statehood, was formed here several years before Tennessee became a state.

The Mountainous East. As the name implies, this area is probably the most rugged of all Tennessee terrain. The 500,000-acre Great Smoky Mountain National Park and its foothill communities provide beauty incomparable to what you'll find elsewhere in the southeast United States.

Throughout the area several museums have dedicated their collections and grounds to the preservation of mountain life, and many communities have preserved that lifestyle by their very existence.

Plateaus and Valleys. Forested and rugged, the Cumberland Plateau rises like a gigantic wall that spans the width of the state, forming the western boundary of the Tennessee Valley.

Although relatively flat, the area has many spectacular streams that have carved out deep gorges in the sandstone, making it one of the best areas in the state for white-water enthusiasts. In fact, the 1996 Olympic Games white-water events took place here.

The Heartland. Also known as Middle Tennessee, the area is a region of gently rolling hills, sloping green meadows, and miles of river and lake frontage.

At the heart of the area lies Nashville, "Music City," the home of the Grand Ole Opry. Musical attractions are popular in this area, as are Tennessee walking horse farms, sour mash whiskey distilleries, and the homes of two U.S. presidents.

The Western Plains. An area of fertile bottomlands and dense hardwood forests, the Western Plains region is bordered on the east by the Tennessee River and on the west by the Mississippi.

A few of the state's most colorful folk heroes—frontiersman Davy Crockett, train engineer Casey Jones, and *Walking Tall* sheriff Buford Pusser—have strong roots here, as do *Roots* author Alex Haley and the King of Rock 'n' Roll, Elvis Presley.

The 520-mile-long state is divided into six telephone area codes, 423, 731, 865, 901, 931, and 615; about half of it lies in the eastern time zone and half in the central zone.

Although care has been taken to ensure accuracy in all listings in this book, visitors are advised to call ahead before traveling any great distance. Life throughout Tennessee is slow-paced and mellow, so if a day appears to be going a bit slow, it isn't uncommon for a proprietor to close early and go fishing. Phone numbers and admission prices have been included in listings where appropriate.

Most of the attractions are open on a year-round basis, but some cut operations a bit during the winter months.

Before venturing forth, you may want to contact the state tourism bureau and load up on brochures and maps of the areas you plan on visiting. In the material you receive from the state, there will be a list of local tourism bureaus that will be able to provide even more specific information.

Write to the Tennessee Department of Tourist Development, Wm. Snodgrass/Tennessee Tower, 312 Rosa L. Parks Avenue, 25th Floor, Nashville, TN 37243; call (615) 741–2159; or visit www.tnvacation.com.

Tennessee Facts

STATE SYMBOLS

Bird:	Mockingbird
Insects, two of them:	Firefly and ladybug
Gem:	Tennessee river pearls
Tree:	Tulip poplar
Rock:	Limestone
Wildflower:	Passionflower
Flower:	Iris
Songs, five of them:	"My Homeland, Tennessee," "When It's Iris Time in Tennessee," "My Tennessee," "Tennessee Waltz," and "Rocky Top"
Animal:	Raccoon
Amphibian:	Tennessee cave salamander
Reptile:	Box turtle
Butterfly:	Zebra swallowtail

Bed-and-Breakfast Inns

Bed-and-breakfast inns can be found throughout the state. Many are listed in this book. Here are a few contacts to call for information on more locations:

- **Natchez Trace Bed & Breakfast Reservation Service,** information on lodging along the Natchez Trace Parkway, (800) 377–2770
- **Bed and Breakfast Association of Tennessee,** www.tennesseeinns.com

SELECTED TOURISM WEB SITES

Chattanooga
www.chattanoogafun.com

Cherokee National Forest
www.fs.fed.us/cherokee

Gatlinburg
www.gatlinburg.com

Historic Rugby
www.historicrugby.org

Knoxville
www.knoxville.org

Memphis
www.memphistravel.com

Middle Tennessee Visitors Bureau
www.antebellum.com

Nashville
www.nashville.net
www.visitmusiccity.com

Northeast Tennessee Tourism Association
www.netta.com

Pigeon Forge
www.mypigeonforge.com

Smoky Mountains and Townsend
www.smokymountains.org

State of Tennessee Tourism
www.tnvacation.com

Tennessee Department of Environment and Conservation
www.state.tn.us/environment/

Tennessee Farm Winegrowers Association
www.tennesseewines.com

Tennessee Overhill Heritage Association
www.tennesseeoverhill.com

Tennessee State Parks
www.state.tn.us/environment/parks/

Tourism Association of Southwest Tennessee
www.tast.tn.org

Upper Cumberland Tourism Association
www.uppercumberland.org

THE FIRST FRONTIER →

Corner of the Frontier

Bristol is about as far north as one can go in the state and stay in Tennessee. In fact, about half the city is in Virginia. The state line runs down the middle of State Street in the heart of the downtown shopping district. But other than the small state markers embedded in the street between the double yellow lines, there's little evidence that the city has two mayors, two city councils, and two telephone area codes.

A big, old-fashioned neon sign forms an archway across State Street, near Randall Street, and proclaims BRISTOL IS A GOOD PLACE TO LIVE. It was erected in 1910 as a symbol of unity between the two Bristols. Arrows point to the Tennessee and Virginia sides.

Although Nashville, about 300 miles to the west, gets credit for being the center of country music, it was here in Bristol that the **Carter Family** and **Jimmie Rodgers** recorded the first country-and-western music that was distributed nationwide. That recording took place on August 2, 1927, and put the area on the musical map. A monument honoring those musical pioneers stands at Edgemont Avenue and State Street.

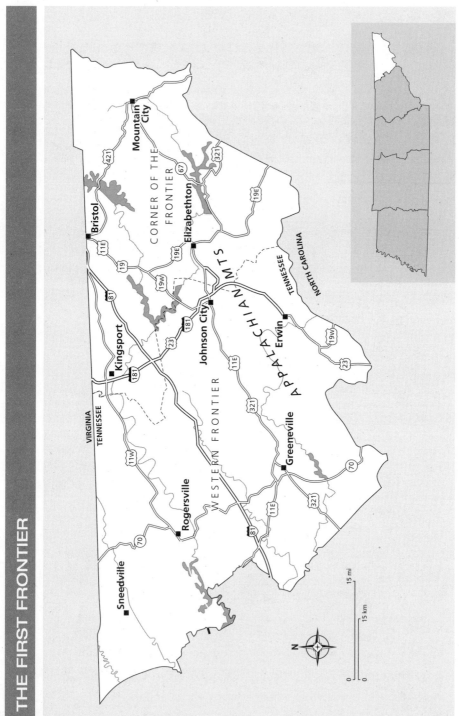

Farther down State Street, a large mural on the side of a building presents a visual memorial to that event.

The performing arts are alive and well in Bristol at the historic ***Paramount Center for the Arts.*** It's a circa 1931 theater restored to its original Art Deco style and is now listed on the National Register of Historic Places. Theatre Bristol calls the Paramount home for its own productions, and the venue is the site of other touring shows and concerts, as well as local meetings and seminars. It's a great place to watch a show. The Paramount Center is located at 518 State Street. Call (423) 274–8920 for a schedule, or visit www .theparamountcenter.com.

Tennessee Ernie Ford was born Ernest Jennings Ford on February 13, 1919, in Bristol, and before he became the booming voice behind many hit country songs, including "Sixteen Tons," "The Shot Gun Boogie," and "Mule Train," he was a radio staff announcer and a bombardier during World War II. He was elected to the Country Music Hall of Fame in 1990 and died in October 1991.

Today the house where Ernie Ford was born has opened as a lasting memorial to the city's favorite son. Located on Anderson Street, the home is garnished with memorabilia of his long musical and television career. The home isn't open on a regular basis; call the Bristol CVB, (423) 989–4850, for hours and more information, or visit www.bristolchamber.org.

Southwest of Bristol, Johnson County is surrounded by the hills of the Appalachian Mountains, and the businesses and attractions reflect that way of life quite nicely. Throughout the county you'll see small handwritten signs hanging from mailboxes advertising handmade quilts or birdhouses for sale.

In ***Mountain City*** about the only thing you won't find are crowds. Within a few-block area of the downtown section, you'll find numerous antiques and gift shops selling a variety of neat things.

AUTHOR'S TOP TEN PICKS

Tennessee Ernie Ford Home	Tennessee Wilderness Road
Bays Mountain Park	Trade Days
Kissing Bridge	Appalachian Fair
Unicoi County Heritage Museum	Cooper's Gem Mine
Archie Campbell Days	Heritage Days (Rogersville)

A great place to start your East Tennessee mountain trek is at the ***Johnson County Welcome Center & Museum,*** located on U.S. Highway 421 in Mountain City. In addition to maps, brochures, and great stories from the attendants, there's a historical museum with a large selection of Native American and pioneer artifacts. One of the coolest exhibits is Jessie Murphy's wedding gown. Jessie married Robert Ferdinand Wright on June 7, 1905, in Mountain City. Along with the dress are her shoes and pictures of the church and wedding party. The center is open daily year-round and on Sunday afternoon from March through December. For information call (423) 727–5800, or log on to www.johnsoncountychamber.org.

South of Mountain City on US 421 is ***Trade,*** the oldest unincorporated community in the state. It's the spot where, in 1673, the first English-speaking white man set foot on Tennessee soil. Situated on an old buffalo trail, the community flourished as a resting place for those traveling the three major paths through the wilderness that crossed at this point.

By the 1790s the area had a country store, a post office, a blacksmith shop, and a handful of cabins, and today it's about as low-key as it was then—no big signs and no souvenir shops. ***Trade Days*** are held each June, when the entire county comes out to celebrate the heritage of the area.

Wilderness Road, one of the three major paths that converged at Trade, continues through East Tennessee to Cumberland Gap, where it heads northward into Kentucky and on to the "Great American West." Today the ***Tennessee Wilderness Road*** tour follows as closely as possible the original trail of the pioneers. The leisurely drive along the path takes you through a landscape of spectacular valleys dotted with church spires, old towns, and, if you take the time to explore on your own, plenty of unique experiences. Use the designated roads as your main route, but don't hesitate to follow a few side roads now and then to experience even more. There is also a full-color brochure and map, *America's First Frontier* tour, available for this part of the state. For more information call the Northeast Tennessee Tourism Association at (800) 468–6882; their Web site is www.netta.com.

In ***Kingsport*** early travelers through the area exchanged their Virginia currency for Tennessee money at a stagecoach stop known as the ***Exchange Place.*** Today the small farmlike village and crafts center is open Thursday through Sunday during the warmer months. If you visit on a Thursday, you're likely to see a group of ladies working on a quilt. The ***Fall Folk Arts Festival*** and an open-house celebration take place during the last weekend of September. There are a lot of really neat traditional Christmas events here as well, including a Yule log burning. The village is located just off U.S. Highway 11W at 4812 Orebank Road. Admission is free. Give them a call at (423) 288–6071, or visit www.exchangeplace.info.

Unlikely as it may seem, a major U.S. boatyard was in operation along the Holston River in Kingsport in 1802. William King's boatyard had a reputation for quality that stretched as far as New Orleans. On the hill across the stagecoach road from the yards was the always busy **Netherland Inn,** an inn and tavern where the likes of the state's three presidents, Andrew Jackson, Andrew Johnson, and James K. Polk, whiled away hours with their friends. The inn has been restored and is open to the public as a museum. Several other buildings on the property, including a shop and wagon shelter, have also been restored. A log cabin that was moved here from Virginia and served as Daniel Boone's home from 1773 to 1775 is now a children's museum; it is a must if there are any small travelers with you. Start your visit at the Log Cabin Visitors Center and Gift Shop, located behind the inn. The former boatyards are now a city park that stretches for miles down the river. Open weekends only, May through October. Admission is charged. To find out more, call (423) 246–7982; their Web site is www.netherlandinn.com.

Within the city limits of Kingsport, tucked away between Holston River Mountain and Bays Ridge, is the secluded and tranquil **Bays Mountain Park.** The 3,000-acre city-owned facility has a wildlife park, a planetarium, a wildlife tour on the 44-acre lake, a natural-history museum, 22 miles of hiking trails, and the unique **Harry Steadman Mountain Heritage Farmstead Museum.**

The museum contains a collection of old tools and implements the founders of the area used in their daily lives. "It gives you a great feel of the hardships and the size of the tasks they were faced with," Valerie Wood of the park staff said. "Everything was donated to us from local families." In the park there's an unusual gray wolf habitat and a snake habitat.

yumyum

The first Cracker Barrel Old Country Store and restaurant opened in Lebanon more than 30 years ago, and there are now 582 locations nationwide, with 50 of those in our own state. That means you're never far from a great plate of country cookin'!

The park is a great way to spend a quiet, laid-back afternoon away from the crowds usually associated with natural parks of this size. The park is located 3 miles off Interstate 181 at Bays Mountain Road, and it is open daily during the summer; open weekends only off-season. Their entrance fee is $3 per car. For more information contact the park at (423) 229–9447, or visit www.baysmountain.com.

The city fathers of **Blountville** say that there are more original log houses along their city's main street than in any other town in the state. Whether that's true or not, there are a great many vintage buildings to see here. One of those, **The Deery Inn,** played an important part in the frontier era of this part of the state. Built during the late 1700s, the building is actually three buildings: a two-story hewn-log house, a three-story cut-stone house, and a two-story frame structure, all built adjacent to one another and joined together. It's now a private residence, but the architecture can still be appreciated from the sidewalk.

Everyone gets a chance to relive the old panning days when they stop by **Cooper's Gem Mine.** Here you can buy a $4 or $7 bucket of ore and take it out back to the stream, step up to the flume, wash away the sand and dirt, and what you find, you can keep! The shop is open year-round and sells specialty crafts and jewelry; the sluice is usually open from March through October. Closed Sunday. It's located at 1138 Big Hollow Road. Call them at (423) 323–5680, or check out www.coopersgemmine.com.

A walking-tour map of Blountville is available, and most of the buildings are decorated and open to the public around Christmas.

Perhaps one of the most historically significant structures in the state is **Rocky Mount,** a two-story log cabin in **Piney Flats** near Johnson City. Built in 1770, Rocky Mount is the oldest original territorial capitol in the United States and one of the oldest buildings in the state.

OTHER ATTRACTIONS WORTH SEEING

Bristol Caverns
Bristol,
(423) 878–2011
www.bristolcaverns.com

Dickson-Williams Mansion
Greeneville,
(423) 787–0500

Farmhouse Gallery & Gardens
Unicoi,
(423) 743–8799

Hands-On! Regional Museum
Johnson City,
(423) 434–HAND
www.handsonmuseum.org

Museum of Ancient Brick
Johnson City,
(800) 414–4661
www.generalshale.com

Tipton-Haynes Historic Site
Johnson City,
(423) 926–3631

Wetlands Water Park
Jonesborough,
(423) 753–1553

It was the capitol of "The Territory of the United States south of the river Ohio" from 1790 until a new capitol was built in Knoxville. With two stories and nine rooms, pine paneling, and real glass windows, the structure was a mansion by frontier standards, and it quickly became a gathering place for people across the entire frontier.

Today the house is open to the public daily, as is the adjoining ***Overmountain Museum,*** which shows the early life of the area. First-person interpretation provides visitors with a true sense of what was taking place in 1791. Guides talk with you as they would have in that year and stay in character for your entire visit. The museum is on U.S. Highway 11E, and their contact number is (888) 538–1791.

Sycamore Shoals, the first permanent settlement outside the 13 colonies, was a muster point for the Overmountain Men on their way to the battle of King's Mountain. Today it is a State Historic Area and offers a museum, along with a reconstructed Fort Watauga that interprets the role this area played in the early settlement of what is now Tennessee and in the expansion of America's western boundary. An outdoor drama, *The Wataugans,* is presented during mid-July.

There are plenty of hiking trails here among the park's 45 acres, and there are several boat launch ramps for the lake. Beautifully shaded and peaceful, this is truly an off-the-beaten-path mixture of history and recreation. It's on U.S. Highway 321 in Elizabethton. Call (423) 543–5808, or visit www.sycamore shoals.org.

One of the state's remaining original covered bridges crosses the Doe River in downtown ***Elizabethton*** and is the focal point for the city's riverside park. Built in 1882, ***The Kissing Bridge*** (as the locals call it) is the oldest such structure in the state. The ***Covered Bridge Celebration*** takes place the first week of June. Activities include concerts, a crafts show, an antique car show, and kids' games and contests. Call (423) 547–3852; you can also find out more at www.tourelizabethton.com.

agreatname

The name "Tennessee" originated from the old Yuchi Indian word *tana-see,* meaning "the meeting place." White men traveling the area in the 1700s associated the word with the name of a Cherokee village and as the name of a river in Cherokee Territory.

For many years a tall Fraser fir tree on Elk Street near downtown Elizabethton was considered the tallest such tree in the world. Then the gloomy day came when officials found it was only the second tallest. But since the tallest is never decorated at Christmas, they now decorate the fir in Elizabethton, making it the tallest *decorated* Fraser fir in the world. While you are in the area, pick up a free walking-tour map of downtown Elizabethton; there are some great buildings here. Maps are available at the chamber of commerce on East Elk Avenue.

About 20 miles southeast of Elizabethton on Route 143 is **Roan Mountain State Park.** The park itself lies at the foot of Roan Mountain, one of the highest peaks (6,285 feet) in the eastern United States, but that's not what makes this park so special. On the side of that mountain is one of the largest rhododendron gardens in the country. More than 600 acres of color bloom each June, making the area a striking display of pinks and purples. The Rhododendron Festival, held in mid-June, features native arts and crafts, mountain music and dancing, local food festivals, and wildlife tours. The park is the best place in the area to view fall foliage. A campground and cabins offer overnighters grand vistas of the mountains.

Walking and hiking trails line the mountain with numerous scenic overlooks. The **Dave Miller Homestead,** a preserved farm, is located in a hollow atop Strawberry Mountain. The Miller family first settled in the area around 1870 and for generations lived in virtual seclusion. Today the farm is preserved intact and serves as a model of early Appalachian life. The park is open year-round; the homestead is open only Wednesday through Sunday during the warmer months. Admission is free. Call them at (800) 250–8620.

Farther down US 321 toward Johnson City is the **Sinking Creek Baptist Church,** the oldest church congregation in the state, having been established in 1773. Next to its new church building, built in the 1960s, is the congregation's former place of worship, a log church built in 1783. It has been renovated, and many of the logs are from the original church. Occasionally the old log church is host to weddings and Sunday services, weather permitting. Reece Harris, pastor of the congregation for more than 40 years, told me that the sight of the log church provokes "a sense of pride knowing that Christians have been on this creekbank for a long time." Call the church at (423) 928–3222 or check out www.sinkingcreek.org.

Johnson City resident John Tipton was a member of the 1776 Constitutional Convention, and today the home he built in 1784 is a significant piece of restored history. At the **Tipton-Haynes State Historic Site,** ten original and restored buildings still stand on the property. A cave and a spring on the property were resting places for the early white explorers, and it is believed that Daniel Boone set up a hunting camp near the spring. The cave can be visited today. The site is open year-round at 2620 South Roan Street. Need more information? Phone them at (423) 926–3631 or visit www.tipton-haynes.org.

While walking through Johnson City, notice the great brick sculptures, created by Johnny Hagerman, a brick sculptor for General Shale Brick. The company, headquartered here, has plants throughout the South and Midwest and is the nation's leading brick maker.

Make sure you're in town when it's time for lunch, and make your way over to 3301 North Roan Street to the **Dixie Barbeque Company.** What a selection of smoked meat meals and sandwiches you'll find here! Owner Alan Howell is quite the host and is willing to tell you everything you need to know in order to enjoy the meat he serves, which ranges from sliced pork and pork ribs to smoked chicken. Try the smoked chicken sandwich with Howell's own East Tennessee sauce. Wow!

At any one time, there will be seven or eight sauces to choose from—most of them made by Howell himself. "If it doesn't have a label on it, that means I made it," he said. Open Monday through Saturday, 11:00 a.m. to 9:00 p.m. Contact them at (423) 283–PIGS.

South of Interstate 81, on Highway 36 headed toward Johnson City, is the little community of **Boone's Creek.** Daniel Boone loved this area, and he came back often to hunt. On one of his trips he brought along William Bean, who liked the area so much he decided to settle his family here in 1769, thus becoming the first permanent white settlers in Tennessee. He built his first cabin on the site of Boone's hunting camp next to Boone's Creek. A monument now marks that spot.

Inside the chapel at **Boone's Creek Christian Church** are several rooms of artifacts from Boone, William Bean, and other pioneers of the area. The **Boone's Creek Museum** is not open on a regular basis. The chapel is at the corner of Highway 354 and Christian Church Road. Call (423) 282–0248 or go to www.boonescreekcc.org.

Out on Old Gray Station Road, off Highway 36, is a small waterfall that Boone once hid under to escape the Indians. The waterfall has eroded over time, but you can still see it right after you turn onto Old Gray Station Road. Approximately 2 miles farther down the road, you'll see a historic marker showing where Boone carved his own monument into a beech tree: D. BOON CILLED A BAR IN 1760. The tree is now dead, but a short walk off the highway will take you to the spot, which is fenced in.

Western Frontier

The Unicoi County seat community of **Erwin** probably holds the distinction of being the only town ever to put an elephant on trial for murder, find it guilty, and carry out the death penalty.

"Murderous Mary," a circus elephant who trampled her owner to death, was hanged from a railroad derrick before 5,000 spectators in 1916. Newspaper

TOP ANNUAL EVENTS

Covered Bridge Celebration,
Elizabethton, mid-June,
(423) 547–3850

National Storytelling Festival
Jonesborough, early October,
(800) 952–8392

Rhododendron Festival,
Roan Mountain State Park, mid-June,
(800) 250–8620

Unicoi County Apple Festival
Erwin, early October,
(423) 743–3000

The Wataugans Outdoor Drama,
Elizabethton, mid-July,
(423) 543–5808

Heritage Days
Rogersville, mid-October,
(423) 272–1961

Fall Folk Arts Festival,
Kingsport, late September,
(423) 288–6071

clippings and photos of that event are but a few of the interesting items in the *Unicoi County Heritage Museum,* housed in a century-old home on the grounds of the *National Fish Hatchery* on U.S. Highway 23.

The hatchery was established in 1894, and the ten-room superintendent's residence was constructed in 1903. By the early 1980s the house wasn't being used by the superintendent, so the federal government signed an agreement allowing the county to use it as a museum. In addition to the story of Murderous Mary, various displays highlight local pottery production and the history of local railroading. On the second floor is a replica of the city's Main Street as it looked a century ago. "Grandmother's Attic" holds a collection of quilts, antique dolls, and children's toys, all displayed as they might be in your own grandma's attic.

Outside, the fish hatchery is still in operation and produces about ten million rainbow trout eggs each year. Free tours are available at the hatchery as well as at the museum. Call (423) 743–4712 for the hatchery, (423) 743–9449 for the museum.

Bring your lunch; the entire area is a beautiful parklike setting, complete with a picnic pavilion and restrooms.

A fun event to catch in Erwin each fall is the *Apple Festival,* held the first weekend in October. There is continuous music, dancing, handmade crafts, the famous Blue Ridge Pottery Club Show and Sale, and various local food vendors. Call (423) 743–3000 for more information.

The 16 counties that now make up the eastern tip of Tennessee were at one time united in an effort to become a state by themselves. The framework for the would-be *state of Franklin* was set when about 30,000 white settlers crossed the Appalachian Mountains and founded several settlements in this area, which was a part of North Carolina at the time.

Leaders met in *Jonesborough* and created a bill of rights for their new state and requested that the lawmakers of North Carolina allow its creation. They refused, but Franklin, under the leadership of John Sevier, continued the battle for several years, until 1788. Several skirmishes between Franklin and North Carolina militia took place in the area.

Although never recognized as an official state, Franklin operated like a sovereign government with an assembly, administered justice, and negotiated treaties with Native Americans.

Eight years after the fight for the quasi state ended, Sevier became the first governor of the state of Tennessee, which incorporated the former boundaries of Franklin. Jonesborough, chartered in 1779, 17 years before there was a Tennessee, holds the distinction of being the oldest incorporated area in the state. And thanks to an ambitious restoration effort, much of the city appears as it did more than a century ago. Jonesborough was the first Tennessee town placed on the National Register of Historic Places.

There are more than 27 points of interest on the walking-tour map of the historic downtown area, including the historic *Chester Inn,* where a young Andrew Jackson stayed while working on his law degree in 1788. Now owned by the state of Tennessee, the inn houses the Storytelling Foundation International. A gift shop on the first floor offer a wide variety of storytelling tools, including books and tapes. Call this historic inn at (423) 753–2171.

Many of the old buildings along the main streets now house a wide array of specialty shops. One particular structure, the *Old Town Hall,* at 144 East Main Street, was restored in 1982 and contains about 50 crafts-oriented shops.

The Hawley House Bed & Breakfast is located on Lot #1 and is the oldest house in the state's oldest town! Built in 1793, the house offers three bedrooms with private baths and a full breakfast. Prices range from $110 to $160 per couple. Call (423) 753–8869 or (800) 753–8869, or go to www.hawley house.com.

The *Jonesborough History Museum,* at 117 Boone Street, is located inside the visitor center and is a good place to start your visit to this historic area. Brochures, maps, and a short film will get you started in the right direction. The museum is open daily. Call (423) 753–5961 for the visitor center; (423) 753–1015 for the museum.

There are two great festivals in town you won't want to miss. An old-fashioned, family-oriented July 4 celebration known as *Historic Jonesborough*

The Bad-Shot President

Once, a long time ago, a small crowd of onlookers followed a fiery lawyer named Andrew Jackson from a courtroom in Jonesborough to a nearby meadow, where Jackson and his opponent, attorney Waightstill Avery, squared off, and a duel began.

Crack! A pistol shot rang out. Crack! Another shot.

Yet both men still stood, unharmed. Each dueler, it seems, had fired into the air, and a deadly conclusion was avoided. Moments later, the two adversaries shook hands.

Jackson went on to become the seventh president of the United States.

Days features arts and crafts, Southern cooking, and clogging. In early October, the *National Storytelling Festival* is a celebration of the country's top storytellers. Call (423) 753–2171 or (800) 952–8392; their Web site is www.story tellingfoundation.com.

If you're in this part of the state during late August, be sure to visit the *Appalachian Fair*, which is held at the fairgrounds in Gray. This six-day event is the largest fair in East Tennessee and features one of the best carnival companies in operation today, the Great James H. Drew Exposition. There are all kinds of live Appalachian crafts demonstrations, farm and home exhibits, and various agricultural exhibits and competitions. This is truly an old-time country fair, complete with demolition derbies, mud drag racing, baby shows, baking contests, and top-name country music entertainment. For more information call (423) 477–3211.

Contrary to the myth started by Walt Disney, Davy Crockett was not born on a mountaintop in Tennessee; he was born along the banks of the Nolichuckey River, near the mouth of Limestone Creek. Today that birth spot, just outside the small community of Limestone, is preserved as the *Davy Crockett Birthplace State Historical Area.*

Born in 1786, David (he never signed his name *Davy*) went on to become the "King of the Wild Frontier." His name and legend can rightfully be claimed by many areas in the state. He was born here in the east, he ran a gristmill in middle Tennessee, and he was elected to Congress from western Tennessee.

But here is where it all began. A reproduction of his birthplace cabin has been constructed, with the cornerstone of his original cabin on display. Probably the most unusual aspect of this park is the monument erected in the late 1960s by a local civic organization. In honor of Crockett's stature as a national hero, each of the 50 states is represented in the wall of the monument. Stones native to each state are incorporated in the wall and engraved with the respective state's name.

The park, located off US 11E, has a campground, swimming pool, picnic facilities, and a visitor center. Open year-round; phone the park at (423) 257–2167.

Fifteen minutes down US 321 is the county seat city of **Greeneville,** which happens to be the only Greeneville in the United States that uses that third e in its name.

It was to this city that an 18-year-old boy moved in 1826 to establish a tailor business for himself. Several years later that boy, Andrew Johnson, became the country's 17th president. Today Johnson's Greeneville years are highlighted at the **Andrew Johnson National Historic Site,** in the downtown section. His small tailor shop has been preserved and is inside the site's visitor center. Across the street is the brick home in which Johnson lived from the early 1830s to 1851. On Main Street is the Homestead, his home from 1851 to 1875, during which time he was vice president and then president of the United States. The cemetery where he and his family are buried is a few blocks away. All four attractions are open every day except Christmas, Thanksgiving, and New Year's Day. The visitor center is located at the corner of College and Depot Streets. The visitor center and Homestead are free. Phone them at (423) 638–3551.

A walking-tour map of Greeneville is available that highlights 36 historic areas or structures of the community.

Greeneville's **Tusculum College,** founded in 1794, is the oldest college south of the Ohio River and west of the Allegheny Mountains. It was the 28th college founded in America, is the oldest college in the state, and is the oldest coed college associated with the Presbyterian Church.

Eight buildings on the campus were constructed between 1841 and 1928 and make up the college's historic district. A walking tour of the campus is included in the city's walking-tour brochure.

The college's **Andrew Johnson Library and Museum** is the state's largest presidential library and houses a great many of the president's books, papers, and manuscripts, as well as those of his family. In addition, the library houses almost 200 original Civil War–era newspapers from throughout the country. This historic site can be reached at (423) 638–1111.

On US 11W, look for **Pal's** drive-through restaurant. You can't miss any of the 21 Pal's drive-throughs, all of which are located in East Tennessee and southwestern Virginia. While the restaurants probably don't stand out if you see them every day, those of us from outside the area should surely appreciate the unique architecture.

In fact, each location is vernacular architecture at its finest. There is no doubt what the restaurant sells: Huge hot dogs, fries, hamburgers, and soft drink containers bedeck each of the little square buildings. Colorful and fun, the buildings stand out from the urban clutter. The food and service are pretty good, too! Their Web site is www.palsweb.com.

Tennessee's first newspaper was printed in **Rogersville** in 1791, and to celebrate that fact, the **Tennessee Newspaper & Printing Museum** has been established in the city's old railroad depot, just down the street from the Hale Springs Inn. Located at 415 South Depot Street, at the railroad. Their contact number is (423) 272–1961.

taxmoneyatwork

There are 53 Tennessee state parks, with 886 miles of hiking trails to walk, 394 species of birds to watch, 18 waterfalls, and 2,950 campsites. For specifics, phone them at (888) 867–2757 or go to www.tnstateparks.com.

Most of the old structures in downtown Rogersville have been restored, and the entire district is listed on the National Register of Historic Places. A walking tour of the historic district includes the **Hawkins County Courthouse.** Built in 1836, the building is the oldest original courthouse still in use in the state. You can view the entire walking tour, including information on each site, online at www.rogersvilleheritage.org.

Most of the Main Street retail businesses now sell antiques or crafts, but there are still a few old-time offices and clothing stores along the way.

There's a fascinating natural phenomenon a few miles outside Rogersville on Ebbing & Flowing Spring Road that you won't want to miss. The **Ebbing & Flowing Spring** is one of only two known springs in the world to flow and stop at regular intervals. The underground hollow is filled slowly with water. As it nears the surface of the ground, a suction is formed and the water begins to be siphoned out of the ground into the spring basin. The siphon continues to drain the hollow until it dries up, breaking the siphon and stopping the flow. It then fills up and starts all over again. This has happened for at least the past 200 years at two-hour-and-47-minute intervals. The water remains at a constant 34 degrees.

Legend claims that any couple drinking from the spring at the height of its flow will marry within the year. The flat rock nearby was a favorite courting spot and the site of many marriage proposals.

The **Ebbing & Flowing Spring School** was built in the early 1800s by families of its first students. Generations of the Amis family, the original land grant owners of the land, were taught here until the dismissal bell rang for the last time in 1956.

The Ebbing & Flowing Spring United Methodist Church met in the school when it was organized in 1820 until a permanent church was built between the school and the cemetery in 1898. It still stands today with its original timbers and interior and is used regularly by the congregation.

From the center of Rogersville, head east on old US 11W (not the bypass) for about a mile to Burem Road. Bear right at the Amis House historical marker, and go a little more than 2 miles and turn left on Ebbing & Flowing Spring Road, a narrow country road. You'll go by ruins of a stone mill on your right. In less than a half mile, you'll come to a stream crossing the road. Immediately to your left is the spring. The road on your right leads to the church and school. You can contact them at (423) 272–1961 or www.rogers villeheritage.org.

Plan your visit to Rogersville in mid-October. That's when the popular **Heritage Days** take place. All the activities are reminiscent of a harvest celebration at the turn of the 20th century.

Out on US 11E at Highway 66 is the little community of **Bulls Gap.** Named after local gun maker John Bull, who settled here in the mid-1790s, this natural gap in Bays Mountain later became a strategic location when the railroad through here was completed in 1858. During the Civil War both the North and South wanted to control the railroad through the mountains; as a result, Bulls Gap was the site of several skirmishes.

Even though the area has more than 200 years of history and architecture going for it, the event that put it on the map more than anything else was the birth of comedian Archie Campbell, who went on to become a member of the Grand Ole Opry in Nashville and to star on the long-running television show *Hee Haw*. He died in 1987.

Today a reconstruction of his birthplace is open in the town park alongside the Caboose Museum. A fun time to visit is during Labor Day weekend, when **Archie Campbell Days** take place. In addition to the Campbell complex, there's an Old Town historic-district walking tour featuring nearly 30 structures. Campbell's birthplace is located 2.5 miles off exit 23 of I–81, at 139 South Main Street. Call (423) 235–5216 for further information.

Located off Highway 31, 7 miles south of Sneedville, is **Elrod Falls,** one of the great hidden treasures of this sparsely populated county. Flat Gap Creek cascades more than 100 feet to the lower pool, where swimming is permitted in the cool, deep water. Take the unnamed gravel road off Highway 31 at the sign for the falls and follow it approximately 1 mile to a small picnic area. Park there; the walk is a very short, easy one to the lowest of the three falls. Need more information? Call (423) 733–4524.

Places to Stay in the First Frontier

BLOUNTVILLE

Rocky Top Campground
496 Pearl Lane
Cable TV; pets allowed
(423) 323–2535
www.rockytopcampground
.com

BRISTOL

Bristol Lodging
111 Holiday Drive
Restaurant, lounge, exercise, pool
(423) 968–1101
www.bristollodging.com

ERWIN

Nolichucky Gorge Campground
1 Jones Branch Road
Showers, flush toilets, fishing
(423) 743–8876

GREENEVILLE

General Morgan Inn
111 North Main Street
Restaurant, room service, fireplaces
(423) 787–1000
www.generalmorganinn
.com

JOHNSON CITY

Carnegie Hotel & Spa
1216 W. State of Franklin Road
Hotel built to elegance of original Carnegie Hotel, circa 1891
(423) 979–6400
www.carnegiehotel.com

Doubletree Hotel
211 Mockingbird Lane
Restaurant, lounge, pool
(423) 929–2000
www.doubletreejohnsoncity
.com

JONESBOROUGH

Hawley House Bed & Breakfast
114 East Woodrow Avenue
Built in 1793; private baths, full breakfast
(423) 753–8869
www.hawleyhouse.com

Historic Eureka Inn
127 West Main Street
Private baths, continental breakfast, private garden terrace
(423) 913–6100
www.eurekajonesborough
.com

KINGSPORT

Fox Manor B&B
1612 Watauga Street
In old neighborhood; private baths, full breakfast
(423) 378–3844
www.foxmanor.com

LIMESTONE

Davy Crockett Birthplace State Park (camping)
Off US 11E
Hiking trails, playground, scenic riverside
(423) 257–2167

Home Place Bed & Breakfast
132 Church Lane
Quiet, private in small rural town; run by historic local family
(423) 921–8424

MOUNTAIN CITY

Prospect Hill Inn Bed & Breakfast Inn
801 West Main Street, Highway 67
Circa 1889 mansion; private bath, fireplace, Jacuzzi; balcony with mountain view
(423) 727–0139 or (800) 339–5084
www.prospect-hill.com

Places to Eat in the First Frontier

HAMPTON

Captain's Table
2285 Highway 321
Overlooking Lake Watauga; specialty is seafood, also steaks and chicken. Open seasonally
(423) 725–2201

JOHNSON CITY

Dixie Barbeque Company
3301 North Roan Street
Selection of smoked meats
and sandwiches. Open
Monday through Saturday,
11:00 a.m. to 9:00 p.m.
(423) 283–PIGS

The Firehouse Restaurant
627 West Walnut Street
In circa 1900 building,
firefighting memorabilia;
pit-cooked barbecue, ribs,
steaks. Lunch and dinner
daily
(423) 929–7377
www.thefirehouse.com

Gourmet & Company
214 East Mountcastle Drive
Fresh croissants, pasta,
salad, and sandwiches.
Lunch and dinner daily.
(423) 929–9007
www.gourmetandcompany
.com

Harbor House Seafood
2510 North Roan Street
Seafood, chicken, steak
Open daily 11:00 a.m. to
9:00 p.m.
(423) 282–5122
www.harborhousejc.com

JONESBOROUGH

The Cranberry Thistle
103 East Main Street
In the historic district.
Soup, sandwiches
Open daily 8:00 a.m. to
7:00 p.m.
(423) 753–0090
www.thecranberrythistle
.com

THE MOUNTAINOUS EAST →

Of Lincoln and Boone

The quaint little village of **Cumberland Gap** rests just a few miles from one of the most historic natural passageways of all time. Much of the westward movement of early America came through this V-shaped indentation in the Appalachian Mountain chain, a wall of rock that stretches from Maine to Georgia.

It was 1775 when Daniel Boone and his 30 axmen hacked out the Wilderness Road through the gap to open up the "western frontier" and the fertile farmlands on the other side. It was the first road platted by a white man in the state. That byway became a major thoroughfare and later was a four-lane paved highway for decades.

Now the Cumberland Gap Tunnel, which opened October 18, 1996, takes U.S. Highway 25E through the mountain instead of up and over the top. With the rerouting of that busy and noisy highway, the area on the mountain surrounding the original road is being restored to resemble, as closely as possible, the path used by the pioneers of the late 1700s.

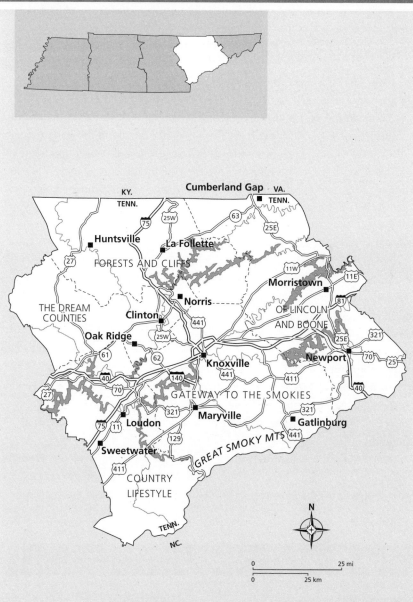

Cumberland Gap

KY.
TENN.

VA.
TENN.

75   25W   63   25E

Huntsville   La Follette

27   FORESTS AND CLIFFS

11W   Morristown   11E

Norris   OF LINCOLN
AND BOONE   81

THE DREAM
COUNTIES   Clinton   441

Oak Ridge   25W

61   62   Knoxville   25E   321

40   140   441   Newport   70   25

27   70   GATEWAY TO THE SMOKIES   411   40

321   Maryville   321

75   11   Loudon   Gatlinburg

129   441

Sweetwater   GREAT SMOKY MTS

411   COUNTRY
LIFESTYLE

TENN.
NC.

N

0   25 mi
0   25 km

At the top of the gap, a marker in the ***Cumberland Gap National Historic Park*** shows where the states of Kentucky, Virginia, and Tennessee meet. It is said that from the top, those three states, plus Georgia and North Carolina, can be seen on a clear day. A visitor center and museum are part of the park. Find out more by calling (606) 248–2817, or visit their Web site at www.nps.gov/cuga.

To reach the park's visitor center, go through the tunnel to Middlesboro, Kentucky. Inside the center is an informative museum about the park, the gap, and early life in the area. A good way to see the terrain of the mountains is to drive 4 miles up to the Pinnacle, where you'll park in Kentucky, walk into Virginia, and overlook the village of Cumberland Gap in Tennessee. You can look down on the actual gap where Daniel Boone came through, and you'll see the old highway that follows the original Wilderness Road.

When old US 25E was built over the gap, much of it followed the Wilderness Road and was paved. Now that the tunnel takes all the traffic, that portion of 25E has been closed, all the paving removed, and the road restored to a primitive condition. The original dirt Wilderness Road, which can be seen from the Pinnacle, was reopened to foot traffic in mid-2002; we can all now walk exactly where those early settlers trekked.

A fun, albeit somewhat tiring, side trip while you're in this area takes you to the mountaintop village where Sherman Hensley lived until 1951.

In 1904 he decided to get away from it all and moved, along with several relatives, to the mountaintop a few miles from Cumberland Gap. They all became self-sufficient when the rest of America was learning to rely more on one another for basic needs.

Since 1965 the National Park Service has restored parts of the ***Hensley Settlement,*** including three houses, several barns, many of the fences, the schoolhouse, and the cemetery. The public is invited to visit. It's not an easy

AUTHOR'S TOP TEN PICKS

World's Largest Stalagmite	Hensley Settlement
Moonshine Capital of the World	The Lost Sea
Davy Crockett's marriage license	Museum of Appalachia
Ripley's Davy Crockett Mini-Golf	Rugby's Utopian Community
Mel's Diner	Dollywood

place to get to, but what an adventure it is! The most popular way of getting there is on foot via a 3.5-mile path up the side of the mountain, or you can be shuttled there by park-operated vehicles. The settlement is free to visit. Call (606) 248–2817 for directions and a schedule of special events.

Deep in the mountain, directly underneath the historic Wilderness Road, is **Cudjo's Caverns,** the home of the **"Pillar of Hercules,"** one of the world's largest stalagmites. The formation is 65 feet high and 35 feet in circumference, and it is still growing. It's estimated to be 85 million years old. The National Park Service oversees the caverns. A call to (606) 248–2817 will give you more information. The village of Cumberland Gap was founded by English settlers and today shows a strong English influence in its architecture. The downtown section has been virtually untouched by modernization for more than 50 years. The opening scene of a movie was filmed here in 1988, and according to one of the downtown businessmen, only one sign had to be removed to make the village look like a small town of the 1930s.

"Instead of getting bigger, this place is smaller now than it was in the 1960s," said Harvey Fuson, owner of **The Old Drugstore** in the village of Cumberland Gap. From his front door one can look up and see the entrance to Cudjo's Caverns, where he worked as a guide during high school. His shop was built as the town drugstore by his pharmacist father and uncle in 1950.

Located at 515 Colwyn Avenue, Fuson's store today is a combination of pharmacy museum, gift shop, antiques gallery, and ice-cream parlor. He makes the best peanut-butter milk shakes in this part of Tennessee! Asked if he had gotten his fudge recipe from his grandmother, Harvey laughed. "No way; I make fudge the way my grandma wished she could make fudge." Open daily. Call (423) 869–0455 for more information. Other gift, variety, antiques, and craft shops can be found up and down Colwyn Avenue.

On Wilderness Trail at the edge of town is the historic **Newlee Iron Works** iron furnace, built in the early 1820s. It was used to make iron that was shipped off to Chattanooga and to blacksmiths throughout the region. At its peak the furnace created more than 35 tons of pig iron a week. To the left of the furnace is a path that is part of the original Wilderness Road, which you can follow to get up to the historic gap itself.

There's a great Web site for Cumberland Gap and the surrounding Claiborne County area. Log on at www.claibornecounty.com, or call the Chamber of Commerce at (423) 626–4149.

A few miles south on US 25E is Harrogate, the home of **Lincoln Memorial University.** Founded in 1896 as a living memorial to President Abraham Lincoln, the school's charter mandated the establishment of a museum to house memorabilia of the Lincoln era. Today the Lincoln Library and Museum

ALSO WORTH SEEING

Forbidden Caverns,
Sevierville,
(865) 453–5972
www.forbiddendcaverns.com

Dinosaur Walk Museum,
Pigeon Forge,
(865) 428–4003
www.dinowalk.com

Great Smoky Mountains National Park,
Gatlinburg,
(865) 436–1200
www.nps.gov/grsm

Farragut Folklife Museum,
Farragut,
(865) 966–7057

James White's Fort,
Knoxville,
(865) 525–6514

Museum of East Tennessee History,
Knoxville,
(865) 215–8830
www.east-tennessee-history.org

on the campus houses the third-largest collection of Lincolniana and Civil War items in the world.

One of the most historic items in the museum is the ebony cane the president was carrying on the night he was assassinated. A lock of Lincoln's hair is also on display. The school itself is beautiful and is a nice tribute to mountain life in East Tennessee. Take time to walk through the campus. Admission is charged for the museum; contact it at (423) 869–6235.

High atop Clinch Mountain, about 5 miles out of Bean Station on US 25E, you'll find *Clinch Mountain Lookout Restaurant.* It's not much to look at and the signs are falling down, but don't let any of that scare you away. The eatery is home to the famous vinegar pie. What a taste sensation! As the story goes, lemons were hard to get during the Depression, so vinegar was substituted for lemons in pie making; some liked the taste so much, they never switched back.

Joining vinegar pie on the menu are ostrich burgers from a local farmer, hamburgers, and steaks. Breakfast is served all day. The outside tables have an astounding view of the valley and the Clinch River far below. It's open seven days a week at 7:00 a.m. Call (865) 767–2511 or go to www.clinchmountain lookout.com.

When Andrew Johnson came to Tennessee to establish a tailor shop, he spent a few months in Rutledge before relocating to nearby Greeneville. A reproduction of Johnson's first shop has been built and is located in front of *Grainger County Courthouse,* on the original site.

A few blocks away is the circa 1848 ***Grainger County Jail,*** the oldest standing brick jailhouse in Tennessee. Restored by the county's historical society, the facility now houses the society and serves as a public meetinghouse for the area's clubs and organizations. Inside, the original metal stairs and wall partitions are intact.

In the 1790s Davy Crockett's dad opened a small, six-room tavern near present-day ***Morristown.*** That's where little Davy spent his early years. In the 1950s a reproduction of that tavern was built on the original site, and today the ***Crockett Tavern and Museum*** serves as a frontier museum honoring the Crockett family and other early Tennessee pioneers. The tavern is full of period utensils and furnishings. It's located at 2002 Morningside Drive. Open Tuesday through Saturday, 11:00 a.m. to 5:00 p.m., May through October. Phone this special historical site at (423) 587–9900.

The first patented flying machine in America was developed by Melville Murrell, a Morristown preacher. Patented in 1877, a good while before the Wright brothers' flight, the ***Murrell Flyer*** flew several hundred yards under bicycle-type power. Parts of the original flyer, including its wings and some of the frame, are on display at the city's Rose Center. A video presentation features interviews with some of Murrell's descendants and several photos of the plane itself.

Built in 1892 and saved from destruction in 1975 by a community action group, the ***Rose Center*** was the area's first school. It now serves as a community cultural center and includes a history museum, art gallery, exhibit space, and gift shop. For specific information phone (423) 581–4330 or visit www .rosecenter.org.

TOP ANNUAL EVENTS

Winterfest,
November through February, Pigeon
Forge, Gatlinburg, Sevierville
(800) 251–9100

Dogwood Arts Festival,
month of April, Knoxville,
(865) 637–4561

**Townsend in the Smokies Spring
Festival,**
late April/early May, Townsend,
(865) 448–6134

**Festival of British &
Appalachian Culture,**
mid-May, Rugby,
(888) 214–3400

Del Rio Days,
crafts and food, late October, Del Rio,
(423) 625–9675

Each October, the **Mountain Makins Festival** is held on the grounds of the Rose Center and features one of East Tennessee's finest juried crafts shows. Two music stages spotlight various forms of local mountain music and other activities. Call (423) 581–4330.

Downtown Morristown is a busy business center, and there are several antiques and collectibles shops along Main Street.

Cosby was settled in 1783 by a corn farmer searching for a quiet, peaceful life. Corn remained the main crop for many years, and it didn't take long before the discovery was made that it was easier to transport corn in the liquid form known as moonshine. For many years the area was known as the **Moonshine Capital of the World.**

Apples are now considered one of the area's biggest cash crops, and there are five or six major orchards that sell directly from their farms. Also, many smaller orchards have been planted and produce excellent crops. Look for APPLES FOR SALE signs along the roads.

doubleletterduo

Tennessee and Mississippi are the only two states having three sets of double letters in their names. And they border each other!

One of the most popular year-round apple producers of the area is the **Kyle Carver Orchards,** located on U.S. Highway 321 South, about 5 miles from Interstate 40. The best time to visit is between mid-August and December— that's when most of the action takes place. They grow and sell many different varieties of apples on the farm and are known widely for their fresh fried apple pies. For $2 you get a huge, tasty, magnificent, and hot fried treat. Forget your diet. You can't find pies of this quality just anywhere!

Along with their apples, the Carvers also sell grapes, peaches, fresh vegetables, honey, jellies, jams, apple butter, molasses, cider, and other seasonal items. Ice cream and several apple products, including both fried and baked apple pies, are available. A candy store features locally produced chocolate candies and other homemade delicacies. The barn is open daily year-round 8:00 a.m. to 6:00 p.m. The orchards can be reached at (423) 487–2419.

Carver's Apple House Restaurant is located in the barn. According to Irene Carver, who runs the eatery for the family, the menu is "great country cooking," and "everything" is made from secret recipes and "that's why it's all so good." Well, secret or not, the chicken potpies are exceptional! Of course there are a lot of apple products on the menu, including apple fritters, apple pie cake, fried apples, and baked apple pies. The restaurant is open daily 8:00 a.m. to 8:00 p.m. Call (423) 487–2710.

The Tales of a Quilter's Husband

John Holloway is a quilter's husband. His wife, Maria, is owner of Holloway's Country Home quilt shop on US 321 near Cosby. John defines his position as "a sad individual whose only outlet is driving from quilt shop to quilt shop—except when the grass needs cutting." We don't know if he really feels that way, but maybe he does.

In any case, he certainly has a sense of humor. When Maria wrote a cookbook containing her favorite recipes and short stories about her special quilts, she asked John to put in a few of his own favorite recipes. He contributed 19 to her book, **Windows of My World.** The names alone are wonderful, but John's true humor comes out in his instructions for each. He admits about halfway through that all the recipes aren't his; some came from Jake, the resident squirrel who visits him in his workshop each day.

In addition to A Quilter's Husband's Groundhog Stew, where he explains how to catch a groundhog, he recalls how he learned to make A Quilter's Husband's Raccoon and Corn. "Walking through the woods one day, I came upon this raccoon. While holding him at gunpoint, I demanded that he tell me why he had been stealing my corn. He complied by giving me his recipe."

He explains how to gather mushrooms in his Mushrooms a la Jake. "An elf told me once that the best time to pick mushrooms is when you can walk under them. I guess that works great for elves, but we big people need another standard. Mine is when they are big enough to eat, go for it."

Maria includes an eclectic mix of recipes in the book, including a nice selection from her family's Portuguese heritage. The book is available at the shop or by calling (423) 487–3866.

Down the road from Carver's is a historical log cabin that houses **Holloway's Country Home.** Boasting that it has the largest selection of vintage quilts in the area, the shop also features locally woven and embroidered afghans, some of which sell for as low as $12 each. If you're a quilt maker, the shop carries a full line of fabrics, quilt kits, and supplies.

Headed up by Maria Holloway, the shop employs 40 full-time quilters to help keep her custom-made quilt inventory to more than 100 at any one time. Next to the rustic log cabin store, Maria has created a quilter's getaway, a kind of bed-and-breakfast for quilters. "It's a retreat where people can come and concentrate on nothing but quilting," she said. Located at 3892 US 321, just a few miles off I–40. Take exit 435 for Newport, and head toward Cosby. The shop is open daily, 9:00 a.m. to 5:00 p.m. Call first during winter, as they may close at times, at (423) 487–3866; online at www.hollowaysquilts.com.

The **ramp** is an onionlike vegetable native to the foothills of the southern Appalachian Mountains. The odd-looking plant has been described as the "vilest-smelling, sweetest-tasting vegetable in the world." Early settlers attributed special medicinal qualities to the ramp.

Raw, parboiled, fried, or scrambled in eggs, it was regarded as a necessary spring tonic to ward off the sluggishness of winter. In the 1950s Cosby introduced the ramp to the rest of the world when it established its first annual spring festival in the plant's honor. Each May thousands come here for the annual **Cosby Ramp Festival** to enjoy activities and eat truckloads of ramps.

In the county seat city of **Newport,** the **Cocke County Museum** is located upstairs in the Community Center building. Among items on display are many from Grace Moore, an internationally known opera singer and movie star who was born in the southern part of the county. Downstairs are the chamber of commerce and tourist information offices. This is a good place to start a tour of the county—at 433 Prospect Avenue, where access is free; call (423) 623–7201 or go to www.cockecounty.org.

One of the classiest bed-and-breakfast inns in this part of the state is located just outside Newport off English Mountain Road. **Christopher Place,** which classifies itself as an "Intimate Resort," is a true Four Diamond Smoky Mountain resort. *Vacations* magazine named the inn "one of the Top 10 romantic inns in America." Great views of the mountains, big and hearty breakfasts, and a nightly four-course dinner by candlelight are only a few of the amenities. Others include a heated pool, tennis courts, billiard room, fitness room, sauna, and a library filled with books, music, and movies.

Nine different rooms, all with private baths and luxurious furnishings, range in price from $175 to $350 per night. If you're looking for the best mountain view the inn has to offer, ask for the Camelot Room. Call (423) 623–6555 for specifics and availabilities; online go to www.stayatchristopherplace.com.

If you're looking for more of a rustic, off-the-beaten-path place to stay, you're only 15 miles away when you're in downtown Newport. To find **Meadow Creek Mountain Rustic Resort,** head out on US 321 to Parrotsville, the state's third-oldest town. Then you'll turn left, then right, then left, and then at the fork, you'll . . . well, you get the picture. This place is way out there in the proverbial boonies. It's located deep in the beautiful Cherokee National Forest on 100 acres of pristine mountain property.

There are ten individual cabins, sleeping anywhere from two to 12 per night. These are full-size cabins, each with bedrooms and private baths, air-conditioning, fireplaces, a gas grill and a hot tub on a private deck, satellite TV, and a kitchen. You can bring your own horse, or you can rent one from

Diane and Charlie Phillips, the proprietors of this fun, unique getaway and giddy-up resort.

In-season prices per cabin start at $110. You can grab some grub at the resort's Barnyard Cafe or create some fixin's in your own kitchen. For exact directions and reservations: (423) 623–7543 or www.meadowcreekmountain.com.

Located next to the popular Lake Douglas, *Dandridge* holds the distinction of being the only town in the United States named for *Martha Dandridge Washington,* George's wife, and today has a well-preserved downtown historic district to be quite proud of. Self-guided tour maps are available throughout town and at the *Jefferson County Museum,* located on the first level of the circa 1845 county courthouse. One of the unique holdings of this regional history museum is *Davy Crockett's marriage license.* Admission is free, and the museum is open during courthouse hours. Phone them at (865) 397–4904.

This community was quite the crossroads through the years. It was a regular stop for boats carrying provisions up and down the French Broad River, it was a major stage stop, and it was a road traveled by the stock traders operating between Tennessee and the Carolinas. As we know, wherever travelers gather, there will always be an abundance of taverns. Today three are still standing in Dandridge.

Almost swallowed by the waters when the Tennessee Valley Authority (TVA) dammed the river to create Lake Douglas in the early 1940s, Dandridge was saved thanks to local protests and the intervention of President Franklin Roosevelt. The million-dollar dike of native stone that holds back the waters today serves as backdrop to many of the historic buildings along Main Street. The lake dominates the outdoor activities in Dandridge as well as the entire county. The yacht club holds a July 4 boat parade, various fishing tournaments run throughout the year, and the lake is always dotted by the colorful sails of pleasure boaters enjoying themselves.

As a result of the dam and the abundance of water, the TVA built a hydroelectric plant that is still in operation today.

If possible, plan your visit to the area for the first Saturday in October. That's when *Jefferson City's Old Time Saturday* festival takes place. This one-day event mixes entertainment and food with a festive open-air market featuring local arts and crafts. Find out more at (865) 475–9071.

The *Glenmore Mansion* is considered by many architects as an almost perfect example of second-empire Victorian architecture. Built in 1869, the 27-room, five-story mansion is fully furnished with antiques of the period. In eastern Tennessee, where most historical preservation efforts are saved for pre-1850 architecture, it's good to see the preservation of the Victorian era.

The mansion is located at 1280 North Chucky Pike in Jefferson City. It's open Saturday and Sunday afternoons from 1:00 to 5:00 p.m., May through October and for special events. Call (865) 475–5014.

Great Smoky Mountains National Park

As the most visited national park in the country, with ten million visitors a year, the **Great Smoky Mountains National Park** is hardly off the beaten path. But the 500,000-acre facility is so large and has so many nooks and crannies that it isn't difficult to get away from the madding crowds.

There are established camping areas throughout the park, but camping is also permitted in the undeveloped regions. Special backcountry permits are needed for that.

The Sugarland Visitors Center, located 2 miles inside the park from Gatlinburg, has maps and other information about the entire park, as well as exhibits on what one will most likely see during a visit.

Featuring more species of plants than any other area on our continent, this official **International Biosphere Reserve** is a true gem in Tennessee travel opportunities.

Within the boundaries there are 16 peaks towering above 6,000 feet, including **Clingman's Dome,** which, at 6,643 feet, is the highest point in Tennessee. For information and a list of events, call (865) 436–5615; also go to their Web site at www.nps.gov/grsm.

One of the park's most unusual attractions is **LeConte Lodge,** a great (but rugged and rustic) place to stay while in the mountains if you enjoy walking. In fact, that's the only way you can get there, and it's not the easiest walk you'll ever make. The lodge rests atop the third-highest peak in the park, making it the highest guest lodge in the eastern United States. The shortest (and steepest) hike to the lodge is 5.5 miles long, which is about a four-hour hike for a person in good condition. Once there you'll find no electricity, phones, or showers—just a great view and wonderful food. Rates start at $100 per adult, per night, and include dinner and breakfast. Call (865) 429–5704 or check out www.lecontelodge.com.

Gateway to the Smokies

The tourist destination city of **Gatlinburg** is located near the main entrance to the park and is considered its main gateway. Souvenir and craft shops and various attractions line the main streets, while honeymoon houses and motels line the backstreets.

Gatlinburg officials have put together one of the most helpful tourism Web sites in the state: www.gatlinburg.com. You can also call (800) 565–7329 for information. Among the attractions here you'll find something to please everyone. The parkway strip is lined with fun, colorful, and often macabre things to see and do. Don't miss *Ripley's Believe It or Not!,* up from the *Guinness World Records Museum,* across from the *Sky Lift,* and under the *Space Needle.*

High atop Mt. Harrison, overlooking Gatlinburg is the *Ober Gatlinburg Amusement Park and Ski Resort.* It's a fun, year-round facility that has a mountain resort feel to it even though it's just up the mountain from Gatlinburg's touristy downtown area.

In the summer there are amusement rides, an alpine slide, a water ride, miniature golf, go-karts, and other outdoor fun. In the winter there is snow skiing. Indoors, and open year-round, is a large ice-skating rink, shops, a lounge, restaurants, and a wonderful little fudge maker!

Gatlinburg's Municipal Black Bear Habitat is located here and provides some great close-up views of the bears. There is also a Black Bear gift shop, museum, and a short film on the species.

A quick but somewhat expensive way to get to the top is via the celebrated tramway. It's free if you have ski lift tickets, and it takes you directly to the top of the mountain. If you have a car full and want to save some money, you can drive to the top and park directly adjacent to all the activity.

The tram is at Traffic Light #9. If you want to drive, go to the end of the parkway; just before you enter the national park, turn right for Ski Mountain Road. Go to the end, and there it is. Call (865) 436–5423; their Web site is www.obergatlinburg.com.

If you're looking for some of the best fine artwork and crafts the state has to offer, a drive through the *Great Smoky Arts & Crafts Community* is a must. It's an 8-mile auto loop that features dozens of independent artists and craftspeople with cafes, restaurants, and lodging sprinkled throughout. Many shops are grouped with others in large complexes, while some are set off by themselves.

Designated as a Tennessee Heritage Arts & Crafts Trail, the community was established in 1937. Along the route, artisans whittle, paint, sew, cast, weave, and carve to create original pieces of art, such as candles, baskets, quilts, brooms, pottery, jewelry, dolls, ceramics, scrimshaw, leather, stained glass, fine photography, and just about anything else you can think of. In all, there are 78 stops. Most of the shops are open daily during the summer. They may close completely during the winter or at best have reduced hours of operation. Call first! (Speaking of calling, you're in the mountains here and there's a very good chance your cell phone won't work, so plan accordingly.)

A good place to start (and finish) the loop is 3 miles out of Gatlinburg from Traffic Light #3, on US 321. You'll see a big green sign with GREAT SMOKY ARTS & CRAFTS COMMUNITY printed in white letters with arrows pointing the way. Turn left onto Glades Road near McDonald's, and the art-venture begins.

You'll definitely want to stop at the **Glades Center,** one of the first major complexes on the right, at King Road. There are nine shops here, and across the street in the Morning Mist Village, there are nearly 25 more arts and crafts shops.

However, before you start your journey through all the shops, stop by the **Mountain Visions Gallery,** owned by Steve and Terri Shoemaker. Steve is a nationally known nature photographer who now specializes in unique scenes of the Smoky Mountains. Some great stuff on the walls in this shop! Steve is also a good one to know if you're looking for some expert advice on quiet hiking trails; he'll be glad to point the way. The gallery is at 600 Glades Road, No. 6; call (865) 430–1994, or go to www.mountainvisions gallery.com.

What started as a co-op for female artists, the **Cliff Dwellers** is now owned by six women who represent approximately 66 other local artists, both male and female. Their building was originally built in downtown Gatlinburg in 1933 and moved to its current location in 1993. On special days you might find a craft demonstration by a participating artist in anything from glass working and painting to creating wooden bowls on a lathe. This is one of the most interesting stops along the trail. Their address is 668 Glades Road. Find out more at (865) 436–6921.

At the end of Glades Road, just around the corner on Buckhorn Road, is Hemlock Village, with several different shops. The largest is **Highland Craft Gallery,** which represents more than 70 different artists offering an eclectic selection of fine crafts. By the way, a photo of many of the represented artists hangs on the wall, so you can see whom you're buying from! Phone them at (865) 430–8951.

And if you're still hungry, check out the charming **Wild Plum Tea Room** in a log cabin setting, just past Hemlock Village at 555 Buckhorn Road. Open only for lunch, this popular eatery, known for its signature chicken salad and Wild Plum Tea, is a peaceful and relaxing stop along the way as you ponder what great art must find its way into your suitcase. You can contact them at (865) 436–3808. Farther down the road, on your left just before you get back to US 321, be sure to stop at **Turtle Hollow Gallery** and **J. Allen Gallery**— both of whose art offerings could go up against any big city gallery. They represent unique, top-quality artisans featuring traditional and contemporary crafts—many of them a one-of-a-kind. Call (865) 430–5904.

The community sponsors three annual shows, all held at the Gatlinburg Convention Center at Traffic Light #8 in downtown Gatlinburg, with free admission. For more information check out the community's Web site: www .artsandcraftscommunity.com.

Since parking is at such a premium in Gatlinburg, perhaps the best deal in town is the 50-cent ride on its rapid transit system, the trolley. During peak season the entire city can become one large parking lot, so find a place to park on the edge of town or at your hotel and rely on the trolley.

The nation's earliest Fourth of July parade takes place on the streets of Gatlinburg each year at 12:01 a.m. July 4. Floats, bands, and huge helium balloons go by as more than 80,000 annually gather for the "Midnight Parade."

The **Hillbilly Golf Course** may well be one of the most unusual miniature golf courses in the world. To get to the first hole, you must ride an incline up to a point 300 feet above the city. Two 18-hole courses, with all sorts of mountaineer hazards, including a genuine outhouse and a moonshine still, are carved out of the mountainside. It's near Traffic Light #2; for more information call (865) 436–7470.

If you happen to be a Ripley's fan, Gatlinburg is heaven. Five of the company's top attractions are located in the city, including its newest, the high-tech and high-fun **Davy Crockett Mini-Golf** course, located at Traffic Light #1. Here you'll find two 18-hole courses with animated figures and interactive holes. Where else can you be chided by a couple of old crows if you miss a putt? This neat place stands out from all the other miniature golf courses in the area! Open year-round, weather permitting. Call (865) 430–8851.

Moving on down the parkway toward the Great Smoky Mountains National Park, on your right at Traffic Light #5 you'll find the world-acclaimed **Ripley's Aquarium of the Smokies.** The fun starts here as you drive up. It's one of the most amazing structures in the state, and there's a real sense of arrival. Inside, there are many great exhibits, including a moving walkway under a large habitat that houses sharks (some up to 11 feet) and thousands of colorful tropical fish. Another fascinating exhibit contains jellyfish highlighted by special lighting and classical music. You'll rarely see anything more calming and surreal in your life! Open daily, year-round. Need more information? Phone (888) 240–1358 or go to www.ripleysaquariumofthesmokies.com.

At Traffic Light #7 is **Ripley's Believe It or Not! Museum** of the weird and unusual. From shrunken heads and matchstick sculptures to vampire killing kits and pieces of the Berlin Wall, the odditorium has one-of-a-kind items. There are original Robert Ripley cartoons, and you'll get a chance to see clips of the *Ripley's Believe it or Not!* television show featuring Dean Cain. A fun place for everyone in the family! Open daily, year-round. Call (865) 436–5096 or www.ripleysgatlinburg.com.

Ripley's Moving Theater and **Ripley's Haunted Adventure** are located next to each other at Traffic Light #8. Both are open daily, year-round. You'll ride along with the 3-D film at the Moving Theater, which is quite fun. Remember to hold on, and eat lunch afterward, not before! Get a chance to explore your nightmare at the Haunted Adventure. Created on the site of the old Grimsby & Streaper Casket Company, the haunted house has live actors and classy scare techniques and is quite a long walk through. They suggest you hold hands to keep from getting lost. Not a bad suggestion. Call (865) 436–9763—if you dare!—for the Moving Theater and (865) 430–9991 for the Haunted Adventure or check out www.ripleysgatlinburg.com.

The **Peddler Restaurant** has the best view, the best ambience, and the best salad bar (can you say smoked oysters?) of any restaurant in town. Located at 820 River Road, the restaurant and bar are located on the edge of the river, and even if you're not lucky enough to get a window table, you still have a lot to look at. People come from all over for the steak, huge salad bar, and grilled fresh salmon. The place is always busy, and although they don't take reservations, you can call ahead and get your name placed on the waiting list. If you get there and there's a long list, go back to the lounge, which also offers great river views. If you find a table you like there, go ahead and order and enjoy your meal in the bar. It's the same menu as the dining room. The locals love this place, and it has been locally owned and operated since 1977. Their number is (865) 436–5794.

Known for romantic wedding chapels, Gatlinburg and the Smoky Mountains have plenty of opportunities for those looking for a memorable wedding. If you're looking for something quite different and a bit funky and fun, call the Hillbilly Minister and he'll arrange a true **Hillbilly Wedding** for you. The minister says he offers a "nontraditional and no-frills approach, yet with reverence and dignity." He'll come to your hotel or cottage, or he can suggest a great location in the mountains. Call him at (865) 436–3817.

And speaking of memorable, a great home base while you're enjoying the area is one of the nearly two dozen bed-and-breakfasts in the Smokies. They are all unique, with different amenities, and all offer spectacular breakfasts. Find a listing of the best at www.smokymountainbb.com.

With hundreds of nationally known craftspeople living and working around the Smoky Mountain region, you can only imagine the scope of arts and crafts, paintings, furniture making, and wood carvings you'll find at the **Gatlinburg Craftsmen's Fair,** held twice a year at the Gatlinburg Convention

Center (Traffic Light #8). There's a weeklong summer event in late July and a two-week fair in mid-October.

In addition to local and regional craftspeople, the best from around the country also take part in these events, and there is always live music, from bluegrass to mountain music, being performed on the trade show floor. Admission is charged. Find out more at (865) 436–7479 or www.craftsmensfair.com.

Head north on U.S. Highway 441 out of Gatlinburg, go through a part of the national forest, and 5 miles later you'll be in *Pigeon Forge,* where a 50-cent trolley ride with 50 stops helps you avoid traffic congestion. Similar to Gatlinburg in its attractions, this city's main draw is country singer Dolly Parton's theme park, *Dollywood.* Country music prevails in the park, as do country crafts and good country cooking.

Even if you're one who doesn't like theme parks, chances are very good you'll love this place, which is more of a trip into mountain culture than it is an amusement ride park. Craftsmen's Valley offers a shady walk through a genuine holler past all sorts of working craftspeople, chefs cooking in huge cast-iron skillets over open fires, and a winding brook. The steam train takes you on a 5-mile journey to the top of the ridge and back and is one ride you definitely need to take. The Thunderhead wooden roller coaster offers a 100-foot drop at speeds of 55 mph! Whew!!!

There are plenty of other great rides, but most people don't come to Dollywood for the rides. The live shows, as you can imagine, are quite well done, with many of Dolly's relatives performing. Food? Did I mention that the food here is about the best you'll find at any theme park in the world? Great Southern cooking at its finest! Throughout the year there are special festivals inside the park, including a traditional Smoky Mountain Christmas celebration and a fall Harvest Festival. A summer concert series features more than 40 top names in country music.

"In by 3, next day free" is the policy here. Travel into the area, pay to get in, and have a nice relaxing dinner at one of the park's restaurants. Leave, get a good night's rest, and come back the next day for free!

Next door is *Dolly's Splash Country,* a waterpark that opened in 2001. You won't find a tropical theme here. No pastels or palm trees. Instead you'll find a re-created Smoky Mountain watering hole, complete with waterfalls, winding streams, and plenty of earth tones and rustic architecture. It's a fun and laid-back way to cool off.

Dollywood is open from spring through the first week of January; the waterpark is open from May through Labor Day. A money-saving combo pass is available if you want to go to both parks. Call (865) 428–9488 or (800) Dollywood, or visit www.dollywood.com.

If you haven't driven through Pigeon Forge lately, you're in for a surprise. Where the Music Mansion used to be at 100 Music Road, there is now an upside-down building. That's right. **WonderWorks** looks as though it has been picked up and tossed upside down. Sure makes you wonder. And that's the whole point. Everything in WonderWorks is fun and has some sort of educational purpose.

Opened in June 2006, WonderWorks mixes fantasy and reality. It's a place where the unexplainable comes to life and natural mysteries are explored. This is done with sophisticated graphic and audio techniques. WonderWorks even has a tale to explain how it came to be. The story is pure fantasy, of course. Legend has it that an experiment on a remote island off the Atlantic coast went awry. During an attempt to harness the power of a man-made tornado, the giant swirling vortex spun out of control and took on a life of its own. The energy vortex was so powerful that it sent the entire structure skyward, hundreds of miles away, where it landed upside down in the heart of Pigeon Forge. The attraction has more than 100 interactive, hands-on exhibits. It also offers a great dinner theater. The Hoot 'n' Holler Dinner Show serves a family-style meal of salad, bread, lasagna, shells with cheese, chicken parmesan, and strawberry shortcake—along with an old-fashioned vaudeville show with plenty of singing, dancing, comedy, and audience participation. Call (865) 868–1800, or visit www.wonderworkstn.com.

Sounds of "Silent Night" fill the air. Santa Claus greets children of all ages. Stockings are hung by the chimney with care. And glittering Christmas trees brighten the winter night. Scenes like this are familiar during the holiday season. But at **The Inn at Christmas Place,** it is Christmas every day. Opened June 15, 2007, the new Smoky Mountain destination has been drawing visitors no matter the season. The Inn at Christmas Place is open year-round and filled with all the joys of the holiday season—no matter what the weather may be outside. Featuring the mountain-village architecture of the European Alps, the inn offers luxurious Old World charm including copper crowned turrets, a stone terraced courtyard, two large ponds with natural stone waterfalls, and landscaped gardens.

Uniformed bellmen and caroling figurines welcome guests through custom-etched glass doors into a holiday wonderland. Guest rooms also are clad in holiday finery, including two- and three-room suites with full-size decorated trees, fireplaces, two-person whirlpools, and private balconies overlooking the courtyard. A stay at the inn includes a complimentary breakfast with country style buffet items and an omelet bar. Located across the parkway from **The Incredible Christmas Place and Village** shops, the inn is within easy walking distance of many Pigeon Forge attractions. For guests who appreciate the inn's decor so much that they would like to add it to their own homes, most of the items are sold at The Incredible Christmas Place and Village shops. Not surprising, since the Biggs family who started The Incredible Christmas Place more than two decades ago are also owners of The Inn at Christmas Place. Call (888) 465–9644 or check out the Web site at www.innatchristmasplace.com.

If you're a real Elvis fan, you can get a good fix by visiting the ***Elvis Museum,*** where you'll see the King's last limousine, his *Double Trouble* tuxedo, and the one-of-a-kind "TCB" (Taking Care of Business, his motto) ring he designed and wore throughout his career. The ring alone is valued at more than $250,000. Of course there is a full line of the wonderfully kitsch Elvis souvenirs in the gift shop, along with plenty of CDs, cassettes, videotapes, and DVDs. There is an admission fee for the museum but none for the gift shop. Located on the parkway, 1 block south of Ogle's Waterpark. Call (865) 428–2001. (For much more on Elvis see the Memphis listing in the last chapter of this book.)

The ***Dixie Stampede*** has an interesting concept for a dinner theater. While eating a Southern feast, patrons watch a live show in the central dirt-covered arena. The Western Show features 30 horses, Conestoga wagons, pig racing, bull riding, steer wrestling, and a bunch more good-old-boy activities. For added flavor the Northerners sit on one side, the Southerners on the other. Reservations are sometimes necessary. Call (865) 453–4400 or (800) 356–1676, or go to www.dixiestampede.com.

Another feature of the Dixie Stampede is the ***world's largest stick-horse collection,*** which is displayed throughout the venue. An offhand comment is what started it all. Dan Cavanah had a friend in Seattle with many fine horses. When he retired, Cavanah told his buddy that he would gather an even larger herd, the biggest in all of Florida. When he got home from visiting Seattle, Cavanah received a gag gift from his pal—a stick horse to get him started on his herd. That was in 1990. Since then, Cavanah has collected more than 500 stick-horse pieces. In November 2002 he was honored by the *Guinness Book of World Records* for having the world-record stick horse collection.

As his collection increased, Cavanah decided he wanted to display his stick horses where others could enjoy them. After checking out various places, Cavanah settled on Dixie Stampede in Pigeon Forge. With its horse-related show, Cavanah figured his make-believe mounts would fit right in. The stick horses were delivered to Dixie Stampede in April 2004. The amazing collection is displayed everywhere inside Dixie Stampede, from the theater to the entrance hall to the carriage room and from the lobby to the gift shop. There's a Davy Crockett stick horse, an orange one autographed by country singer Tammy Wynette, a Lone Ranger stick horse, Gumby's horse Pokey, Roy

A Veterans' Thank-You

Pigeon Forge throws a big party each August to say "thank you" to our country's military veterans. The city is loaded with activities, including a land and air parade, lectures, educational forums, keynote speeches by well-known American veterans, a military history book fair, static aircraft displays, canteen dances, war story storytelling, and a huge picnic. The two-week **Celebrate Freedom** event is sponsored by the city of Pigeon Forge, with help from the University of Tennessee and the Center for the Study of War and Society. Contact them at (865) 453–8574 or www.my pigeonforge.com.

Rogers's Trigger, and many more. Some have wheels that make a galloping noise, while others have reins with bells, yarn manes, and moving mouths. A 1950s model is battery operated to make a whinnying sound. Call (800) 356–1676 for information.

Another unique dining opportunity in Pigeon Forge is **Mel's Diner,** where the good ole days of rock and roll are featured on the menu, on the walls, and on the jukebox. Located at 119 Wears Valley Road, one road west of the parkway, in an authentic stainless-steel diner, Mel's features a fun, tasty menu. The half-pound burgers are called Jukebox Heroes, and among the offerings are the Beach Boy Basic Burger, the Chubby Checker Cheeseburger, Marilyn's Mushroom Burger, and the Little Deuce Coupe Cajun Burger. The Sandwich Favorites include the Hot Diggity Dog, the Bette Davis B.L.T., James Dean Grilled Chicken, and the Doo Wah Diddy Philly Chicken Cheese. Starters include Fonzarelli Cheese Sticks, Potsy's Potato Salad, Ralph Malph Nachos, and Chachi's Cheese Nachos. The kid's menu is called Little Anthony's, and the wonderful thick and creamy milk shakes can be found under the Shake, Rattle & Roll heading.

Next to the vintage jukebox is a sign that reads IF MUSIC IS TOO LOUD, YOU'RE TOO OLD, and near the cash register a sign proclaims IF YOU THINK YOU HAVE A RESERVATION, YOU'RE IN THE WRONG PLACE. This is a fun, quality eatery. Open daily. Call them at (865) 429–2184.

The country's first indoor skydiving simulator, **Flyaway,** bills itself as America's "most unique" sports attraction. You suit up and ride in a vertical wind tunnel with wind speeds up to 115 mph, and as you float and fly in the air current, you're never more than 5 or 6 feet from a padded landing spot or from the arms of your personal flight attendant. Each flyer receives training, and the entire experience will last about an hour. A video machine is running so that you can take your experience home with you and impress your friends.

The flight costs $27.95, plus tax, and anyone under 18 must be accompanied by a parent. Located at Traffic Light #5, 3106 Parkway. Call them at (865) 453–7777 or (877) 293–0639; www.flyawayindoorskydiving.com.

Elvis Presley's Mercedes-Benz is just one of the 30 cars on display at the *Smoky Mountain Car Museum.* Al Capone's bullet-proof Cadillac is here, as is Sheriff Buford Pusser's Oldsmobile patrol car. Hank Williams Jr.'s silver dollar car and one of James Bond's 007 cars are also on display. Open seasonally, daily during summer peak periods. This fascinating museum is on 2970 Parkway, next to the Mountain Breeze Motel; call (865) 453–3433.

Applewood Farms is located just off US 441 at 230 Apple Valley Road, right where Pigeon Forge and Sevierville meet. Part of a working apple orchard, the barn was converted into a cider mill in 1981, just in time to attract people from 45 different states and ten foreign countries who were in the area visiting the 1982 *World's Fair* in nearby Knoxville. Owners Bill Kilpatrick and Bon Hicks knew they had something going and started to expand.

Today, in addition to the cider mill, they have a bakery, a winery featuring apple and other fruit wines, an apple butter kitchen, a fudge kitchen, a candy factory, an ice-cream factory specializing in apple-flavored ice cream, a smokehouse, a Christmas and candle shop, and a gift shop featuring crafts, gifts, and souvenir items. In 1987 their old farmhouse home was turned into the *Applewood Farmhouse Restaurant.* On the menu you'll find traditional items such as prime rib and steaks, but you'll also find a local favorite, fresh Smoky Mountain trout. One of the favorites is trout cake, made from crumbled trout mixed with cheese and onions. But save room for some wonderful apple

Hike with a Personal Guide

If you've thought about hiking in the Smokies but thought you didn't know enough about the mountains or about hiking, here's a unique opportunity to enjoy the area on foot. Liz Domingue, owner of *Outdoor Adventures,* located in the Wears Valley area of Sevierville, is a noted naturalist and wildlife biologist who has hiked the world over in the name of environmental science. She teaches environmental education for the University of Tennessee's Smoky Mountain Field School and for several other environmental organizations.

Give her a call and she'll custom-fit a hike to your interests and skill level. She is an expert on the salamanders, frogs, and birds of the Great Smoky Mountains and can talk with you about the cultural as well as the natural history of the mountains as she points out all the various flora and fauna. She also knows where all the neatest views and waterfalls are located. Prices start at $50 per day per person for groups of five or more. Reach them at (865) 774–5885, or visit www.justgetoutdoors.com.

dessert. The homemade apple pies are always a favorite, but the apple fritters, accompanied by homemade apple butter, are also high on the list for apple lovers. Located across the road from the Little Pigeon River, there are plenty of huge shade trees to sit under while you wait your turn. There was such a demand for their food that the owners decided to build a second eatery on the property in 1995 so that they wouldn't have to turn away so many hungry friends. Now the *Applewood Farms Grill* offers the same menu, plus some lighter options for those who want to sample the different foods without digging into a full meal. Open daily for breakfast, lunch, and dinner. There are special meals and hours for Thanksgiving and Christmas. Call (865) 453–9319 or go to www.applemillciderbarn.com for more information.

About 4 miles north on US 441, or the *Dolly Parton Parkway,* as they call it around here, is the downtown section of Dolly's hometown, *Sevierville.* Stop and ask about her and you'll be amazed at how many "good friends" this lady has. Less commercial than the other communities along US 441, the downtown section has retained most of its small, mountain atmosphere. On a walking tour of 26 historic landmarks, you'll get to see a life-size bronze statue of Dolly.

Billing itself as the World's Largest Live Reptile Zoo, the *Rainforest Adventure* takes you on a fun journey into the mysteries of the world's rain forests. In here you'll find hundreds of cool-looking species in natural habitats. Look close, because they'll be looking back at *you!* There are snakes, gators, amphibians, spiders, and scorpions and several live shows daily. Open daily year-round, 9:00 a.m. to 5:00 p.m. Located in Governor's Crossing, across from Wal-Mart. Call (865) 428–4091.

Heading to *Knoxville* from Sevierville on U.S. Highway 441/411, you'll pass an abundance of antiques and craft shops, potteries, and souvenir and gift shops. When the highways split, continue on US 441 into Knoxville until you cross the Tennessee River. That big golden ball you see high in the air to your left as you cross the river is the *Sunsphere,* the 300-foot-tall centerpiece of the 1982 World's Fair.

Adjacent to the fair site is the *Knoxville Museum of Art,* with a fine permanent collection as well as 12 exhibitions a year to choose from. On most Friday nights during the year, a special Alive After Five program features jazz and blues music from 5:30 to 8:00 p.m. The $8 admission gets you the music and access to the exhibits. A cash bar and light appetizers are available. The museum is open Tuesday through Sunday. For more information call (865) 525–6101.

A great way to start a visit in Knoxville is at the *Gateway Regional Visitor Center,* located downtown on the riverfront. The complex serves as an orientation and link not only to Knoxville but to a region within a radius of 100 miles. Inside, there are three main exhibit areas; outside, waterfalls and native plantings show the botanical and geological diversity of the area. There's a lot of cool stuff to learn here! A boardwalk along the river provides great views, and a restaurant offers an eclectic menu. Open daily. The center's phone number is (800) 727–8045; their Web site is www .knoxville.org.

Across the street from the Gateway is the ***Women's Basketball Hall of Fame.*** It's located under the huge 30-foot-wide, 20,000-pound orange basketball. Although I have never counted them, officials say there are 96,000 pebbles on that ball. I'll take their word. Inside the entranceway is a spectacular 17-foot-tall, three-player bronze sculpture. There are exhibits, videos, and memorabilia from all facets of women's basketball—from collegiate to professional. Open daily except Thanksgiving, Christmas, and Easter. Admission is $7.95 for adults, $5.95 for seniors and children ages six to 15. Call (865) 633–9000, or go to www.wbhof.com.

See the Warbirds

The *Tennessee Museum of Aviation* is home to resident warbirds and is intended to be patriotic, educational, and entertaining. It certainly achieves all three! Even if you're not particularly interested in aviation or war history, this is a compelling, emotional stop. We guarantee you'll end up with a couple lumps in your throat.

Located in a 50,000-square-foot hangar next to the Gatlinburg–Pigeon Forge Airport, along Dolly Parton Parkway in Sevierville, the museum has a collection of functional warbirds, including two rare P-47D aircraft, a P-47 Thunderbolt, a Mig-17, and a T-6 trainer. Planes will be flown in, flown out, and rotated in the exhibit lineup.

Exhibits include a comprehensive historical timeline, uniforms, memorabilia, plane engines, and jeeps. Among the prized possessions is the Congressional Medal of Honor presented to aviator general Jimmy Doolittle in 1942. Also on display is an in-depth look at the roots of flight through the eyes of the Wright Brothers; it showcases their first ten years of flying experimentation, complete with models of nine of the planes they built during that time.

The mission of the privately owned museum is to preserve an understanding and appreciation for the aircraft and those who flew them to change the course of American history. There is a gift shop, and the museum is also home to Tennessee's Official Aviation Hall of Fame. Open daily, year-round. Just call (865) 908–0171.

The museum's Web page is one of the neatest sites I've ever seen. There is plenty of music, plenty of action, and a great deal of information about the museum at www .tnairmuseum.com.

Knoxville is the site of the main campus of the **University of Tennessee,** where the Volunteers play their football games in the 95,000-plus-seat **Neyland Stadium.** It's only natural that tailgate partiers would adapt to the unique position of the stadium next to the Tennessee River. The Volunteer Navy, as it is called here, starts gathering as early as the Thursday before a Saturday game, and by game time as many as 300 boats have tied up. The only traffic these folks have to contend with is walking across the street to the stadium. Washington State is the only other major college stadium in the nation accessible by water.

Colorful "Big Orange" football is king in the fall, but the pinks and whites of flowering dogwood dominate the city's attention each spring. City officials estimate that about a million such trees bloom in their city each year. A Dogwood Arts Festival is held annually during late April with arts, crafts, and other activities. There are six designated "dogwood trails" in the city for self-guided tours. Free bus tours leave from the festival grounds at Market Square Mall.

You won't find any chain stores or nationally known restaurants in the **Old City area** of Knoxville. What you'll find is a several-block area of one-of-a-kind shops, restaurants, bars, and music clubs that feature everything from jazz to reggae.

The hub of the Old City is at the junction of Jackson Avenue and Central Street in the northeastern section of downtown Knoxville. The area is a product of the period when the railroad made the city a center for commerce by delivering merchandise to the many huge 19th-century brick warehouses in the neighborhood.

The Old City's charm adds a perfect backdrop to various festivals and events during the year, including a Blues Fest and Rib Cook-off, a Halloween Carnival, and an Oktoberfest. Don't miss the fun: Call (800) 727–8045, www .knoxville.org.

In Morningside Park, near downtown, is the largest statue of an African American in the United States. The 13-foot-tall bronze statue honors Tennessee's own **Alex Haley,** author of numerous novels, including *Roots*. Designed

Birthplace of a Phrase Maker

"Damn the torpedoes! Full speed ahead." That well-known command was given by David Farragut, a Civil War admiral of the Union navy during the battle of Mobile Bay. He was born in Knoxville, and today the community where he grew up is named for him.

for interaction, the statue depicts Haley with an open book as if he's reading to children; it's a popular setting for photos. Phone (800) 727–8045 or visit www.knoxville.org.

Dedicated in 1998, the **War Dog Memorial** commemorates all the dogs that served during World War II. It's located in front of the University of Tennessee's Veterinary Hospital at 2407 River Drive. A touching memorial, it can be reached at (865) 974–5869.

The **Bijou Theatre,** Knoxville's third-oldest building, is on the National Register of Historic Places and is a fun place to attend a concert or a live stage production. Located at 803 South Gay Street, the restored relic houses all sorts of events, plays, and concerts throughout the year. Call (865) 522–0832, or go to www.knoxbijou.com.

The **Three Rivers Rambler** train excursion is one of the best in the South. The 90-minute trip aboard a vintage train pulled by a 1925 Baldwin steam engine, affectionately known as *Lindy,* runs parallel to the Tennessee River, providing some great views. It passes through the historical areas of the city, past industrial plants, and through farmland.

Where the Holston and French Broad Rivers converge to form the head of the Tennessee River, the train crosses the Holston River on the historic Three Rivers Trestle. On the way back, the engineer will usually slow way down or stop on the trestle, allowing passengers to take in a fabulous view!

There is food and drink in the club car, and passengers are permitted to bring a picnic lunch if they desire.

You can choose to ride in a plush circa 1925 Pullman car, a circa 1932 enclosed passenger car, or an open-air gondola car. Adult rates are $20 to $26. The train loads at Volunteer Landing, downtown on the Tennessee River, and runs Saturday and Sunday from late March through December, except for home football game Saturdays. For more information call (865) 524–9411, or go to www.threeriversrambler.com.

East Tennessee's preeminent fair, the **Tennessee Valley Fair,** takes place in early September each year in Chilhowee Park, 4 miles east of downtown. There's top-name entertainment, livestock and agriculture shows, carnival rides, and plenty of great old-time fair flavor. Admission is charged. Call (865) 637–5840 to find out more.

Another example of the old-time company town is found along U.S. Highway 129 south of Knoxville. Incorporated in 1919, the city of **Alcoa** was created by the Aluminum Company of America (ALCOA). Corporate offices are in Pittsburgh, but the southern plant opened in 1913 in a town called North Maryville. Six years later, with the financial help of the corporation, the city was created and its name changed.

Sam Houston, Davy Crockett's good friend, came to Blount County with his family when he was 14 years of age and in due time developed a fascination for the lifestyle of the neighboring Cherokee Indians. Soon he was adopted by the Cherokees, who called him The Raven.

He left the Indians to take a teaching position in a one-room schoolhouse near Maryville. He had little formal education but had read every book he could get his hands on, had won every spelling contest he entered, and could recite large portions of Homer's *Iliad* from memory. His teaching career lasted one term. In March 1813 he gave up teaching to enlist in General Andrew Jackson's army to fight the Creek Indian War.

The schoolhouse where he taught still stands and is considered the oldest original schoolhouse in the state and the only building left having a close association with this famous soldier and statesman. Built in 1794, the school now houses many Houston artifacts, including a pair of lead knuckles with his name carved in the soft metal. The guide at the **Sam Houston Schoolhouse** speculates whether he used them to keep order in the classroom.

The site also includes a visitor center and museum exhibits. It's located 6 miles north of Maryville on Sam Houston Schoolhouse Road, off Highway 33. Open year-round; admission for adults, $1; children under 10, free. For further information call (865) 983–1550.

Before the Smoky Mountains became a national park in 1935, the little community of **Townsend** was a major lumbering center. The Little River Railroad and Lumber Company, headed by Col. W. B. Townsend, set up mills and harvested logs from the rich, fertile forests that are now federal lands.

Today very little of that heritage exists except in memory and old photos. In the center of town you'll find the **Little River Railroad and Lumber Company Museum.** Among its memorabilia are a restored Shay Engine No. 2147 that was used locally during the early 1900s and an L&N Class NE Little Woody vintage caboose.

A restored train depot serves as a museum that's filled with memorabilia and photos of early railroad and lumbering industries. It's open daily during the summer; weekends during April, May, and September. Admission is free. Need more information? Call (865) 428–0099, or go to www.littleriver railroad.org.

Sandy Headrick is one of the dedicated group members that run the museum, and she can be found across the street at the resort facility she owns and operates with her husband, Don. The Tudor-style **Highland Manor Inn** has a classy country inn atmosphere. The views from the balconies offer a spectacular vista of the Smokies, and several rooms have private whirlpool baths. It's located up on a hill, off US 321, near the center of town. In-season

room rates start at $79.50. Call them at (865) 448–2211; their Web site is www
.highlandmanor.com.

Townsend calls itself "The Peaceful Side of the Smokies," referring to the
fact that it is still quite laid-back and low-key, while the cities on the other
side of the mountain, Pigeon Forge and Gatlinburg, are bustling tourist mag-
nets. However, there is still a great deal to do here, especially if you love the
outdoors.

You're only 8 miles from one of the national park's premier attractions
when you're in Townsend. *Cades Cove* was a thriving mountain community
in the 1850s with about 685 residents and 15,000 acres of usable farmland
under cultivation. Today the area is as it was then, with original buildings in
original locations, so visitors can get a true sense of the spaciousness of early
mountain life. An 11-mile self-guided auto loop tour gives the best idea of
the culture of the region. Most homes, churches, and stores are open to the
public.

The *Foothills Parkway,* which runs from US 321 near Walland for 17
miles, is a magnificent stretch of road that provides some great scenic pull-off
opportunities that give you superb panoramic views of the mountains.

While it's always beautiful around here, our favorite time to visit is in the
spring. Wildflowers seem to be growing everywhere you look! The mountains and valleys are carpeted with mountain phlox, dwarf irises, trilliums,
and pink lady's slippers. Dogwoods, redbuds, and azaleas also add their
color. The temperatures are usually comfortable, and the hiking and biking
are superb!

If you're interested in hopping on a horse and doing some trail riding
in the mountains, give the expert horsemen at the *Davy Crockett Riding
Stables* a call at (865) 448–6411. They are located at 505 Old Cades Cove
Road.

Billing itself as the "greatest sight under the Smokies," the *Tuckaleechee
Caverns* is a fun diversion if you get tired of always going up into the mountains. Here's your chance to go *under* things. It's always 58 degrees, and
some of the formations and cave rooms are quite spectacular. These lovely
caverns are open March through November and located off US 321. Call (865)
448–2274.

The Townsend Visitor Center on Lamar Alexander Parkway is the place
to start your visit to this part of the state. In addition to having just about all
the information you need, the Carl Koella Exhibit Center has local artists and
craftspeople demonstrating their skills most every day.

For additional information on the Townsend side of the Great Smokies,
call (800) 525–6834, or visit www.townsendchamber.org.

Country Lifestyle

Sequoyah was an uneducated, crippled Cherokee half-breed who was shunned by his peers for much of his life until, in 1821, he introduced an alphabet to his people. It was so easy to learn that soon thousands were using it. Before long the Cherokees were more literate than most of the white men living in the area.

Sequoyah is the only man to single-handedly develop and perfect an alphabet. In doing so he endowed an entire nation with learning. The story of Sequoyah is told in the **Sequoyah Birthplace Museum,** which is located south of Vonore on Highway 360 and is owned and operated by the Eastern Band of Cherokee Indians. The only Indian-operated historical attraction in Tennessee, it's located on the shores of Tellico Lake, 37 miles south of downtown Knoxville on Highway 360.

The museum is dedicated to this brilliant Native American, but it also tells a great deal about the Cherokee as a nation. Displays range from Native American artifacts to a present-day *Blondie* comic book written in the Cherokee alphabet. An adjacent gift shop offers a wide variety of Cherokee crafts, works of art, and related books. Open daily, year-round; admission for adults, $3; children under 12, $1.50. Their phone number is (423) 884–6246.

Along U.S. Highway 11 a few miles from Sweetwater lies the little town of **Niota,** which you may remember from national news reports a few years back. It was put on the map when the town was run by an all-female government. Coincidentally, this was the home of Harry Burn, the Tennessee legislator who cast the deciding vote to ratify the amendment to the U.S. Constitution that gave women the right to vote.

The main attraction here is the **Niota Depot,** the oldest standing railroad depot in the state. Built in 1853, the building now houses the town offices. If you'd like a tour, stop by and someone will take you on a guided walk through the historic building. You can contact them at (423) 568–2584 for more tour information.

Along Highway 68, just outside Sweetwater, you'll find something quite amazing "under the beaten path." It's the **Lost Sea,** an attraction that the *Guinness Book of World Records* calls **America's largest underground lake.** It's a four-and-a-half-acre "bottomless" lake 300 feet underground.

The 55-minute tour is an easy walk down to the lake. There's not a single step to concern yourself with, since all paths are sloping and include handrails. Glass-bottomed boats take you out onto the water, and white trout will gather around the boat as you approach their end of the lake. The tour guides are

Trade Faire Follies

Trade fairs during the 18th century were the commercial centers of an English community. Streets were filled with vendors and craftspeople selling all sorts of essentials. Puppet shows were presented for the kids and theatrical plays for the adults. Farmers would bring their oxen to trade and their handiwork to sell.

In America trade fairs were abundant throughout most of the colonies and were originally set up to resemble those in Britain. However, it wasn't long until Americans came up with their own version of this annual social event. Sporting challenges, including fistfights and running races were held; fortune-tellers foretold ladies' dreams for the coming year; and circus performers and Gypsies would appear for both fun and profit.

It's not often in today's society that one gets the opportunity to walk among the sights, sounds, and smells of those early social gatherings. However, early each September, more than 100 reenactors regularly gather at Fort Loudoun State Historic Area to put on an early trade fair, both for their own fun and for the public's education.

At the **18th Century Trade Faire,** you can sample the foods and the crafts of the 1700s, enjoy period musical entertainment, and see how good we really have it today! You'll have the opportunity to interact with costumed reenactors—from British and French soldiers to ladies with small children—all who will be more than happy to talk with you and explain the way of life they are re-creating.

It all takes place at the 1,200-acre **Fort Loudoun State Historic Area,** one of the earliest British fortifications on the Western Frontier, built in 1756. Today the area houses an interpretive center offering information and artifacts excavated from the ruins prior to the fort's reconstruction. Numerous other unique events take place on the grounds during the year, including a warm and wonderful Christmas celebration. Located 30 miles south of Knoxville, off US 441 in the town of Vonore. Call (423) 884–6217, or go to www.fortloudoun.com.

local and have quite a few interesting stories to tell. They might even try to scare you a few times as you walk along.

The Lost Sea has been designated as a Registered Natural Landmark by the U.S. Department of the Interior because of the lake phenomenon and the abundance of rare crystalline formations throughout the cavern system. Open year-round; admission for adults, $17.95; children six to 12, $7.45. Call (423) 337–6616 or go to www.thelostsea.com.

Eugene Morgan is in the museum business now and he loves it. The **Museum from the Past** is his creation and is regularly open on weekends and during the week by chance. On display is his personal collection of 20 years' worth of acquiring everything from South American pottery to a 5.3-foot-long chain saw to a genuine Tennessee moonshine still.

Most of his collection of 1,300 items is out on tables and shelves, and he encourages you to touch them or pick them up. He'll even show you how the things worked.

"I had to get special permission from the government to put up the still. I think they thought I might want to put it in action," he laughed as he told the story of how he acquired it. The permission letter is tacked to the door of the still, located down a short path from the museum in deep woods. Morgan is a cordial host, and he'll be more than happy to spend time with you explaining every item inside and outside his main building. He has built his own blacksmith shop and has devised an old-time round pump to pump water out of the creek up to his bathrooms.

It's located 4 miles south of Madisonville, on Highway 68. Watch for signs along the road and the old stoplight in his front yard. Open during the warmer months, weekends only. For more information call (423) 442–4833.

Back in 1958, members of the Tellico Plains Kiwanis Club started talking about the lack of roads from Monroe County across the mountains into North Carolina. That put plans in motion, and in 1996 *The Cherohala Skyway,* also known as the Ribbon in the Sky, opened as a $100 million, 51-mile scenic stretch of pure, uninterrupted mountain beauty. It runs along the ridge for a portion, down into the valleys for a while, and provides amazingly colorful vistas from 5,000 feet up, from the dogwoods and redbuds in the spring to the oranges, reds, and browns of the fall.

herewecome

Tennessee earned its nickname, the Volunteer State, by its remarkable record of furnishing volunteers in the War of 1812 and the Mexican War.

The road is one of only 20 National Scenic Highways in the United States and gets its unusual name from a combination of the two national forests where it begins and ends, the Cherokee in Tennessee and the Nantahala in North Carolina.

In *Tellico Plains,* enter the Skyway via Highway 165. There are plenty of brochures out about the road, and you can see some stunning photographs of the highway at www.monroecounty.com. Or call (800) 245–5428.

The Tellico Ranger Station of the Cherokee National Forest is located just off the Skyway. Built on the site of an old Civilian Conservation Corps camp, the visitor center is located in a building built by the CCC in the 1930s. An exhibit area has a display of CCC items, including photos, caps, coats, and equipment. The folk here know the area quite well and can help you custom-build a day in the forest. There are plenty of maps and brochures, as well as a gift shop. Open Monday through Friday 8:00 a.m. to 4:30 p.m.

To reach the ranger station, take the Skyway out of town; the river will be on your right. Approximately 5 miles out of town, you'll see Forest Service Road 210 forking off to the right and continuing along the river. Take it; the station is less than half a mile down the road on your left. The river will still be on your right. Get more information at (423) 253–2520; www.southernregion.fs.fed.us/cherokee.

It may be wise to fill up your tummy before heading to the mountains, and in Tellico Plains, the popular *Tellibala Cafe* is the place to do it. There's an enormous selection, but if you're stopping for lunch, try the country-ham sandwich or the chicken-fried steak. You'll find them on the menu under "Luncheon Favorites." Located at 128 Bank Street, it's open every day but Monday for lunch and dinner. Call (423) 253–2880 for hours.

For more information on this area, call (800) 245–5428, or you can log on at www.monroecounty.com.

The people of the Coker Creek area are still shouting, "There's gold in them thar hills!" The community has been celebrating the *Autumn Gold Festival* each October since 1968 to highlight the area's two forms of gold—the golden color of the leaves as they turn each fall and the gold that can still be found in the creeks of the area. The festival salutes the gold-mining heritage of the region, which goes back to the late 1820s.

Organizers bring down a few truckloads of dirt from the mountain gold mines so that festivalgoers have a better chance of finding some real gold when they participate in one of the major events, panning for gold. There are also board splitting, syrup making, gospel and country music, and arts and crafts. The festival is held at *Coker Creek Village,* on Highway 68 a few miles from North Carolina in the Cherokee National Forest area.

Coker Creek Crafts Gallery is located 1 block off Highway 68 on Hot Water Road. Turn onto Hot Water across from the fire station in town. Owned by Ken and Kathleen Dalton, the business specializes in high-quality crafts and visual arts. The Daltons' baskets are widely known and are in craft collections and museums all over the country. Closed January through March, it's open the rest of the year Tuesday through Saturday. Phone the gallery at (423) 261–2157.

The *Crosseyed Cricket* advertises that it's more than "just a place to stay." Located on Country Lane a few miles from exit 364 on I–40, about 20 miles southwest of Knoxville, the Cricket is a restaurant/public fishing/camping complex in a beautiful rural setting.

The restaurant is located in a 150-year-old operating gristmill and an adjacent 50-year-old log cabin overlooking the lake. The specialties are rainbow trout and channel catfish, both caught and cleaned fresh every day from the lake. Hush puppies, coleslaw, homemade pies, and fried chicken round out the menu.

Leave room for dessert! Owner Jim Lockwood says they are constantly adding new homemade desserts to the menu. Among the traditional favorites are black bottom pie and banana crème pie. Also served on a regular basis are toll house pie, grasshopper pie (chocolate mint), and lime cheesecake pie.

There are two fish-out lakes, one for the trout and one for the catfish. Public fishing is allowed, and you pay by the pound for what you catch. They'll provide everything you need, including bait, for free if you didn't bring your own. If you wish, they'll clean your catch and send it over to the restaurant, where it will be cooked to your taste. Otherwise they'll pack it in ice and you can take it home with you. There are 47 campsites on the far side of the lake. There's no need to have a fishing license either; they have one that covers anyone who fishes their lakes.

In October you can climb aboard a hay wagon and take a ride up to the top of the hill to the pumpkin patch, where you can pick out your choice from the thousands growing in the field. There's a flat fee for the ride, which includes your choice of a pumpkin. From Thanksgiving through Christmas, the Christmas Tree Plantation is open. You can choose from several thousand trees to cut down. Bone saws are provided, or you may bring your own. Fishing privileges and the restaurant are closed November through February, but camping is open year-round; everything is closed on Sunday. For more information call (865) 986–5435 or visit www.crosseyedcricket.com.

Roane County is dominated by the Tennessee Valley Authority's (TVA) *Watts Bar Lake.* With 783 miles of lakefront, water-oriented activities are quite popular. Numerous marinas with boat rentals are scattered throughout the county. Once on the lake, island hopping is a popular activity. Hundreds of small islands make perfect secluded areas for picnicking and swimming.

Watts Bar Lake is one of several TVA lakes throughout the state that make up the chain called the *Great Lakes of the South.* Many families live on the lake in houseboats. One colony is located just west of Kingston off U.S. Highway 70.

The *TVA steam plant* in *Kingston* has free tours. There's no way you can miss it; just follow the roads to the big stacks. Elsewhere, a driving tour of the county has been developed, as has a backcountry trail driving tour. Brochures and maps for both are available from the Roane County Visitors Bureau, 1209 North Kentucky Street, 1 block north of I–40. For tour information contact them at (865) 376–4201 or (800) FUN–INTN; www.roanealliance.org.

The *Old Courthouse Museum,* located, as you can imagine, in the old county courthouse, features local and state history from prehistoric time

Fainting Goats and Other Cool Mammals

Legend has it that a stranger from Nova Scotia brought a few goats to Tennessee in the early 1880s that were said to have "fits" when they became scared. The kids from those goats were sold, and before long the descendants of those four goats found their way across the United States.

Known today as **Tennessee Fainting Goats** (or nervous goats, in some areas), the breed reacts to loud noises and to being scared. "Their joints lock up and they fall over. They don't actually faint," said John Presswood, who now raises the breed along with other exotic and miniature animals on his farm. "Once the goats hit the ground, they will usually start coming back; within a minute they are usually back on their feet."

John has a passion for the off-the-beaten-path type of animal. In addition to "regular" farm animals, he raises miniature horses, deer, and donkeys, along with pygmy goats, baby doll sheep, doves, pigeons, and Siberian chipmunks. "I love the chipmunks," he told me. "They are white with tan stripes, and they are real easy to tame. If you work with them a little bit, they will eat right out of your hand."

Located in Roane County south of Kingston, **Presswood Farm** is open to visitors. It's a working farm, not a petting zoo, so what you see out here is for real! In fact, if you like an animal and want to take it home with you, John will probably sell it to you. If you'd like to visit John, give him a call at (865) 376–4479; he'll give you directions to the farm.

to World War II. The building, with tall white columns, is only one of the seven remaining antebellum courthouses in the state. Located at the corner of Kentucky and Cumberland Streets in Kingston. Open Monday through Friday 8:30 a.m. to 4:30 p.m. Free. Call (865) 376–9211, or visit www.roanetn heritage.com.

Fort Southwest Point in Kingston is the only fort in the state that has been reconstructed on its original foundation. The completed sections of the fort so far include the barracks, blockhouse, and more than 250 feet of palisade walls. A separate building houses the welcome center and the **Fort Southwest Point Museum.** Work began on the site in the early 1970s, with a lot of work still to do, according to officials.

The fort is located on a 30-acre hill overlooking Watts Bar Lake. Take Highway 58 south out of town; go 1 mile and the fort is on your right. Call (865) 376–3641.

West of Rockwood off US 70, high atop "the mountain" (as locals call it), is a Forest Service–run fire tower. Although visitors are not supposed to climb to the top of the tower, the picnic area around the bottom offers a magnificent bird's-eye vista of Rockwood and Watts Bar Lake. There are several shaded picnic tables and barbecue grills for the public to use. Open daily during daylight hours only. If you're driving through Rockwood during the Christmas season and see a huge star shining brightly to the west, this is where it's plugged in.

The Dream Counties

During the 1880s and 1890s, **Oliver Springs** was a central railroad town for the local coal miners. The area was booming by 1895 when the Oliver Springs Hotel opened and created a strong demand for passenger rail service to the area. As a result, the town built a new rail depot in 1896 to serve the increased needs.

That depot still stands today and is the home of a museum that highlights the area's growth to fame and fortune, although the hotel burned in 1905 and was never replaced, and the town hasn't had passenger service for decades. The town's library is located in the restored depot. A reconditioned caboose sits out back, as do several other large pieces of local memorabilia. Located on the corner of Winter's Gap Road and Walker Avenue; free admission. You can reach the depot at (865) 435–2509.

In 1942, as World War II was raging, President Franklin D. Roosevelt approved the proposal by Albert Einstein to proceed in making a secret weapon. The Army Corps of Engineers chose an isolated 60,000-acre site here in Anderson County. Within one year, three defense plants were built and a **Secret City** for 75,000 people was cut out of the wilderness.

Throughout the war years **Oak Ridge,** the name given the community, remained under direct supervision of the government and was surrounded by a tall barbed-wire fence. Only a handful of the workers knew the true nature of the project, and all were sworn to secrecy. It was not until the dropping of the first atomic bombs in 1945 that the inhabitants behind the fence learned that they had been members of an important team of the famed Manhattan Project. **Oak Ridge National Laboratory** produced the uranium 235 and plutonium 239, the fuel necessary for the atomic bomb.

shhh!don'ttell anyone

The **World War II Secret City Festival** takes place in late June each year and features tours, diverse entertainment by national acts, a WWII reenactment, arts and crafts, and children's activities. Call (865) 425–3610, or visit their Web site at www.secretcityfestival.com.

The fences came down in 1949 and the city was incorporated. Today more than 4,000 buildings exist as a link to this era of secrecy. All three plants are still there, but the main emphasis in Oak Ridge now is energy research.

The original graphite reactor, the oldest continuously operated nuclear reactor in the world, is open to the public and is located in the Oak Ridge National Laboratory. A map of the 38-mile self-guided motor tour of the entire area is available at the visitor center, 302 South Tulane Avenue; (865) 482–7821; www.oakridgevisitor.com. Since September 11, 2001, some areas have been closed to the public.

Next to the visitor center, the U.S. Department of Energy has developed one of the world's largest energy exhibitions. The **American Museum of Science and Energy** includes interactive exhibits, live demonstrations, computer displays, and filmed interpretations. All forms of energy and their relationship to humanity are explained. One favorite demonstration, especially of the young, makes a person's hair stand straight up on end. Open year-round 9:00 a.m. to 5:00 p.m.; closed on Sunday morning, Monday, Thanksgiving Day, Christmas Day, and New Year's Day. Closing time is extended by one hour in June, July, and August. Admission fee is $5 for those 18 years of age and over, $3 for those six through 17, $4 for senior citizens, and free for kids under six. Contact by phone is (865) 576–3200; on the Web at www.amse.org.

The story behind the creation of the living areas of Oak Ridge is an amazing one. Five home designs were created and assigned to workers according to family size and job importance. Neighborhoods centered on the Town Site, which was designed to offer shopping and recreation. The high school, multifamily housing, and the hospital were also built near the Town Site. Now known as Jackson Square, a walking-tour of that original town site is available. You can get information on the tour at the visitor center.

bringhome dinner

The Clinch River has the highest trout catch rate of any stream in the eastern United States.

Within Oak Ridge's city limits on Highway 62, the University of Tennessee has established a forestry experiment station. The arboretum is open to the public and has four designated nature walking tours. More than 800 species of plants grow here naturally, and most of them are labeled for easy identification by visitors. Specific information about the experimental work being done is available at the visitor center. Call (865) 483–3571; www.forestry.tennessee.edu.

For more information on Oak Ridge, contact the convention and visitors bureau at (800) 887–3429, or visit their Web site at www.oakridgevisitor.com.

For information on Norris and other parts of Anderson County, call (800) 524–3602, or sign on to the truly Southern Web page, www.yallcome.org.

The *Appalachian Arts Craft Shop* is located on Highway 61 about a mile after it crosses Interstate 75. The center was started in 1970 to "enrich the souls and pocketbooks of low-income people." Today the nonprofit organization that runs the center works with local people to preserve traditional Appalachian crafts and techniques. All types of crafts are available. The center is open 10:00 a.m. to 6:00 p.m. Monday through Saturday and 1:00 to 5:00 p.m. Sunday. Calling (865) 494–9854 will get you further information.

Less than a mile down the road from the crafts center is the *Museum of Appalachia.* Founded by John Rice Irwin in 1960, the museum is considered one of the most authentic representations of early Appalachian mountain life. Dozens of cabins and buildings have been moved here and preserved in the spaciousness of their original locations. More than 250,000 items are on display. Live music and demonstrations abound as employees go about living and working in a mountain village. *Roots* author Alex Haley said he loved the museum so much that he "built a home in sight of it." He lived across the street until his death in February 1992. Open daily, year-round; admission for adults is $15.95; children six to 12, $5, and senior citizens $12. Call (865) 494–7680.

If you can, plan your visit during one of the three "authentic" annual events: July 4th Celebration, Tennessee Fall Homecoming in October, or Christmas in Old Appalachia.

The nearby city of *Norris* is a great little community. Planned and built by the Tennessee Valley Authority (TVA) in 1934 as a demonstration of sound community development, the town features a greenbelt, a town forest that protects the city's water supply, and houses placed in a parklike atmosphere. Now an independent municipality, Norris has preserved its original look. Brochures and information are available at the police and fire departments.

The Tennessee Valley Authority Act was signed into law by President Franklin Roosevelt on May 18, 1933, and within a few weeks the TVA's first flood-control project, the Norris Dam, was started. As the oldest TVA facility, the dam is open to visitors on occasion, although the entire operation is now run by remote control. No tours are given, but you can drive across and get some great photos.

The dam and the lake are part of the *Norris Dam State Park,* as is the *Lenoir Family Museum.* Made up primarily of Helen and Will G. Lenoir's "junk" collection, items in the state-run facility date from prehistoric times to the present. The place is filled with artifacts that visitors are encouraged to pick up and touch. As the guides walk visitors through, they tell stories that bring the items to life. Many of the stories are more fun than the items themselves.

To get the full benefit here, take the tour first and listen to the stories, then go back through and look at the displays at your own pace.

The museum's most treasured artifact is a European barrel organ with tiers of hand-carved wooden figures. Research shows it was made in Germany in 1826 and probably brought to America by a traveling showman. Admission is free. Open daily during summer; weekends only for the rest of the year. Call (865) 494–9688.

Outside, the TVA has gathered two additional buildings. The *Cosby Threshing Barn,* built in the early 1800s, was one of the first threshing barns to be built in the United States. It's full of pioneer machinery, including a wooden treadmill made in 1855. Across the field from the barn is a 1798 gristmill where corn is ground during the summer months. A gift shop is on the upper level. The entire setting is very rustic and just a short distance from the dam and a picnic area.

If it's rugged wilderness and wild white water you're looking for, follow U.S. Highway 27 north to *Wartburg* and the *Obed Wild and Scenic River.* The area is managed by the National Park Service and the Tennessee Wildlife Resources Agency and consists of four streams within the same watershed. Over the years they have carved their way through the landscape and have created beautiful gorges, some as deep as 500 feet.

capitaldujour

Four cities have served as Tennessee's state capital:

Knoxville, 1796-1817

Kingston, 1807, for one day only

Murfreesboro, 1817-1826

Nashville, 1826 to present

During the rainy season, from December through April, the streams provide some of the finest, most technical white water in the nation. Some primitive camping is allowed. The visitor center for the area is located at 208 North Maiden Street, next to the Federal Building in Wartburg. Get further information at (423) 346–6294 or www.nps.gov/obed.

Frozen Head State Natural Area was named for a 3,324-foot peak in the Cumberland Mountains, the top of which is often shrouded in ice or snow. You enter this peaceful area through a vestige of densely forested, unspoiled mountain terrain. A vintage fire tower, which is accessible only by a walking trail, offers a spectacular panorama of this majestic part of the state. The park is located off Highway 62, east of Wartburg. Contact the park at (423) 346–3318; www.state.tn.us/environment/parks.

A great way to see the Scott County area is by horseback, and the folks at the appropriately named *Tally Ho Stables* can help you get saddled up.

You can rent a horse here and join in on one of the several different trail rides offered. They claim they have more than 150 miles of developed horse trails to explore. An hour ride will cost you $20; two hours, $30; half day, $50; and an all-day eight- or nine-hour journey will cost $80. They also have two-day or more pack trips. Located at 6334 Grave Hill Road, just outside of Oneida. Call the stables at (423) 569–9472.

Of the three utopian experiments in Tennessee during the late 1800s, **Rugby's** was the largest and has left us with the most evidence of the dreamers' struggles.

Today 20 of the 70 original buildings of **Rugby's Utopian Community** still stand and have been preserved or restored. A few are still inhabited by descendants of the original settlers.

In 1880 English author-reformer Thomas Hughes launched this colony with the dream that it would be "a centre in which a healthy, reverent life shall grow." At its peak in 1884, the population was about 450. Today Rugby has about 85 residents.

Hughes's vision of a utopian existence in the wilderness of Tennessee brought a taste of British culture along with it. Most of the settlers were young British of good family, and today their colorful Victorian legacies line the streets, making Rugby one of the most unusual communities in the state.

A journey through town should begin at the old Rugby Schoolhouse, which now serves as a museum and visitor center. In addition to the school, historic buildings open to visitors include the Christ Church, Episcopal, with its original hanging lamps and 1849 rosewood reed organ, and the **Thomas Hughes Free Public Library,** which still contains what is regarded as the best representative collection (7,000 volumes) of Victorian literature in America.

Two historic structures have been restored and now offer overnight accommodations with historical accuracy. The **Pioneer Cottage** and the **Newbury House Inn** are available with prior reservations.

If you're into ghosts and stories of haunting, you'll get your fill during your tour of Rugby's historic district. If your guide doesn't talk about the various sightings through the years, make sure you ask. Rugby is located on Highway 52 a few miles west of US 27. Structures are open year-round except for Thanksgiving Day, Christmas Eve, Christmas Day, and New Year's Day; during

January, tours are by appointment. Housing, shops, and a restaurant are open year-round. Phone (423) 628–2441 or go to www.historicrugby.org.

Approximately 1 mile west of Rugby on Highway 52 is the **Grey Gables Bed and Breakfast Inn.** The magnificent home was built in 1990 for the purpose of setting up a classy inn that would combine the best of Victorian English and Tennessee country heritage. Decorated with country and Victorian antiques, the inn reflects the grace of the English and the cordiality of this area.

Innkeepers Bill and Linda Brooks Jones, along with their children, not only have a great ten-bedroom inn, but you'll have to loosen your belt a few notches after you've eaten a couple of meals with them. In fact, Linda's cooking has gone over so well, and so many people were asking for her recipes, that she has written her own cookbook, called *The Table at Grey Gables.* She was born and raised in the area, and the cookbook has not only recipes but also historical narrative about Rugby and her relationship with the locals through the years.

If you look around, you'll see a few photos of former President Jimmy Carter and his wife, the inn's most famous boarders to date. They stayed here on June 17, 1997, and Linda has some great, fun stories about the visit. If it's available, she may let you have the bed the famous couple slept in.

In addition to the great hospitality and the yummy cooking, the hosts offer a full array of activities and themed events. Rates include an elegant evening meal and a hearty country breakfast. Reservations are required; rates are $125 double occupancy, $80 single occupancy. Call Linda or Bill, and they'll send you a calendar that highlights their special themed weekends. Wheelchair accessible. You can reach them at (423) 628–5252; www .rugbytn.com.

In addition to their bed-and-breakfast duties, Bill and daughter Tiffany run the **R. M. Brooks General Store,** on Highway 52 just west of Grey Gables. Linda's grandparents started the store in 1930, and it has remained in the family since. The village post office was tucked away in a corner of the store for years, and when it moved, Bill made sure that the old-time postal feel of the mailboxes remained. The family wants to keep it a "typical, working country general store" where you can buy sandwiches, hoop cheddar cheese, mousetraps, soup, and just about anything else. Plus they have a selection of antiques and local crafts on sale. As in most establishments of this type, you'll find a good supply of local characters sitting around the potbellied stove just about any time you drop in. The general store is open Tuesday through Sunday 10:00 a.m. to 5:30 p.m. For more information call (423) 628–2533.

Forests and Cliffs

The 673-acre *Cove Lake State Recreational Area* is located on the banks of Cove Lake, near *Caryville.* Established in the 1930s as a recreation demonstration area by the TVA, the National Park Service, and the Civilian Conservation Corps, the lake is home to more than 400 Canada geese each winter. Surrounded by the towering Cumberland Mountains, the park is perhaps more popular with visitors in the winter than the summer. Open daily year-round, the park is visited by nearly one million people each year. The *Cove Lake Restaurant* has a full menu of country-cooking favorites and seats about 115. Their schedule changes seasonally, so call (423) 566–9701.

The restaurant, the ranger's station, and the masonry fences around them were built by the Civilian Conservation Corps.

Christmas in the Park is an annual event that county residents look forward to. The celebration features all sorts of music, lights, and decorations throughout the park. The walkways and roads are lined with candles. In the summer the park offers an Olympic-size swimming pool, tennis courts, and 4 miles of paved hiking trails. Phone for details at (423) 566–9701.

This entire county has been described by many as one big natural museum. Ruggedness is the key word here, and one access to that ruggedness is through the *Big South Fork National River and Recreation Area,* www .bigsouthforkpark.com.

Authorized by Congress in 1974, the park has been frequented mainly by those who have been willing to explore the wilderness on its own terms. During the last few years, more roads, overlooks, and river access sites have been built, opening up the 100,000-acre park to less adventurous visitors.

The Big South Fork River cuts a course through one of the most spectacular chasms east of the Mississippi. The gorge is rimmed by towering bluffs of weathered sandstone rising as high as 500 feet. It's considered to be one of the best white-water rivers in the East. In all, there are more than 80 miles of prime canoeing waters within the park.

Camping is permitted just about anywhere in the park, and mountain bikes and four-wheeled off-road vehicles are permitted on designated trails and roads. There are three developed campgrounds and the *Charit Creek Hotel,* www.charitcreek.com, which offers dormitory-style housing with bunk beds. There is no electricity here, and no vehicular traffic is allowed. Call for further information, (865) 429–5704.

The most comfortable way to see the rugged terrain and the river is aboard the *Big South Fork Scenic Railway.* The three-hour narrated trip leaves from the historic coal-mining town of Sterns, Kentucky. The 7-mile trip takes you down gently to the bottom of the gorge, through a massive tunnel, and along high rock ledges. It then hugs the banks of the river, where you might catch a glimpse of white-water aficionados. Call the railway at (800) 462–5664 or visit www.bsfsry.com.

One of the most scenic highways in this part of the state connects Jellico with La Follette. Although it seems much longer, U.S. Highway 25W curves and twists for 29 very interesting miles. The road offers some spectacular views as it follows the canyons through the mountains. This route is a great alternative to interstate driving, but you'll need to adjust your speed to the road conditions, and you'll probably want to pull off a couple of times to enjoy the scenery. Several bitter skirmishes were fought around here during the Civil War.

Since 1760, treasure hunters have searched this area for the legendary Swift's Silver Mines, where John Swift and his crew mined silver, minted coins, and took it all back to the colonies. The operation ended during the Indian Wars. Several years later, Swift came back but due to his failing eyesight was unable to locate his mines, which he insisted were still full of silver. Nobody has found those mines yet.

Places to Stay in the Mountainous East

CARYVILLE

Cove Lake State Park (camping)
US 25W
Restaurant, hiking trails, lake, fishing
(423) 566–9701

CUMBERLAND GAP

The Olde Mill Bed & Breakfast
603 Pennlyn Avenue
Buffet style country breakfast; antique/Victorian furnishings
(423) 869–9839
www.oldemillbbinn.com

DANDRIDGE

EconoLodge
531 Patriot Drive
Pool, fireplaces, cable TV
(865) 397–9437

GATLINBURG

Great Smoky Mountains National Park
Camping in undeveloped areas
(865) 436–5615
www.nps.gov/grsm

LeConte View Motor Lodge
929 Parkway
Fireplaces, indoor and outdoor pools
(865) 436–5032

KNOXVILLE

Volunteer Park (camping)
9514 Diggs Gap Road
Grocery, pools, showers, phones
(865) 938–6600

LENOIR CITY

Crosseyed Cricket
Paw Paw Road
Restaurant, fishing, camping (year-round)
(865) 986–5435
www.crosseyedcricket.com

PIGEON FORGE

Twin Mountain Outdoor Resort (camping)
304 Day Springs Road
Pool, river tubing, laundry room
(865) 453–8181
www.twinmountainrvpark.com

RUGBY

Grey Gables Bed and Breakfast Inn
Highway 52
Great food, themed weekends, country/Victorian decor
(423) 628–5252
www.rugbytn.com

SEVIERVILLE

Hidden Mountain Resorts
Condos, cottages, and log cabins
(865) 453–9850

Oak Tree Lodge
1620 Parkway
Private balconies, fireplaces, pools
(865) 428–7500
www.theoaktreelodge.com

TOWNSEND

Highland Manor Inn
Highway 321
Tudor-style, balconies, private whirlpools available
(865) 448–2211
www.highlandmanor.com

Places to Eat in the Mountainous East

BEAN STATION

Clinch Mountain Lookout Restaurant
US 25E at the summit
Vinegar pie, ostrich burgers, breakfast all day
Open daily for early breakfast, lunch, and dinner
(865) 767–2511
www.clinchmountainlookout.com

COSBY

Kyle Carver Orchards
On US 321 South, 5 miles from I–40
Country cooking with many apple dishes
Open daily year-round, 8:00 a.m. to 8:00 p.m.
(423) 487–2710

CUMBERLAND GAP

The Tomato Head
12 Market Square
Award-winning gourmet pizza, salads, sandwiches
Monday: lunch only
Tuesday through Sunday: lunch and dinner
(865) 637–4067
www.thetomatohead.com

GATLINBURG

Applewood Farmhouse Restaurant
US 441, entrance to Smoky Mountains National Park
Great view of the Smokies, country rustic atmosphere; bountiful breakfast served until 2:00 p.m.
Open daily for breakfast, lunch, and dinner
(865) 453–9319

Peddler Restaurant
1110 Parkway
Steaks, salmon, best salad bar in town; on the river with great views
Open year-round; dinner served nightly
(865) 436–5794

KNOXVILLE

Webb's Country Kitchen
602 Colwyn Avenue
Country-style cooking—greens, taters, pintos
Closed Monday
(423) 869–5877

PIGEON FORGE

Dixie Stampede
Located on the parkway
Watch a live show while eating a Southern feast
(865) 453–4400
www.dixiestampede.com

Mel's Diner
119 Wears Valley Road
Rock and roll featured on menu, walls, and jukebox
(865) 429–2184
www.meldinerspf.com

Old Mill Restaurant

2934 Middle Creek Road
Southern cooking, fish,
chicken, steak
Next to 1830 Old Mill
attraction at Traffic Light #7
Open daily for breakfast,
lunch, and dinner
(865) 429–3463
www.old-mill.com

SEVIERVILLE

Applewood Farmhouse Restaurant

230 Apple Valley Road
fresh trout, trout cake,
apple pie

Applewoods Farm Grill

offers lighter options across
the street
(865) 453–9319

SWEETWATER

Dinner Bell

I–75 and Oakland Road
(exit 62)
Home cooking, nightly
buffet, country atmosphere
Open daily at 6:00 a.m.
Breakfast, lunch, and
dinner
(423) 337–5825

Upper Cumberland

In a valley surrounded by the Cumberland Mountains a few miles from the Kentucky border, **Sergeant Alvin York,** one of America's most celebrated military heroes, was born and reared. Except for the two years he spent in World War I, Sergeant York spent his entire life in these mountains. But those two years put York in the history books and this part of the state on the map. Today the ***Alvin York State Historic Area*** commemorates his life and career.

York's one-man firefight with the German army in France's Argonne Forest on October 8, 1918, is now legendary. As a patrol leader, he killed 25 German soldiers and almost single-handedly captured another 132. As a result he received more than 40 Allied decorations and worldwide publicity.

His modest upbringing here in the Tennessee mountains and his refusal to cash in on his popularity by selling out to the media won the hearts of millions, and he returned to the valley as a bona fide hero.

York died in 1964, and four years later the state bought a large portion of land that included his family farm and the mill

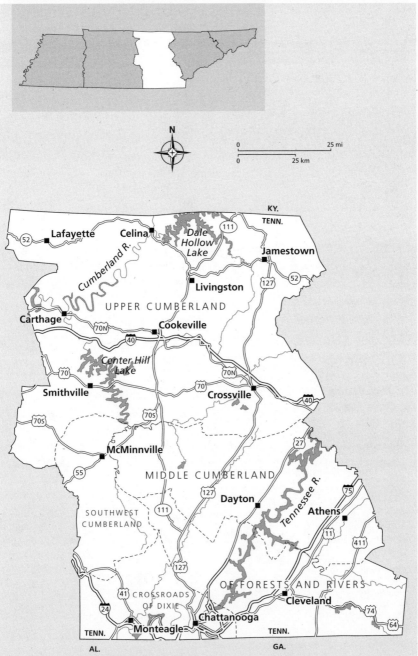

KY.
TENN.

52 Lafayette   Celina   111   Dale
                                  Hollow
                                  Lake   Jamestown

Cumberland R.   127   52

                    Livingston

UPPER CUMBERLAND

Carthage   70N   Cookeville

            40

Center Hill
Lake   70N

70

Smithville   70   70   Crossville   40

            70S

            70S

McMinnville   27

MIDDLE CUMBERLAND

55   75

                    127
            127   Dayton
SOUTHWEST   Athens
CUMBERLAND   111
                                         11   411

                    127

OF FORESTS AND RIVERS

41 CROSSROADS
24   OF DIXIE   Cleveland   74
                                              64
TENN. Monteagle   Chattanooga
AL.   TENN.
                             GA.

World's Longest Outdoor Sale

The 450-mile U.S. Highway 127 Corridor Sale starts in Kentucky; runs through the Tennessee towns of Jamestown, Allardt, Clarkrange, Crossville, Pikeville, Dunlap, Whitwell, and Chattanooga; and ends somewhere in Alabama.

All along US 127 from the Kentucky to the Alabama state line, you'll find rural front yards loaded with items; in the cities you'll find sidewalks filled with merchandise. It's an almost endless supply of trash and treasures, and you'll find just about anything you'd ever want. Please be careful: US 127 is quite busy during the sale. Watch out for traffic and always use your turn signals if you are going to pull over. Held one weekend in August, Thursday through Sunday. Call (800) 327–3945, or go online at www.127sale.com.

that he once operated. The exhibits are fine, but the real reason to visit this area is the park ranger, York's son, Andy York. He's often here, and he'll be more than glad to spend some time with you and tell you all sorts of stories about his famous father and the family's ties to the area. It's not too often that you get to meet a genuine hero's son whose business it is to talk about his father's life. It's a unique opportunity to put history into perspective.

The area is about 9 miles north of Jamestown on U.S. Highway 127 and is open daily. Call (931) 879–6456.

Jamestown was popular with Native Americans and early travelers because of the many freshwater springs that came up through the sandy soil. In fact the original name of the community was Sand Spring. One of the early settlers here was John M. Clemens, the father of Samuel Clemens, better known as Mark Twain. On Main Street, just off the courthouse square, *Mark*

AUTHOR'S TOP TEN PICKS

Highland Manor Winery

Great Pumpkin Festival and Weigh-Off

Muddy Pond

Homesteads

Russell Stover Candy Factory Outlet

Rhea County Museum

Horsin' Around Carving School

Tennessee's Badlands

Ocoee Whitewater Center

International Towing & Recovery Hall of Fame and Museum

Twain Spring Park is on land adjacent to the Clemens homestead and still has a small spring that was once the source of water for the early residents. Although there is no evidence that Samuel Clemens ever visited here, he was conceived here. He was born five months after his parents moved to Missouri.

Three miles south of Jamestown on US 127 is the *Highland Manor Winery,* which has the distinction of being the oldest licensed winery in the state and the first American winery to be awarded the International Gold Medal for Quality in Madrid, Spain. This is one of 17 commercial wineries in the state. (See Grundy County in the Southwest Cumberland section later in this chapter and Montgomery County in the Heartlands chapter for additional fruit-of-the-vine experiences.) The winery is open daily for tours and tasting; call (931) 879–9519, or go to www.highlandmanorwinery.com.

Some huge pumpkins are grown each year in the area around Jamestown, and the pumpkin is king for a weekend early each October when the *Great Pumpkin Festival and Weigh-Off* is held in nearby Allardt, southeast of Jamestown on Highway 52. The folks here have turned pumpkin and gourd competition into a reason to play. On Saturday morning the weigh-offs begin to find the year's champion. Pumpkins from all over show up on the back of pickup trucks. We were amazed at our first sight of an 800 pounder!

In addition to all the noteworthy gourds, pumpkins, watermelons, and squash, dozens of local craftspeople set up in Bruno Gernt Park to sell their unique products. There's also music, an antique tractor show, a quilt show, a street dance, a bake sale and auction, a parade, and of course plenty of pumpkin-flavored goodies! Admission to all this great, rural slice of life is free. Call (931) 879–7125.

In the heart of the Upper Cumberland region, *Livingston,* the county seat, is rapidly becoming known for its quality crafts outlets. The downtown area around the historic courthouse is known as Court Square and is home to many retail shops, antiques stores, and crafts stores.

Counted among the antiques stores in downtown is the *Antique Market,* at 116 North Court Square. Inside you'll find more than 50 booths and two large rooms full of everything from fabulous antique jewelry to postcards to oak furniture. It's open seven days a week. For more information call (931) 823–4943. Hungry? The *Apple Dish,* with a nice selection of soups, salads, and sandwiches, is located inside the Antique Market and offers not only great home cooking but also tremendous home-baked desserts, including Italian cream cake. Call (931) 823–3222.

Livingston throws a great party during July, and it is Hometown USA at its finest. The *Overton County Bluegrass Festival* fills the city square with

OTHER ATTRACTIONS WORTH SEEING

Creative Discovery Museum,
Chattanooga,
(423) 756–2738

Cumberland County Playhouse,
Crossville,
(931) 484–5000
www.ccplayhouse.com

IMAX 3-D Theater,
Chattanooga,
(800) 262–0695
www.tennesseeaquarium.com

Key Park Log House,
Lafayette,
(615) 666–5885
www.maconcountytn.com

Virgin Falls,
Sparta,
(931) 836–3552

music, food, arts and crafts, and a lot of good-neighbor howdy's. Call (931) 823–6421.

Down in the southeast corner of Overton County is *Muddy Pond,* a small Mennonite community that happens to be way off the beaten path. Entrance to the community is off Highway 164, about halfway between Crawford and Monterey, or off Highway 62, 1 mile west of Clarkrange. In either direction you'll have a nice paved road for several miles before the gravel road begins.

There are several retail shops located back here, and many of the farmers sell fresh eggs and bread out of their homes. A horse-powered mill creates the product at the Sorghum Mill, where the owners also sell homemade bread and fried pies. The Muddy Pond Variety Store makes its own sorghum and carries produce and vegetables as well. The Baken Haus is a homestyle bakery with great breads and pies; and the Muddy Pond General Store has sorghum, cheeses, meats, quilts, pottery, outdoor furniture, and a large variety of gift and household items. Most of the businesses are open Monday through Saturday. Phone them at (931) 445–7829.

There are a great many houses, fences, walls, and buildings around Crossville made of the famous Crab Orchard stone—a brownish beige stone that is quarried along U.S. Highway 70 in the small community of Crab Orchard. The quarries are located along the north side of the highway and show years and years of mining operations.

Crab Orchard was a pioneer outpost in the 1700s, and those on a westward trek would stop here for a rest after going through the mountains and climbing onto the plateau. The crab apple trees were numerous, and the

Indians caused no problems. It was a comfortable respite. In his 1985 novel, *Jubal Sackett,* Louis L'Amour wrote fondly of the area.

A few miles east on US 70 is the **Ozone Falls Natural Area,** where old-growth forests dominate. The highlight here is the magnificent 110-foot-high waterfall where Fall Creek cascades into the deep gorges below. Park in the pull-out area along the highway, and you'll only have about a fifth of a mile walk to the top of the falls. *Be very careful.* There are no guardrails or railings. If you follow the path, you'll walk right over the edge! Also be wary of slippery stones that you might step on as you lean over to take a look. Nearby Cumberland Mountain State Park is in charge of the area. You can find out more at (931) 484–6138.

Looking for some great cheddar cheese? **Simonton's Cheese House,** located behind the chamber of commerce on West Avenue North in **Crossville,** is known throughout this part of the country for its three-pound hoop of cheddar, made from grade A milk. It's sold here along with other specialty cheeses, jams, jellies, teas, candies, and hams. They carry more than 60 domestic and imported cheeses in all! Simonton's Cheddar even has a cheer: "Red as an Apple, Yellow as Gold, I am Delicious, I am Told . . . TRY ME!" Simonton's is open Monday through Saturday 9:00 a.m. to 5:00 p.m. Call them at (931) 484–5193 or www.simontonscheese.com.

Considered one of the South's top professional theater groups, the **Cumberland County Playhouse** is located here in Crossville. With two indoor stages and an outdoor amphitheater, the playhouse features professional theater in an unlikely rural setting and draws audiences from a great distance. Ticket prices range from $18 to $26 for adults for most shows. The theaters

TOP ANNUAL EVENTS

Riverbend Music Festival,
mid-June, Chattanooga,
(423) 756–8687

Fiddler's Jamboree,
early July, Smithville,
(615) 597–8500

White Oak Mountain Bluegrass Festival,
mid-July, Cleveland,
(423) 476–9310

Cherokee Days of Recognition,
first weekend in August, Cleveland,
(423) 478–0339

Fall Heritage Festival,
early October, Carthage,
(615) 735–2093

Celebration of Fine Arts,
early October, Chattanooga,
(615) 385–1094

are located at 221 Tennessee Avenue. Phone them at (931) 484–5000, or go to www.ccplayhouse.com.

The **Stonehaus Winery** offers free nitty-gritty tours daily with all aspects of the winemaking process shown. Unlike a lot of wineries, which give superficial tours, these guys take you from A to Z, from crushing to bottling—and of course they have a tasting counter. In the gift shop there is a large selection of local cheeses to choose from; in the deli they can rustle you up a great sandwich. Visit www.stonehauswinery.com.

However, if you want wine with that sandwich, you'll have to buy a bottle. They'll open it for you and give you a glass, but Tennessee law forbids them from serving it to you. Open Monday through Saturday 9:00 a.m. to 5:00 p.m. and Sunday noon to 5:00 p.m. Located on Genesis Road, at exit 320 off Interstate 40. Contact (931) 484–9463.

The **Vanity Fair Outlet Mall,** located across I–40 from the Stonehaus Winery, has enough shopping opportunities to keep you busy for hours.

South of Crossville, where Highways 127 and 68 split, is the planned community of **Homesteads.** The area, with its quaint little stone houses lining both highways, is often referred to as the "showplace of the New Deal."

In January 1934, following several years of hard times in the area, the local farm agent submitted an application to the government for one of the subsistence projects formulated by the Roosevelt administration. The application was accepted, and work began on the 10,000-acre project.

The plan was to build 250-plus homesteads, each of about 20 acres. The homesteaders were selected following a series of intense background checks and interviews of about 4,000 applicants. Cooperatives were established for the community, and family members went to these to make their families' mattresses, can their families' food, or weave at a loom house.

Today 218 of the 255 houses built are still standing. At the base of the 85-foot-tall octagonal tower that originally served as a water tower is a sandstone building that housed the administrative offices of the project. Today those offices serve as a museum depicting Roosevelt's homesteading project. If you want you can climb the 97 steps to the top of the tower.

Of the 102 New Deal projects nationwide, the Cumberland Homesteads was considered one of the most successful of all. Open daily March through December. A small admission is charged. Call for more information, (931) 456–9663, or www.cumberlandhomesteads.org.

More information on Crossville, Crab Orchard, and the rest of Cumberland County can be found on the chamber of commerce's Web site, www.crossville .com/thechamber, or call (931) 484–8444.

Cannon County is known throughout the state for the number of fine craftspeople it has within its borders. Just about every craft you can think of is created here by superb artists. From potters to folk artists to basket weavers to chair makers, a great many craftspeople call Cannon County home.

Unfortunately, many of the gifted craftspeople don't like you to visit their home workshops unless they know you, preferring instead to sell their crafts through various shops and at craft shows throughout the Southeast. A directory listing more than 100 local craftspeople is available from the Arts Center of Cannon County in **Woodbury.** Call (800) 235–9073, or visit www.artscenter ofcc.com.

The county's craftspeople come out in force for the local **White Oak Country Fair,** held the second weekend in August. Artists from other counties are invited to participate as well, making this a wonderful place to buy items you won't find in too many other locales. The fair is held at the Arts Center of Cannon County on John Bragg Highway (US 70-S), 1 mile west of town.

Check statewide crafts show calendars, or write the **Arts Center of Cannon County,** P.O. Box 111, Woodbury 37190.

Up off Highway 96 at the very top of the county is the little community of **Auburntown,** which claims to have the **"best little fish fry in the South."** In fact, that's a bit modest. It actually has two of the best fish fries in the South. Both are held in the community center, and you'll see a lot of the same people feasting at both. They're the social highlights of the area.

The local Lion's Club has been holding its fry the first Saturday of each month since 1978, when it was first held

soconfusing

Short Mountain in Cannon County is actually the highest point between the Ozarks and the Appalachian Mountains.

as a way to raise money for the club. Since then it has become a tradition. They offer both deep-fried shrimp and northern white bass, along with all the fixin's, for just $7 per person. Call Roger Turney for more information, (615) 464–5210.

The Lion's Club outing was so popular that the local volunteer fire department decided to fry up some fish to make a few bucks. The firefighters hold theirs on the third Saturday of each month and offer chicken along with their fried fish. They charge $8 "for the working man" and $6 for seniors. Call Frank Patrick for the info on the firefighters' fry, (615) 464–4213.

Both fries include homemade hush puppies (worth the trip themselves), white beans, coleslaw, and iced tea and coffee. Both do amazingly well, with the firefighters' averaging nearly 1,200 meals a month; the Lion's Club, a bit less. There's a huge repeat business from month to month from a six-county area. It's a great place to catch up on all the gossip and to meet some great icons of rural America.

Several bed-and-breakfast facilities in the state are also bona fide tourist attractions, and **Evins Mill** in **Smithville** is one of them. James Lockhart built his mill on this spot in 1824 and had a burgeoning business through the late 19th century. Tennessee state senator Edgar Evins purchased the property in 1937, renamed it, and had a 4,600-square-foot lodge built on the bluff overlooking Fall Creek and the mill.

Today the lodge and the rustic cabins built along the bluff serve as a bed-and-breakfast. The restored mill, still with all its workings in place, is a full-service state-of-the-art conference center. The kitchen of the lodge has been turned into a modern operation with a full-time chef who provides lodging guests as well as conferencing business folks with gourmet meals. The huge stone fireplace and the original wood flooring add a neat, homey feeling to the environment. If you want someone else to do the cooking, this is a charming place to spend Thanksgiving Day! Roaring fire in the fireplace, good eating, and some great walking trails will help make the day a fun one for everyone! It's off US 70 on Evins Mill Road, 1.5 miles east of the junction of US 70 and Highway 56. Call (800) 383–2349 or visit www.evinsmill.com.

The internationally famous **Old-Time Fiddler's Jamboree and Crafts Festival** is held on the Smithville Square early each July, and for a country and Appalachian music fan, it's truly a piece of heaven. There are 28 categories of traditional music and dancing, including old-time bluegrass, clogging, buck dancing, old-time fiddle bands, five-string banjo, dulcimer, Dobro, fiddling, and flat-top guitar, all for top prizes. The fiddle players have a fiddle-off to determine the grand champion fiddler. There are also seven categories for musicians under the age of 12. In addition there are more than 300 traditional crafts booths, food stands, and other great things to do and see. This is a great educational experience as well as a fun, unique event to visit. The festival is free. For more information call (615) 597–8500 or go to www.smithvilletn.com.

Back when this part of the state was known as the New Frontier, the Wilderness Road (US 70) was the main route through the state, connecting the frontier settlements to the west and the more civilized areas to the east. The Rock House stagecoach inn and tollhouse were strategically built at the point where an early railroad connection crossed the trail. Built between 1835 and 1839 of Tennessee limestone, the inn soon became a gathering place for the "Who's Who" of the American frontier.

Preserved through the years by caring friends, this piece of Americana is now open to the public on a limited basis. The Rock House chapter of the

Daughters of the American Revolution is the caretaker of the property, now known as the **Rock House Shrine** state historic area. Located on US 70, 4 miles west of Sparta, this historic site can be reached at (931) 657–2021.

A somewhat brief but solemn and touching annual event takes place at **Edgar Evins State Park,** 20 miles north of Smithville on Highway 96. A flag retirement ceremony is held on the Saturday before Memorial Day each year when the park rangers take down the American flag that has flown over the park's office and raise a new one. The local AMVETS and VFW posts come out and take part and provide the honor guard. It's a nice way to honor the veterans. For further information on this ceremony, call (931) 858–2446 or visit www.tnstateparks.com.

While you're here, check out the great Southern-fried catfish at the restaurant down at the park's marina. Located on Center Hill Reservoir, the restaurant is open daily April through October. Call (931) 858–5695 for more information.

Cookeville, Putnam County's seat of government, had two early surges of commerce that resulted in two distinct downtown sections. The town had already established its square and business hub long before the railroads came through. When the rails came to town in 1890, they came through a residential area on the west side of town. That area soon became less residential and more commercial as business shifted from the established area around the courthouse to the new, prospering area around the depot. A large hotel was built, and warehouses and stores soon followed.

By 1910 a new passenger depot had been built, and the area was considered the Hub of the Upper Cumberland. Passenger service was terminated in 1955, but the locals were able to save the depot, which is now on the National Register of Historic Places and the site of the **Cookeville Depot Museum.**

Inside is one of the best re-creations of an early depot in the state. Original fixtures, desks, time schedules, and the like have been preserved through the years. There are four rooms of exhibits, plus a caboose out back with more displays. Open Tuesday through Saturday 10:00 a.m. to 4:00 p.m. Admission

Fun-Filled Region

The region formed by the northern 14 counties in this area of the state is called the Upper Cumberland and is one of the most beautiful areas in the state for rolling hills, waterfalls, and foliage. A listing of sites, heritage trails, waterfalls, lakes, rivers, festivals, and accommodations can be found at www.uppercumberland.org. You can call the Tourism Association at (800) 868–7237.

is free; its location is Broad and Cedar Streets. Contact the depot at (931) 528–8570.

Across the street from the museum, high atop an old dairy, you'll see a big, old-fashioned neon sign advertising Cream City Ice Cream. Atop the sign is a giant ice-cream sundae whose cherry bounces up and down (in neon) when the sign is turned on. The people who bought the location when the dairy closed chose not only to save but restore the sign to its 1950s beauty. Now the sign is lit several times each year, much to the delight of local photographers and nostalgia buffs.

The streets are rolled back in Cookeville the first weekend after Labor Day each year. That's when the ***Tennessee State Championship Barbeque Cook-off*** and the ***Downtown Fall Fun Fest*** run concurrently on the streets around the courthouse. The cook-off is a Kansas City Barbeque Society-sanctioned event and regularly draws 20 to 25 teams from several states. Some of the cooking teams will not only cook for competition but will also vend their products. These, of course, are the teams you cheer on and hang with.

The Fall Fun Fest runs both days and features live entertainment on two stages with a big headline act on Saturday night. One stage is reserved for the local acts that specialize in blues, jazz, and the Latin beat. Along the streets are food vendors and a top-notch crafts fair sponsored by the Tennessee Association of Craft Artists, which holds its big festival in Nashville about three weeks later.

The local PBS television station has a big presence on Saturday with entertainment on its own stage with PBS characters and storytellers. A couple dozen activity booths are set up for the kids.

Considering everything there is to offer, this is one of the most fun-filled weekend events in the state. Check it out; get more information by calling (931) 528–4612 or going to www.fallfunfest.com.

CHOCOLATE ALERT! CHOCOLATE ALERT! The Russell Stover candy factory, located on Chocolate Drive in Cookeville, also has an outlet store. A great selection of Russell Stover candies is offered at less than retail prices. WOW! There are three levels of prices. The first quality level is the exact candy you'd buy at a retail store, but for a little less. The intermediate level is for overstocked items that exceed the company's strict peak of freshness standard but are still of top quality. The seconds are imperfectly shaped or are lacking the standards necessary for them to be included in regular packaging. (Yes, they do give out free samples!) The ***Russell Stover Candy Factory Outlet Store*** is open daily 9:00 a.m. to 6:00 p.m. Take the Cookeville/Algood exit off Highway 111, 3 miles north of I–40, and turn toward Cookeville. Almost immediately take a right onto Chocolate Drive. The store is on your left about 0.5 mile down the road. Attention, all candy lovers: Call (931) 528–6434.

Looking for some truly off-the-beaten-path, funky, laid-back outdoor fun? Cookeville's **Hidden Hollow** fills that bill. The place is hard to explain and is certainly something you don't see every day. Back in 1972 Arad Lee retired in order to live out his childhood dream and transformed an old, 86-acre discarded farm into a fun place to picnic. Among its offerings now are a small petting zoo with deer, rabbits, a 40-pound snake, ostriches, and other birds; a dandy beach complete with kiddie swimming pool; and cane-pole fishing in the pond.

There's a gingerbread house for the kids to play in, a covered bridge, a waterwheel, a wedding chapel, rock gardens, and fountains. But the real uniqueness shows up between Thanksgiving and Christmas when Lee transforms the place into a winter wonderland, most of the time without snow. The 50-foot-high windmill is lit to resemble a Christmas tree, and the hills are alive with thousands of lights and figurines. Located at 1901 Mount Pleasant Road, Hidden Hollow is open daily year-round. Admission is $4, children and seniors $3; swimming and cane-pole fishing are each $1 extra. Call Lee at (931) 526–4038, and he'll be glad to tell you all about his dream come true.

There's definitely artistic magic in a remote hollow in the beautiful hills of northern Jackson County. About 3.3 miles west of Whitleyville, along Highway 56, you'll find North Fork Lane. If you follow that gravel road for about a mile, you'll discover the hideaways of two nationally known potters: Tom and Sally Freestone of **Freestone Pottery.**

Tom and Sally moved here from New England in 1986 and established Freestone Pottery. They had met in early 1985, got married, and decided to start a new life and lifestyle in Tennessee. Tom, an Englishman, was a well-known gristmiller and had earned a reputation for restoring old mills throughout England. Sally was a potter and an art teacher. They both are now full-time potters and can barely keep up with their orders.

They specialize in functional pottery, and what makes their stuff so unique is that each piece has a short Bible verse on it. "They are all happy love and faith verses. None of this doom, gloom, and damnation for us," Sally says with a smile, adding that this work combines her three loves: clay, comforting and inspiring words, and God. Their property, which houses their showroom, home, and studio, has a waterfall and a lot of room to "come on out and have a picnic," Tom adds. Located at 707 North Fork Lane, this unusual pottery store's phone number is (401) 647–1939; www.freestonepottery.com.

Gainesboro is the seat of Jackson County and has several antiques stores on the main square in the downtown area. It also has two drugstores, Anderson & Haile Drugs and Gainesboro Drugs, which still have the old-fashioned soda fountains in operation.

If you think marbles are just for kids, then you haven't met the gang of marble players in **Celina.** For the group of dedicated players around here, the simple ring marble game is unheard of. What they play in "these here" parts is called Rolley Hole.

The game is a team sport, played on a 40-by-20-foot field called a marble yard. There are three holes evenly spaced down the middle. The object of the game is for each team of two to get their marbles into each hole in succession, down the court, back and down again, three times.

The top players make their own marbles or buy them from other local players. The best of the best was **Dumas Walker,** who died in 1991. He was the world champion Rolley Hole player, and people would come from miles to watch him play.

In his memory the **National Rolley Hole Marble Tournament** is held each September in conjunction with the county's Homecoming Day celebration. Players from other Rolley Hole hotbeds, namely, Kansas City and parts of New Jersey, come to Celina to compete in that tourney. In September the national championships are held at the nearby Standing Stone State Park. Several English players usually show up for that one as well. Call (931) 823–6347 for details.

The **Dale Hollow National Fish Hatchery,** just north of Celina on Highway 53, produces yearly about 300,000 pounds of 9-inch rainbow trout, which are used to restock public waterways. They also hatch and ship about 500,000 fingerlings each year.

Most of the public waterways in the Southeast are too warm for trout to breed, hence the need for this facility. Trout fishing is allowed and encouraged

What the Heck Is Poke Sallet?

There are only three **poke sallet** festivals in the United States, and downtown Gainesboro is home to one of them. That distinction is something to be proud of, even though this is basically a festival to celebrate a weed. Poke sallet grows wild in the South and is cooked the same as (and tastes something like) turnip and mustard greens. Events that you won't want to miss include the poke sallet–eating contest, continuous country music, and the outhouse races. (No, not a race to the outhouse, but rather a race of outhouses.) The terrapin (turtle) races are also a highlight. Found locally in the countryside, the terrapins are placed in a circle by up to 60 contestants, and the first turtle to cross the outer line of the circle wins. There are also crosscut saw contests, a hay bale roll, and the Miss Poke Sallet Festival contest. It has been held during early May each year for about 25 years; proceeds from the festival fund the Rescue Squad. Their number is (931) 268–0971.

on most dam and river sites owned by the government, so periodic restocking is necessary.

The hatchery offers self-guided tours, but there are plenty of workers around to answer any questions. The long greenhouse-type building is where the eggs are hatched, and then the small trout are taken outside to spend the rest of their time here in one of the more than 100, 8-by-100-foot concrete raceways.

Feeding times, early morning and late afternoon, are probably the best times to visit. The larger fish are fed food pellets from a truck. A certain amount of food drops down onto a base and then is blown across the water by a current of air. The smaller fish are fed by hand. Open every day year-round; admission is free. Need more information? Call (931) 243–2443.

During the first half of the 20th century, **Red Boiling Springs** was a bustling health and vacation resort known for its medicinal waters. The resort enjoyed its heyday in the years between the world wars, when as many as six large hotels and ten boardinghouses were in business. Today the spa resort feeling hasn't totally vanished. The springs are still here, as are three of the hotels, and you can still get a mineral-water bath. A major flood in the sixties wiped out much of the old-time charm, but the community has rebuilt and has restored much of that ambience.

Brenda Thomas realized back in the early 1990s that Red Boiling Springs still had a life to it and that some of the charm and history of the area could be brought back. She and her husband, Bobby, both born and raised in the area, bought and renovated **Armour's Red Boiling Springs Hotel,** built in 1924. In the fall of 1999, Reba and Laban Hilton visited the inn and decided they wanted to own it. They are now the proud owners of this charming piece of Americana. The owners were quick to assure us that nothing has changed and all the atmosphere that Brenda Thomas created is still there. They also assured me they weren't going to change its name to the Hilton Inn. There are 16 rooms, including two suites, all with private baths. Rates are $49 single, $79 double, and $129 for suites (two persons). All rates include a full country breakfast; dinner is available for an additional $13 per person, plus tax. A treatment consisting of a steam bath, mineral bath, and 30-minute massage is $65; $89 with a 60-minute massage. Located at 321 East Main Street, the proprietors of this rejuvenating stop-off can be reached at (615) 699–2180 or www.armourshotel.com.

Just down the street is a two-story brick hotel, the **Thomas House.** Owned by Evelyn Thomas Cole, who was born and raised in the area, the hotel differs in style from the others in that it has a courtyard and a European feel to it.

This historic hotel was ravaged by fire in 2001 and was closed during much of the renovation. Now there are 14 rooms back in operation, as are the kitchen and dining room. The Thomas House has the only swimming pool in town, and on Sunday from 11:00 a.m. to 2:00 p.m., the dining room is open to the public for an all-you-can-eat buffet—with no reservations required. The room rate is $100 plus tax for a double occupancy, which includes dinner and breakfast. It's located at 520 East Main Street. Call (615) 699–3006 or visit www.redboilingsprings.com.

This town was famous for four types of water: black, red, double and twist, and free stone. Each is quite different in its mineral analysis, and each was considered a "cure" for different ailments. A self-guided-tour brochure of the area is available at the small log cabin visitor center on East Main Street.

Over in **Lafayette,** the county seat, you don't have to have a map to find the biggest loafers in the county. On any fair-weather day, be it in January or June, you'll find a group of men of indeterminate age sitting under an old oak tree on the southeast side of the Macon County Public Square. With knives in hand, these whittlers have become part of small-town life around here. The chamber of commerce likes them because of their almost unlimited knowledge of the area. But you don't have to have kin in the area to ask after; just walk right up and start talking with them. Of course you'll always walk away wondering whether the directions they gave you will really take you where you want to go or whether these good ole boys have played another trick on a city slicker.

While you'll see plenty of bumper stickers in this part of the state that proclaim REELECT GORE IN 2004, it is true that Al Gore failed in his attempt to become the state's fourth resident to become president of the United States. He would have joined the ranks of such statesmen as Andrew Jackson, Andrew Johnson, and James K. Polk. Win or lose, this is still Gore country.

Gore is from the small town of **Carthage,** the county seat of historic Smith County. A good way to start your visit in this area is to stop by the Smith County Welcome Center, located in a log cabin at Mile Marker 267 on I–40, in a rest area just east of the Carthage exit. It's 60 miles east of Nashville and is accessible from both east- and westbound traffic. Inside, you'll find plenty of printed information, plus people who not only know the area but knew Al Gore as a young boy who loved showing his cattle at the county fair. If the weather's cold, sit a spell in the rocking chairs in front of the fireplace; if the weather's nice, take a short walk down to Caney Fork River. It's a pleasant setting.

In downtown Carthage, the circa 1879 courthouse is a must-see. Built in the Second Empire architectural style, the building has undergone extensive renovation and is now listed on the National Register of Historic Places. A lot more history is live and well in Carthage, including the old city cemetery and the circa 1889 Carthage United Methodist Church. The church has amazing stained-glass windows, with several dating back to when the church was built.

In 1936 the **Cordell Hull Bridge** replaced an old toll bridge. Named for the former secretary of state of the United States, who served under President Franklin D. Roosevelt, the bridge's unique steel grid work makes it not only an interesting sight but also a great place from which to view the river valley.

Upriver about 5 miles from Carthage, the 12,000-acre **Cordell Hull Lake** was built by the U.S. Army Corps of Engineers primarily for navigation, hydropower generation, and recreation. Construction began in 1963, and the lake was fully functional in 1973. The power plant visitor center is open every day from Memorial Day through Labor Day. It's located on Highway 263 north of Carthage. There are 11 access areas to the lake with boat ramps, and there are eight different recreation areas, some with camping. Call (615) 735–1023 for additional information.

On Highway 25, about halfway to Hartsville, is **Dixon Springs.** It was founded by Revolutionary War major Tilman Dixon on a military land grant. There are many of the area's original homes still standing, including **Dixonia,** the home of Major Dixon, now a private residence. Call (615) 735–2093 for more information on the area.

If Civil War history fascinates you, here's an unusual chance to find out quite a bit about Gen. John Hunt Morgan and the Battle of Hartsville. A 17-stop self-guided tour of Hartsville starts at the site where General Morgan, known as the **Thunderbolt of the Confederacy,** crossed the Cumberland River with his troops the night of December 6, 1862, and ends at the Hartsville Cemetery, where more than 50 Confederate soldiers are buried.

The general and his men seized the *Hartsville Vidette* newspaper while raiding the town, and they ended up publishing it themselves when they could find the opportunity and paper. The newspaper still publishes and still bears that historic name. The tour brochure is available from the chamber of commerce, 200 East Main Street, Suite 111. Call (615) 374–9243.

Middle Cumberland

It's hard to believe that **Dayton,** a small city 40 miles north of Chattanooga, was probably a household word from coast to coast during the long, hot summer of 1925. That's when the silver-tongued orators William Jennings Bryan and Clarence Darrow engaged in a legal battle in the **Rhea County**

Courthouse. The **Scopes "Monkey Trial"** let the world know that a Dayton outside of Ohio actually did exist. Although John Scopes, a schoolteacher, didn't reach the heights that the Wright brothers of the other Dayton did, he earned himself a place in history.

The Romanesque Revival, Italian Villa-style courthouse was built in 1891 and has been restored to its 1925 vintage. The Scopes trial courtroom is on the second floor and contains the original judge's bench, four tables, railing, jury chairs, and spectator seats.

The **Rhea County Museum** is housed in the courthouse and contains exhibits, photos, and actual newsreel footage of what many still call the first major trial treated as a media event.

Scopes was accused of teaching the Darwinian theory of evolution to a high school biology class in violation of a recently passed Tennessee statute making it unlawful "to teach any theory that denies the story of the divine creation of man as taught in the Bible."

Scopes wasn't even the school's regular biology teacher, but a math teacher filling in. He was fined $100, a fee he never paid. Open at various times during courthouse hours; admission is free. Call (423) 775–7801 for more details.

The Scopes Trial Play and Festival take place each summer in mid-July when a special drama, **The Scopes Trial: Destiny in Dayton,** is acted out in the courtroom where the trial took place. The play is adapted directly from the trial transcript and is presented by Bryan College. A historic homes tour, a crafts fair, an antique car show, and traditional music are all a part of the festival. Of course there's plenty of great Southern cooking available as well.

Like strawberries? If so, plan your visit to the Dayton area during the first or second week of May. That's when the annual **Strawberry Festival** takes place, featuring the "World's Longest (line of people eating) Strawberry Short-cake" and three days of eclectic fun.

Other events include a carnival midway full of rides, a formal ball, various sports tournaments, an arts and crafts show, and the Strawberry Jam, a music festival. Contact them at (423) 775–0361; or go to www.tnstrawberryfestival .com.

An unlikely resident of the wonderfully named Soddy Daisy, Tennessee, is the **Horsin' Around Carving School.** Owner and chief carver Bud Ellis teaches classes, does historic carousel restoration, and enjoys talking about his art. He'll give you a free tour of the place—and for only $1,250 to $1,650, you can sign up, take a course in carving, and take home your own carousel horse. The brass ring is extra.

Ellis is responsible for the restoration and the horse carving on the Coolidge Park Carousel, next to the Walnut Street Bridge in Chattanooga.

Located behind the Wal-Mart at the Soddy Daisy exit off U.S. Highway 27 North, 14 miles north of the Tennessee River. Call (423) 332–1111 or visit www .carouselcarvingschool.com.

Out on Highway 30 is the small community of Meigs, the county seat of **Decatur,** where a historic town square will attract your attention. Unlike many of the older courthouse squares, this one is a bit barren and free of large trees.

But in the shadow of the courthouse, you'll find the area's version of the **Spit and Whittle Gang,** a bunch of old-timers who gather each day to—well, you guessed it.

Codfish dinners are the specialty of the house at **Lee's Restaurant,** 11 miles south of Decatur off Highway 58. The popular eatery attracts people from all over, mostly by word-of-mouth recommendation. The "secret ingredients" in the light batter are what give the fish its great, memorable taste. A children's menu is also available. Other items include steaks, seafood combination plates, and a special vegetable plate for Sunday dinner. Open Thursday and Friday 4:00 to 8:00 p.m., Saturday noon to 8:00 p.m., and Sunday noon to 7:00 p.m. Call (423) 334–5695.

In **Athens,** just off Highway 30, rests **Tennessee Wesleyan College,** a liberal arts school established in 1857. The first building on campus, appropriately called the "Old College" building, is still standing and up until 1989 housed the county's heritage museum.

The structure, built in 1854 and also used as a hospital during the Civil War, faces the quad grounds of the school. Behind Old College on Dwain Farmer Drive, you'll find a marker explaining one of the most poignant legends in Tennessee history.

A wounded English officer from nearby Fort Loudon was befriended by an Indian chief and nursed back to health by Nocatula, daughter of the chief. The soldier, given the name of Connestoga (the oak), was accepted into the tribe and married Nocatula. A jealous suitor attacked Connestoga with a knife. As he lay dying, Nocatula confessed her eternal love for him and plunged a knife into her breast.

The pair were buried together, and the chief placed an acorn in Connestoga's hand and a hackberry in Nocatula's hand, symbolizing undying love. From these there developed two trees that grew intertwined on this spot for more than 150 years.

After these two original trees died in 1957, two others were planted. Those have since died, and today the stumps are all that remain.

The **McMinn County Living Heritage Museum** is located in Athens's old high school building, about a half mile from downtown at 522 West Madison Avenue.

The museum's collection of 19th- and 20th-century quilts is one of the finest in the state. In addition to the permanent display of quilts, a nationally known quilt show is hosted by the museum each year. Check to see when it will be held, as it varies from year to year. For more information on the quilt museum, call (423) 745–0329 or visit www.livingheritagemuseum.com.

There is also a great children's collection that includes china and bisque-head dolls, toys, and clothing, along with school desks, books, and maps dating from 1850. Admission is charged; open daily except Sunday. Call (423) 745–0329.

The *Mayfield Dairy* has been serving the folks in this part of the state for more than 75 years with fresh milk products and some of the best ice cream you've ever sunk your teeth into. The dairy now offers fun tours, which conclude at a gift shop and dairy bar where you can sample (for a price) some of the products you saw being made. Their phone number is (423) 745–2151 or go to www.moospace.com.

The *Swift Museum Foundation* is housed here at the McMinn County Airport, which is also the Swift Aircraft international headquarters. The small planes with the home-built feel to them were first built in Texas in the mid-1940s and today have quite a fanatic following. You can learn the history and see a few of the planes at the airport, but if you really want to get a big dose of them, drop by the weekend before Memorial Day each year. That's when the annual *Swift Fly-In* takes place, usually attracting more than 100 aircraft. Get more information by calling (423) 745–9547 or www.swift museumfoundation.org.

Out on County Road 52, 8 miles west of Interstate 75, Dave and Vicki Rhyne make "fruitcakes for people who don't like fruitcakes." Really, that's their slogan. Dave told me his pecan fruitcakes don't have the raisins or citrus peel that the others do and that his contain 25 percent pecans by weight. Their *Sunshine Hollow Bakery and Exhibition Gardens* pumps out about 10,000 pounds of the holiday treat each year.

When they aren't making fruitcakes, they are out in their greenhouse hybridizing daylilies and hostas. The farm is also home to National Daylily and Hosta exhibition gardens. Right now they grow and sell 1,000 varieties of daylilies and 100 varieties of hostas. They sell them at the farm as well as by mail order. They have a two-and-a-half-acre shade garden and a seven-acre daylily garden, displaying many of their varieties. The public is invited to come out and visit the bakery operation October through December and their plant business May through July. The store sells other items as well, including pecan pralines, chocolate-covered pecans, jams, and jellies. Admission is free. Call (423) 745–4289, or go online at www.sunshinehollow.com.

At the turn of the 20th century, the site of present-day Etowah on U.S. Highway 411 was muddy farmland. Then news came that the Louisville and Nashville Railroad (known as the L&N) was to build a new railroad line between Cincinnati and Atlanta. The land was purchased to build a rail center. Named Etowah, a boomtown soon sprang up, and the **L&N Depot** was built in 1906. It became the community's central point from which social, economic, and cultural activities evolved for many years.

By 1974, passenger travel had declined to the point that the depot was abandoned and sat empty until the town purchased it in 1978. It was restored and placed on the National Register of Historic Places. It now houses a railroad museum that examines what it meant to be a railroad town in the "New South."

You've never seen a railroad depot like this one! As you drive up, the elegant Victorian structure looks more like a hotel or an elegant private home than a railroad depot. It's made of yellow pine and has 15 rooms. The depot is also home to the Depot Gift Shop, but the building itself is the star here.

The grounds around the depot remain a community gathering spot and are the site of several fairs, festivals, and weddings during the year, including a popular old-time July Fourth celebration. The train yard is still active and can provide rail buffs a fun time watching all the switching and maneuvering. Located on US 411 in downtown Etowah. For further information call (423) 263–7840.

The city fathers of Etowah have also purchased the circa 1918 **Gem Theater** and are restoring it to its cultural splendor. At one time the Gem was considered the largest privately owned theater in East Tennessee. Today it has a full schedule of live stage presentations. Located at Seventh and Tennessee Avenues. For information on shows call (423) 263–7840.

There aren't too many museums around that spotlight women in industry, but in the little village of **Englewood** you'll find such a place. This area of the state is unusual in that it was built on textile manufacturing, the one Appalachian industry that employed large numbers of women. The **Englewood Textile Museum** traces the area's textile industry from 1850. Exhibits present examples of different textiles and machinery from 1890 and emphasize the role of working-class women in the mills, their home life, and their role in the development of the community. Located at 17 Niota Street. Open Monday through Saturday noon to 5:00 p.m. Free admission, but help them out by throwing a couple bucks in their donation bucket. Call (423) 887–5455.

Adjacent to the Textile Museum is The Company Store, an antiques and "attic treasures" store. Local crafts and gift items are also available.

Southwest Cumberland

In **Tracy City** you'll find **Henry Flury and Sons** general store, which has had "staple and fancy groceries" for sale since 1905. The proprietors like to call their little establishment the "living museum of mountain life and the gathering place for friends."

Henry Flury and his three sons are all gone now, but Paul Flury, Henry's grandson, runs the store. "I guess you could say I'm the last of the Mohicans," he laughs.

Along with the groceries the store offers fresh meats, hoop cheese, produce, deli sandwiches, deli trays, and hand-dipped ice cream. Call ahead and they'll pack a picnic for you. The old wooden floors and the high ceilings are just what you would think you'd find in a store like this. Feed bags hang from the ceiling, baskets line the top shelves, and old-time items are sitting around the shop. The local folk use the store as a handicraft outlet for their homemade products. Located on U.S. Highway 41 in Tracy City. For further information about products, call (931) 592–5661.

Stay on US 41 and head to Monteagle, where, just across Interstate 24 on U.S. Highway 64/41A, you'll find one of the best places for pit barbecue and hickory-smoked meats in the state. **Jim Oliver's Smokehouse** complex offers a great country store, meeting rooms, a lodge, a motel, a wedding chapel, and his famous restaurant. In all, he has 20 acres full of all sorts of things to do. The motel's swimming pool is a sight in itself; it's in the shape of a ham. Call (931) 924–2268 for additional information.

If you're heading toward **Monteagle,** make plans to stay at the **Edgeworth Inn,** located on the grounds of the historic Monteagle Assembly. The inn, owned and operated by Jeanine Clements and Michael Owens, is a first-class, ten-bedroom bed-and-breakfast. Built as a boardinghouse in 1896, the structure has been completely renovated to its Victorian splendor and offers guests a respite from the real world.

letmomvote

Women today can thank the state of Tennessee for helping them get their right to vote. It was the state's ratification in 1920 that added the 19th Amendment to the Constitution, giving women the vote.

The owners accept no pets, and they ask you to call ahead and make arrangements if you'll be bringing children. Rooms start at $125. They can be reached at (931) 924–4000 or www.edgeworthinn.com.

Grundy County is gaining a national reputation as a mountain crafts center thanks to several artisans whose works are known and in demand from coast to coast. Many of these craftspeople have settled in the center of the county and have established homes and local ties.

In *Altamont* folk artist Ron Van Dyke bought the town's old mill and rebuilt a couple of its buildings. He plans to restore as much as possible. *Greeters Mill* pumped water for the town, ground its corn, cut its wood, and was a major operation until 1968.

On the other side of Beersheba Springs, Phil and Terri Mayhew live and work in an 1850s log cabin. Phil's work with high-fired, functional porcelain pottery is represented by ten galleries in 12 states. Terri creates porcelain and handwrought silver jewelry. Phil, a former arts professor, has developed a porcelain that will fuse at a higher temperature, thus making it more durable and giving it a unique color range.

Although they do some shows and are still represented by some of the country's finest galleries, Phil and Terri do about half of their business out of their home. *Beersheba Porcelain* has no showroom, no fancy gallery, just a lot of great art. In the warmer months they'll have stuff on the front porch; the rest of the year, "we kinda sleep and eat around our business" in the house, Phil said.

The Mayhew cabin is in the historic district, just off Highway 56. They have a small sign out front, so you'll have to look hard or you might miss it. If you do, drop by the Beersheba Springs Market, the only store in town, and the friendly folk there will direct you to the Mayhews. Contact the Mayhews at (931) 692–2280 or www.beershebaporcelain.com.

Beersheba Springs was a bustling resort area during the last half of the 1800s, and its grand hotel, which was built in 1850, is still standing. Down the road a couple of blocks from the Mayhews, the building is now owned by the United Methodist Church and used as a summer meeting facility. The view from the front of the hotel is nothing less than breathtaking.

When the hotel was active, stagecoaches would stop at the foot of the mountain and sound a horn once for each guest they had aboard for the hotel. By the time they reached the top, the hotel's band was ready to greet them. Dinner and a clean room had also been prepared.

The *Beersheba Springs Arts & Crafts Fair* takes place on the hotel grounds each August and is considered one of the best shows in this part of the state. The setting alone sets this show apart from most of the rest. Call (931) 692–3733 for dates and times.

Cumberland Caverns, located about 7 miles southeast of McMinnville just off Highway 8, is the second largest cavern system in the United States, after Kentucky's Mammoth Cave, and is a U.S. National Landmark. Unless you happen to be an expert in this sort of thing, most of the tour through the cave reminds you of just about any other cave journey.

One room here, however, is impressive no matter what your interests are. The Underground Ballroom is 600 feet long, 150 feet wide, and 140 feet high. It is the *largest cave room east of the Mississippi River.* The room's man-made amenities are built alongside the natural formations. Of these constructed features, the most amazing is the dining room, which will seat 500 for a banquet. High above the tables is a 15-foot, 1,500-pound chandelier from a theater in Brooklyn, New York. And all this is more than 300 feet below the hustle and bustle of the real world! Find out more by calling (931) 668–4396 or go to www.cumberlandcaverns.com.

Falcon Rest, in *McMinnville,* is both an elegant bed-and-breakfast and a tourist attraction. In fact, owners Charlien and George McGlothin had so many requests for tours of the house that they now offer daily tours from 9:00 a.m. to 5:00 p.m. for $7 per person. The hour-long tour, peppered with local color and anecdotes, is a great way to learn the personal history of this magnificent Queen Anne–Victorian mansion, built in 1897 by entrepreneur Clay Faulkner for his wife, Mary.

Faulkner promised Mary that he would build her the finest house in Warren County if she would move next to their woolen mill, then 2.5 miles from town. She agreed, and a year later the couple moved in with their five children. In 1946 the 10,000-square-foot mansion was converted into a hospital and nursing home. By the mid-1950s the building had been added onto and named the Faulkner Springs Hospital. Today bloodstains can still be seen on the floor in a couple of spots, and the nursing station now houses some of the modern kitchen equipment.

In his tour of the house, George proudly points out that this was the first house built with central heat and air-conditioning in the county and that its foundation goes 17 feet below ground to solid bedrock. George was born and raised locally, and his sister was born in this house when it was a hospital. As a bed-and-breakfast, the mansion offers seven guest rooms lavishly furnished with period antiques and private baths. Rates start at $105 per room, per night, with a full breakfast. A honeymoon suite, complete with brass bed, has been built in the old kitchen. The house next door has been added to the complex and now serves as a visitor center with a large Victorian gift shop, a tearoom, a Jacuzzi suite, and a wedding chapel. At the end of Faulkner Springs Road, off the US 70 bypass. Call (931) 668–4444, or go online to www.falconrest .travel.com.

Warren County, which McMinnville serves as county seat, is known as the *Nursery Capital of the World.* More than 500 commercial nurseries throughout the county produce trees, shrubs, and plants, many of which are located along the major highways and provide miles of flowering beauty for you to observe as you drive along. Several of the nurseries are open for tours; some have small retail outlets. For a listing of those open to the public, call the chamber of commerce at (931) 473–6611 or go to www.warrentn.com.

Of Forests and Rivers

If you happen to be in this part of the state and are tired of beautiful, lush mountains and forests, trek on over to the *Ducktown* area, a portion of the state often referred to as *Tennessee's Badlands.* Here you won't be surrounded by lush, green vegetation. In fact, you'll be surrounded by a 56-square-mile area of barren red hills, stunted pine trees, and washed-out gullies. This area of raw landscape is similar in looks to the famed badlands area of the Dakotas.

The story about this area, known officially as the *Copper Basin* area of Tennessee, Georgia, and North Carolina, is a fascinating tale of hard work and inadvertent destruction of the environment. The area is steeped in the history of copper mining. Copper was first discovered in 1843 near Potato Creek, between Ducktown and *Copperhill,* and by 1860 copper mining was in full swing and dominated and dictated the lifestyle of the basin for generations until the last mine closed in 1987.

By the time the industry called it quits, there was a 56-square-mile area of denuded red hills shimmering with glowing colors ranging from soft pastels to dark copper hues. The area stood out because of the otherwise lush green of the Cherokee National Forest. From space, NASA photos show the area look-ing like a moonscape.

Through vigorous reforestation programs, most of the area now has some vegetation growing, and it will only be a matter of years before the Copper Basin blends in with the rest of the area. However, some historians are hoping to keep a part of the area barren as an example of their active copper mining heritage.

The copper mining story is told through numerous methods at the **Duck-town Basin Museum** on the Burra Burra Mine site, now on the National Register of Historic Places. Founded in 1978, the museum is located on 17 acres that include the buildings, mining structures, and mechanical operations of the mine site just as they were when it went out of business. The state purchased the museum in 1988, making it the first state-owned historic industrial site.

This is a fascinating part of the state that few residents even know exists. It's also an industry that isn't much talked about in the state. Your visit here should begin at the museum. You'll learn about the industry, why the area looks as it does, why the social life was affected so drastically by the industry, and what part Native Americans played. You'll also get a chance to tour the mine site, but you are not permitted to go underground.

Hoist House, which housed the equipment used to pull men and ore from the mines, is now used as a theater and is where the annual Halloween Ghost Stories storytelling festival is held. This structure and the steam boiler building were two of the first structures built at the turn of the 20th century by the Tennessee Copper Company. Hoist House is open Monday through Saturday, year-round. Adults are charged $3; seniors, $2; children 12 and under, 50 cents. Call (423) 496–5778.

In the quaint little village of Ducktown, around the corner from the museum, is the **Company House Bed & Breakfast.** Built in 1850 by the mine company's doctor, the building has had a colorful past. After standing empty for nearly a decade, the building was purchased by Margie Tonkin and Mike Fabian, who dove in and undertook 90 percent of the massive renovation project by themselves. That was 1994. "It took us two weeks just to figure out where to start and we did it one room at a time," Mike said. Now the structure is listed on the National Register of Historic Places.

Ask Margie and Mike about the renovation and they'll pull out a volume of "before" and "after" photos that will astonish you! They'll also show you photos of the Italian Olympic white-water team that stayed here during the Olympic trials that took place on the nearby **Ocoee River.**

The six bedrooms, all with private baths, are named for area mines and are quite nice, as is the marvelous hearty breakfast the couple puts out every morning for their guests. All rooms are nonsmoking; well-behaved children over 12 years of age are welcome, Margie notes. Rates are from $80 to $90 per room for two adults. Located at 125 Main Street, this peaceful bed-and-breakfast can be reached at (423) 496–5634 or www.companyhousebandb.com.

A great many residential and industrial structures within the Copper Basin are listed on the National Register of Historic Places. More than 200 are listed as part of the **Copper Basin Historic District.** Along with **Ocoee,**

Copperhill, across the Ocoee River from Georgia, was another major town during the copper days. It was the corporate headquarters for the Tennessee Copper Company in 1904 and still resembles the company town that it was.

The storefronts along Ocoee Street and the stone steps that lead to the houses on various levels of the hill above the town offer a glimpse of early life there. As in any company town, the workers lived at street level, closest to the factory or mine. Other employees lived further up the hill in order of importance, most often with the president at the top so that he could overlook the entire operation. Many of those houses are still in use today and are a part of a walking tour of Copperhill's residential area. Maps are available throughout the town.

In 1911 the Grand Avenue Bridge was built across the Ocoee and connected the mining town of McCaysville, Georgia, with Copperhill. Take a walk across the bridge and look for the spot where you can stand with one foot in Tennessee and one in Georgia. For more information on these two historic mining towns, write the Ocoee Region Information Center, P.O. Box 1094, Copperhill 37317.

Farther down US 64, between Ducktown and Cleveland, you'll find yourself driving along the Ocoee River, one of the top ten white-water rivers in the country. You'll also find numerous business establishments that will be more than happy to rent you a raft, canoe, or kayak so that you, too, can experience an adventure of a lifetime. The river is such a good area for white-water events that it was chosen as the site of the white-water competition in the 1996 Summer Olympics, held in nearby Atlanta.

The **Ocoee Whitewater Center,** located a few miles northwest from Ducktown along US 64, was the site of the 1996 Olympic Slalom Canoe/Kayak events and following the games became a visitor center and a hub for both land- and water-based recreation activities in the Cherokee Forest and Ocoee River areas.

Now open to the public, the center houses a gift shop, the Olympic Legacy exhibit, and a conference center. Open daily 9:00 a.m. to 5:00 p.m. during spring, summer, and fall; Friday through Sunday in November through April. Contact the center at (423) 496–5197 or www.r8web.com/ocoee.

Outside, a native flower garden and a magnificent pond have been created. A path has been built along the white-water channel where the races took place, and you can hike or bike the Old Copper Road, a section of which has been restored adjacent to the center.

A walk along the 2.4-mile-long section of the **Old Copper Road** takes you across four footbridges from the 1850s era. Built in 1851, the 33-mile-long road was used to haul copper ore from the mines in Ducktown to the railhead in Cleveland. Most of the original section was destroyed when the adjacent US 64 was built in the 1930s, and this is the only original section still intact. Along the road you'll find an abundance of flora and fauna. Take time to go out on the deck overlooking a beaver pond. Neat place!

If you're not of the adventurous variety or don't have the time, there are several pull-offs where you can experience the danger and the excitement of the white water vicariously. The mostly two-lane road is very busy here, so be careful to pull off the road completely before you take in the beauty.

If you do choose to be adventurous (and you really should), a good place to stop is the **Ocoee Adventure Center,** located on US 64, 3 miles east of the Ocoee Whitewater Center. The proprietor of this outpost worked the river for decades for other people. When he decided to go off on his own, he brought along some of the best river guides in the area.

You'll get a lesson on how to best combat the white-water adventure awaiting you, then you'll be told how you must respect the river itself. "It's a wild, unpredictable ride, and you must be ready to handle everything. This is not an amusement park ride," our guide told us.

With life jackets and helmets in place, you'll climb aboard a school bus for a 4-mile trip down to the river's entry point. There you'll be launched for one great ride through areas of the river with such ominous names as Grumpy's Ledge, Hell's Hole, Tablesaw, and Double Trouble. Call (888) 723–8622 or visit www.ocoeeadventurecenter.com for up-to-date schedules, special events, and prices. The cost here and at most outfitters along the river usually depends on the day of the week you choose for your trip, with Saturday during peak season costing approximately $49 for a half-day journey. It's $39 per person Sunday through Friday. No one under 12 years of age is permitted.

Look closely through the trees on the other side of the river and you'll see the largest wooden flume known to exist in the United States. The **Ocoee Flume** is 5 miles long, 11 feet wide, and 14 feet tall. Originally built in 1912

Rugged and Cool Counties

The **Tennessee Overhill Heritage Association** promotes the counties of McMinn, Monroe, and Polk, and there's plenty of cool stuff to promote in this southeast area of the state! This is where the best white-water rafting and outdoor adventures take place. Plus, some of the most spectacular scenic drives in the state are here. The association has a great Web site where you can order all sorts of specialty brochures, www.tennesseeoverhill.com, or call (423) 263–7232.

by the Tennessee Valley Authority (TVA), it was closed for a few years in the late 1970s and then rebuilt.

Its major function is to divert water from the river to help produce hydro-electric power, but it has also been a savior of the river for the white-water aficionados. With the diversion the flume creates, the TVA can produce their power and the river can still run to the point of whiteness.

The Webb Bros. Float Service in Reliance, along the Hiwassee Scenic River, is not only a professional outfitter, but the **Webb Brothers Store,** in which it is located, is a fun and funky general store to visit.

If it's a peaceful, easy journey down a scenic river you're looking for, here's the place. They rent one- or two-passenger rubber "duckies" that are self-bailing and hard to flip over. Resembling a kayak, they rent for $20 per person, including the 5-mile trip up the river where you're dropped off. You then paddle and float the current back downriver and get out at the store, where you began your journey.

The trip can be direct, or you can stop and swim, rest, or just sit and watch the other boats go by. If you like, pack your lunch and take it along. This is a great first river adventure for smaller children and the weak at heart, and it's a beautiful journey as well.

In addition to its river services, the store sells groceries, prepared foods, snacks, gasoline, and just about anything else you'll need while you're in the area. The store, built in 1955, also serves as the town museum and has photos and memorabilia of early **Reliance.** Entry is free; call (423) 338–2373.

The Webbs is a good starting place for your tour of the **Reliance historic district,** listed on the National Register of Historic Places. You can pick up information and quite a few stories about the area that will make your visit

click&surf

An easy way to find out more about all the corners of Tennessee is to log on to one of the state's best independent Web sites: www.seetennessee.com.

a lot more fun. The district, off Highway 30 along the river, has five principal buildings, including a hotel and the first house to have indoor plumbing. None of the restored structures is open to the public on a regular basis, but they are beautiful to look at. The area is still quite underdeveloped, so a drive through can give you a good idea of what life was like along the river at the turn of the 20th century.

For a spectacular view of the Hiwassee River, you'll want to walk all or part of the **John Muir Trail,** an 18.8-mile-long trail that meanders along the river. Not only are the views of the river fantastic but you'll also see a tremendous amount of wildlife and native plants. Watch for the beaver activity all along the trail. In addition you'll have the opportunity to view ruby-throated hummingbirds, mink, raccoons, and great blue herons. What are those things sunning themselves on the flat rocks in the river? Chances are they are North America's largest salamander, the hellbender.

The trail begins at Childers Creek, near Reliance (follow the signs), and ends near Highway 68 at Farner. If you have your entire family to watch out for, you might want to stick to the first 3-mile section of the trek; it has been designated as an easy walk but still covers some beautiful terrain.

Mention mountain forests and fantastic views, and most people think of the Smoky Mountains. That's why the 620,000-acre *Cherokee National Forest* here in the southeast portion of the state remains virtually untouched by crowds.

More than 1,100 miles of roads have been cut through the dense forest, opening up all sorts of opportunities for outdoor enthusiasts or for those who simply enjoy driving and looking. Take your time; there's a real good chance that no one will be honking and trying to get around you. The Forest Service maintains 29 camping areas, horse trails (bring your own horse), and 105 hiking trails. This area is every bit as beautiful as the Smokies, making it a great alternative that most locals are hesitant to tell too many people about. The supervisor's office can give you more specifics; call (423) 338–5201.

When you're in *Cleveland* you're deep in Cherokee country, and history abounds. This was the geographic center for Native American culture in the Southeast, and there are reminders of that fact throughout the city and county.

The historical area of Cleveland is known as the Downtown Historic Greenway. Johnson Park, in the heart of downtown, is a great place to start a walking tour of the city. There are 20 different historic sites on the tour, including restored churches and buildings. While in Johnson Park, stop by and marvel at the *Cherokee Chieftain,* a wonderful sculpture of an Indian

Celebrating Agriculture

The one-of-a-kind **Polk County Ramp Tramp Festival** takes place each year during the fourth week of April at Camp McCroy 4-H Camp in Greasy Creek, on Highway 30 south of Reliance. The day begins with a trip to Big Frog Mountain to dig, and then you come back to camp and cook and eat the ramps. A popular annual event since 1958, the festival features local bluegrass music along with your ramps. Call (423) 338–4503.

chief carved from a tree by internationally known Native American artist Peter Toth.

To get a better idea of the role the county played in the everyday life of the Cherokee, two self-guided tours have been developed. Maps and additional information are available at the Cleveland Convention and Visitors Bureau, 2145 Keith Street; (423) 472–6587. The Cherokee Heritage Wildlife Tour points out the best locations in the area to view wildlife and allows you to get a good feel for the Cherokee heritage. The Cherokee Scenic Loop Tour begins and ends in Cleveland and takes you throughout the county, where you'll visit many of the areas mentioned in this chapter, including Red Clay and the Ocoee River. Both maps offer a well-organized way to see the best the county and the region have to offer.

One of the state's most forward-looking historical museums is located in the 5ive Points area of downtown Cleveland. Opened in late 1999, the *Museum Center at 5ive Points* incorporates the *Cleveland Bradley Regional Museum* and the *Amanda T. Gray Cultural Center.*

Unlike most historical museums included on our off-the-beaten-path journey through Tennessee, this one is bright and new but merits a few words because of its community-minded, contemporary mission. It's really much more about today than it is about yesterday, and it's way beyond your father's typical stuffy local museum. Hats off to you folks in Cleveland!

The museum center was created to fill four distinct community needs: Create a place to preserve heritage in order to give residents, children, and visitors a sense of the area's rich history; create a showcase for the entrepreneurial spirit that continues to fuel the community; create a cultural center to showcase the talents of residents; and create an anchor for the 5ive Points revitalization project.

Located at 200 Inman Street East, the center opens Tuesday through Saturday at 10:00 a.m. Call (423) 339–5745, or visit www.museumcenter.org.

If you're looking for some great food and want to have a little fun at the same time, head out to the *Apple Valley Orchard,* 351 Weese Road, 10 miles southeast of Cleveland. There you'll visit a farmers' market and bakery that offers a variety of foods. Fresh-baked apple goods don't get any better than this! Open daily from the end of August through December; no admission charge. Call (423) 472–3044.

About 12 miles south of Cleveland, off a series of back roads, you'll find the *Red Clay state historic area.* Red Clay was the site of the last council ground of the Cherokee nation before their forced removal in 1838. It was the site of 11 general councils, national affairs attended by up to 5,000 Native Americans each.

The U.S. government wanted the Cherokees to surrender their eastern lands and move the entire tribe to lands in Oklahoma. The Cherokees fought it for quite a while, but controversial treaties resulted in their losing the land. The journey to Oklahoma, known today as the Trail of Tears, actually began here at Red Clay.

The march, often referred to as the Great Removal, was a wintertime cross-country journey that covered more than 1,000 miles. Reportedly, 4,000 of the 18,000 who were forced to leave perished during the trek. That was almost one-fourth of the entire Cherokee nation.

Today people can drive that same path across the state on the ***Trail of Tears State Historic Route.*** It's marked quite well, and maps that explain the various historical activities along the way are available here at Red Clay. About 80 percent of the original trail is now covered by modern highways.

Here where it all began, a 275-acre state historic area has been developed. The only original part left is the council spring, locally known as the "blue hole." It was this pure running spring that probably attracted the Cherokees to this site in the first place.

Also on the grounds are various reproductions of early Native American homesteads and an interpretive center with displays and historical exhibits.

It's not an easy place to find. Take Highway 60 south out of Cleveland and follow the signs. They are good signs, but often understated in size and can be easily overlooked if you happen to be looking at the cows and horses along the way. If you see a sign that reads WELCOME TO GEORGIA, you've gone about a half mile too far. Open daily; admission is free. Call for more information at (423) 478–0339.

For more information on the Cherokee Mountains, the Ocoee River, Cleveland, and the entire Bradley County area, call (800) 472–6587 or visit the chamber of commerce Web site at www.clevelandchamber.com.

Crossroads of Dixie

Chattanooga, the state's fourth-largest city, with a population of fewer than 160,000, is located along a 7-mile bend in the Tennessee River. The deep ravine along the river is often referred to as the ***Grand Canyon of the South.***

Lookout Mountain is probably the best known of the three major "ledges" that loom over the city. As in any major tourist destination, the beaten path and the unbeaten path catch up with each other here, with the same attraction often offering different things to different people.

A lot of states have large public aquariums, but none can beat the ***Tennessee Aquarium*** here in Chattanooga at One Broad Street next to the Tennessee

River. The location is quite appropriate for the theme of this beautiful facility, which opened in 1992.

Billed as the "world's largest major freshwater life center," the aquarium salutes the state that has more species of freshwater fish than any other state. Few of us will ever have the chance to personally explore the entire length of the magnificent Tennessee River, but here's your chance, and it will take less than two hours. During that time you'll have the opportunity to see more than 9,000 creatures that swim, fly, and crawl—all in their natural habitats.

Through exhibits of live and luxuriant flora and fauna, you can take a journey from the river's source in the Appalachian High Country through its midstream and finally to the Mississippi Delta. A visit to the aquarium is an enjoyable experience for the entire family. Open every day except Christmas and Thanksgiving. Admission is charged. Find out more at (800) 262–0695 or visit www.tnaqua.org.

Adjacent to the aquarium is the ***Chattanooga Visitor Center,*** a great place to start your visit here. Open seven days a week from 8:30 a.m. to 5:30 p.m., the center offers a wide assortment of brochures on the area's attractions, accommodations, and restaurants. Information specialists are on hand and will be glad to point you in the right direction. Among the bright and shiny brochures is a set of four historical and architectural tour brochures. Pick them up, as they offer a vast amount of information on various areas and neighborhoods of the city, places you might otherwise overlook. Inside the center are public restrooms, vending machines, a gift shop, and an ATM.

The city is obviously quite proud of its river heritage. To prove that point, the city founders have created the ***Tennessee Riverpark*** along the mighty Tennessee River, adjacent to the aquarium. Beware; there are some steep grades and a lot of steps, but it does appear to be wheelchair accessible via a series of ramps. The area includes parks, fishing piers, a riverside amphitheater carved out of the bluff under a highway overpass, and playgrounds.

Along the Riverwalk, which runs through the Riverpark, you'll come upon the 2,370-foot-long ***Walnut Street Bridge*** spanning the river. The circa 1891 bridge is considered the longest pedestrian walkway in the world. Once the only way across the river in the city, the structure underwent a $4 million renovation in 1993 and is now a fun place to walk, jog, or sit upon one of

whatadeal forabuck!

The first franchised Coca-Cola bottling plant in the world was built in Chattanooga in 1899 by two local attorneys, who bought the franchise bottling rights for $1 each.

the benches and enjoy a fantastic view of the river far below and the Ross's Landing area of the city.

A fun event takes place on the Walnut Street Bridge in late September each year. The *Wine Over Water Festival* is a wine-tasting event that offers a fine selection of wines, entertainment, and activities.

While tasting the fruit of the vine on the bridge, make sure you walk over to the north shore and visit Coolidge Park, located on the waterfront between the Walnut Street and Market Street Bridges. Located there is a historic carousel that operates most of the year, offering rides for $1.

A stroll farther up the Riverwalk takes you to the *Bluff View Art District,* where you'll find a classy little conclave of arts and dining. The area, on East Second Avenue, high on a bluff overlooking the Tennessee River, is definitely the hippest area in the city.

There among the tall shade trees, you'll find the *Hunter Museum of American Art,* housed in a restored classic revival mansion. It offers the most complete collection of American art in the Southeast. Call (423) 267–0968 or visit www.huntermuseum.org. Nearby, the *Anna Houston Museum* houses the renowned decorative arts collection of Anna Safley Houston.

The *River Gallery* is housed in a turn-of-the-20th-century home and showcases an extensive collection of regional, national, and international fine art and crafts, including paintings, sculptures, and studio art glass. Across the street is the *River Gallery Glass Studio,* where you can watch resident glass artists demonstrate a variety of glassblowing styles and techniques.

The two-acre *River Gallery Sculpture Garden* overlooks the Tennessee River and features 30 pieces of original art placed around a beautifully land-scaped garden. All the art is for sale through the River Gallery.

The *Bluff View Bed & Breakfast* consists of three turn-of-the-20th-century restored homes, all offering spectacular bird's-eye views of the river. Rates start at $115, including breakfast.

Once you've settled into a classy room, get out and walk around the area. It's amazing up here, with everything only a couple of steps away from everything else.

There are five restaurants to choose from. *Tony's Pasta Shop and Trattoria* serves up a classic Italian menu specializing in fresh house-made pastas, sauces, and European-style breads. Open daily year-round for lunch and dinner. The *Renaissance Commons* offers a bountiful Sunday brunch from 11:00 a.m. to 2:00 p.m., and the *Back Inn Cafe* serves upscale cuisine and desserts to die for and has extensive wine and beer lists. Open daily for lunch and dinner, it has terrace dining overlooking the river, weather permitting.

If it's good coffee and a fresh pastry or overstuffed sandwich you're looking for, **Rembrandt's Coffee House** is open all day, every day.

The newest addition to the Bluff View family is the **Bluff View Bakery.** The vision of Bluff View head baker Rob Alexander, the establishment is located in the renovated Powers & Condon building across from the River Sculpture Garden. Here you'll find the famous Bluff View Art District's signature breads, including the ciabatta and the country loaf, and of course a bunch of other really cool baked goods.

For information on everything up here, call (800) 725–8338 or (423) 265–5033 or visit www.bluffviewartdistrict.com.

The popular **Riverbend Festival** takes place along the river each June and usually attracts about a half million people during its nine-day run. It's so spread out, however, you don't usually feel crowded. More than 100 musical artists perform on five different stages, offering up everything from rock, country, and blues to jazz and folk. Of course, there are all kinds of food and drink and other festival-style activities. Get more details at (423) 756–2212 or log on to www.riverbendfestival.com.

Selected as one of the top 20 children's museums in the nation by *Child* magazine, the **Creative Discovery Museum** in downtown Chattanooga is all about child's play. Located at 321 Chestnut Street, the museum is an awesome place to spend time playing and learning. Kids can climb up to a crow's nest, dig for dinosaur bones, see how bees make honey, spray jets of water to spin whirligigs, build robots, make a sculpture, and make music with all types of musical instruments.

The museum's Rooftop Fun Factory is designed to provide hours of fun and education—and it's only one of the choices at the Creative Discovery Museum. The Rooftop Fun Factory takes play outside and opens it up under a big sky. Explore the world of simple machines with sound, movement, and fun galore. Blow soap bubbles and watch as they gently sail through the sky. Turn a wheel to play a pretty tune. Use pulleys to lift yourself off the roof. Work a hand pump up and down to launch balls into the air and make them bounce through a cage. Crank a huge ball into the air and watch as it shakes the roof on its way back down. Call (423) 756–2738 or visit www.cdmfun.org for more details.

In 1916, while steering a Tin Lizzie over a bumpy road, a Chattanooga motorist took a sharp right when he shouldn't have and helped create a major invention. When the dust cleared, John Wiley and his son found themselves unhurt. Their car, however, was submerged in the Chickamauga Creek. Only one wheel peeked above the water. When he got to the closest phone, Wiley called Ernest Holmes, a former student from his business college who now operated a garage and automobile repair shop. Holmes feared it was a hopeless cause, but the ingenious scheme he came up with worked. Using three poles, a pulley, and a chain hooked to the frame of a 1913 Cadillac, Holmes pulled the vehicle back up on the road. From that, the Wrecker King was born. With more and more horseless carriages chugging along the nation's roads, Holmes foresaw a need for handling wrecked and disabled vehicles. In the fall of 1917, the Chattanooga man created the first wrecker in the United States. That tale is recounted at the ***International Towing and Recovery Hall of Fame and Museum*** at 3315 Broad Street in Chattanooga.

At the museum, visitors can see all kinds of spiffy wreckers and towing equipment. A green 1929 Chrysler with a Weaver 3-ton auto crane sparkles everywhere, from its protruding headlights to its glistening black tow hook. Its gold-rimmed tires look as though they have never seen a spot of dirt. Then there's the 1936 Chevy truck emblazoned with the notice IT'S A DIRTY JOB BUT SOMEONE HAS TO DO IT. The wrecker is waxed to the max. Opened in September 1995, the museum was built by the Friends of Towing, an organization boasting over 350 members throughout 21 counties. A Hall of Fame portion of the museum honors people who have in various ways significantly advanced the industry. Call the museum at (423) 267–3132 or visit the Web site at www .internationaltowingmuseum.org.

Children of all ages love a trip to the zoo and the ***Chattanooga Zoo*** at Warner Park is a great place for walking around and animal watching. Located in downtown Chattanooga at 1101 McCallie Avenue, the small seven-acre zoo is ideal for a day's visit. One of its most popular exhibits is the Himalayan Passage, which houses the world's largest indoor red panda habitat. In 2006, the Himalayan Passage was expanded to include habitats for snow leopards and Hanuman languars (Asian primates).

Children never seem to tire of visiting the Ranch Exhibit, where each day is a new adventure. Visitors are welcome to interact with "ranch" animals at a petting zoo. Animals making their home here include goats, sheep, Vietnamese pot-bellied pigs, miniature horses, Sicilian donkeys, dromedary camels, and man's best friend—dogs. The ranch also features tools used by ranchers and farmhands—saddles, bridles, saws, shovels, pitchforks, and more. Children will learn that before tractors and other farm machines were invented, farmers and ranchers used animals to prepare fields for planting, as well as for herding livestock and for transportation. For information, call the zoo at (423) 697–1322.

Chattanooga is one of those cities where there is an abundance of off-the-beaten-path things to see and do. Everywhere you look there are unique and fun experiences. Unfortunately we don't have room to cover them all here.

Call the visitor bureau at (800) 322–3344 for a bevy of additional activities, or visit www.chattanoogafun.com.

Along with all its Civil War history, the area around Lookout Mountain contains a lesser-known fact about an earlier war. History books usually tell us that the American Revolution started at Lexington, Massachusetts, and ended with Cornwallis's surrender at Yorktown, Virginia. Actually, historians currently say that the last engagement between official forces of the war took place on the slopes of Lookout Mountain on September 20, 1782, a year after Yorktown.

The National Park Service must agree with these historians, because it has marked the spot, just off Highway 148 near the foot of the mountain, with a historical marker, calling it the *"Last Battle of the Revolution."*

Farther up the mountain, one of the Civil War's most famous battles was fought. Known today as the "Battle above the Clouds," the fight at Chickamauga Creek and the Battle of Chattanooga are immortalized in the nation's first and largest national military park. The huge *Chickamauga-Chattanooga National Park,* established in 1890, contains more than 400 markers on the battlefield that outline the series of events that claimed 34,000 casualties. The park also contains 666 monuments honoring the men who fought on the grounds.

Just when you think you've seen all the ways that Civil War history can be taught, you walk through the front doors of the *Battles for Chattanooga Electric Map,* and get a huge surprise! This spectacular electronic 3-D battle map of the area's Civil War history features hundreds of lights, 5,000 miniature soldiers, and a computerized sound system and soundtrack. The presentation provides exceptional details of the battles fought here in November 1863. You'll also see a relic and weapons collection, and there's a well-stocked bookstore on hand for further reading about the Civil War. Located across from Point Park, at 1110 East Brow Road. Open daily year-round from 10:00 a.m. to 5:00 p.m., with extended hours during the summer. Admission is $7 for adults, $5 for children. For further information call (423) 821–2812 or visit www.battlesforchattanooga.com.

The visitor center is a good place to start your education on the area's Civil War history. It's located at the top of the mountain across from the entrance to Point Park, the site of the Battle above the Clouds. Call (423) 821–7786.

As you continue to climb Lookout Mountain, you'll pass several other well-known attractions, including the incredible *Ruby Falls.* They are very much on the beaten path but shouldn't be overlooked just because you don't like crowds or don't want to visit a place where everyone else in the world has been first. Open every day but Christmas. Admission is charged. Contact (423) 821–2544 or www.rubyfalls.com.

The **Mountain Memories gift shop** is located on the Scenic Highway, less than a mile up the mountain from Ruby Falls, and if you're looking for some funky stuff, this is the place to stop. The outside of the building is covered with advertising signs, and the porches are overflowing with rustic crafts. They offer the best price around on "See Rock City" birdhouses and bird feeders, and they have one entire area dedicated to beautiful handmade quilts. Located next to the incline tracks, the store is open daily year-round. Call (423) 821–6575.

Many Tennessee natives don't realize that one of the most popular attractions on Lookout Mountain, **Rock City,** is actually across the state line in Georgia.

"See Rock City" birdhouses and painted barn roofs throughout the Southeast have made this attraction a genuine piece of Americana. There's nothing like it anywhere else. Ten acres of natural rock gardens, some with formations looming 20 stories high, and a barren spot called **Lover's Leap,** from which seven states can be seen, are the highlights of the attraction. Twisting paths take you through wonderfully landscaped gardens and narrow crevices. One such crack is thoughtfully named "Fat Man's Squeeze."

The founder, Garnet Carter, first built a hotel on the property and in early 1928 developed a recreational outlet that changed leisure-time activities from coast to coast. Using the natural hills, rocks, hollow logs, and pools of water as hazards, he created a miniature golf course for his guests who didn't want to take the time to play a complete round of regulation golf.

Within a short time various other hotels in the country asked him to design courses for them, and **Tom Thumb Golf** took the country by storm. By 1930 about 25,000 miniature golf courses were operating in the United States, many of which were Carter's courses.

The original course and the hotel are now gone, but several of the small characters that were placed around the course are a part of the Fairyland portion of Rock City. Admission is charged. Call (706) 820–2531 or visit www .seerockcity.com.

Less than a mile from Rock City, at the very top of the mountain, the **Castle in the Clouds Resort Hotel** was built in 1928. Today the old hotel, since restored, is the main building for **Covenant College,** a small liberal arts school. Other buildings on the campus also have historical as well as nostalgic appeal. Drop by and look up one of the school's officials, who love to give tours. Call (706) 820–1560 or go to www.covenant.edu.

If you're a little leery about driving up the mountain, there's a solution. Built in 1895, the **Lookout Mountain Incline Railway** is now a part of the city's transit system. Billed as the "World's Steepest and Safest Incline Railway,"

See Rock City

That's a phrase you've seen painted on the roofs and the sides of barns throughout America. Have you ever wondered who painted most of those barns? Clark Byers can be given that credit. As the Depression drew to a close in the 1930s and more and more tourists began hitting the nation's highways once again, Rock City Garden's owner, Garnet Carter, enlisted Byers to paint the barns as unique billboards. Legend has it that when Byers asked what he was supposed to paint, Carter gave him a slip of paper with three words: See Rock City.

Farmers welcomed the new paint jobs on their barns, and Carter enjoyed the increased business the signs brought to him. Being a creative person, Byers often added mileage and the best route to the attraction on his own. The barns can still be seen as far north as Michigan and as far west as Texas. The barns became legendary, and today birdhouses can be purchased with See Rock City on their roofs, and modern billboards for the attraction are in the shape of a barn (or birdhouse) with the famous words on top. There are also several new books that feature the barn art. For more information visit www.seerockcity.com.

it has a 72.7 percent grade near the top. At the top of the mile-long ride, the upper station has been developed into a small retail village, which happens to have some of the best ice cream in the Chattanooga area. For more details call (423) 821–4224.

At the foot of the "other side" of the mountain, the west side, at 400 Garden Road in Lookout Valley, the ***Chattanooga Nature Center*** is an environmental education facility. This is a great place for your family to learn about the wonders of nature through interpretive activities. It features passive solar-design buildings that house a wildlife diorama, a touch-and-feel discovery room, and interactive exhibits. There's a 1,200-foot boardwalk out over the wetlands, with interpretive signs along the way. Contact them by phone at (423) 821–1160 or on the Web at www.chattanooganaturecenter.org.

Next to the nature center, the ***Reflection Riding*** is a 300-acre nature preserve and botanical garden that are absolutely beautiful during the spring. That's when all the wildflowers are in bloom. A 3-mile loop meanders through the area, and you can either drive, walk, or ride a bike along the path. You might spot some deer or wild turkeys as you enjoy the flora of the park. Both facilities are open year-round. Admission to both the Chattanooga Nature Center and Reflection Riding is $6 for adults and $3 for children four to 12. Call (423) 821–9582 or visit www.reflectionriding.org.

Pardon me, boy, is that the ***Chattanooga Choo Choo***? Down in the city, the Choo Choo is one of the most unusual shopping areas in the state. Located at the old Terminal Station, 1400 Market Street, the complex features a Holiday Inn with several of its rooms in restored train cars, landscaped gardens, and myriad Victorian-era shops and restaurants. This has to be the coolest Holiday Inn of all times! It's a train, it's a song, and, yes, it's a hotel! All play on the train theme. Call (800) TRACK–29 or go online at www.choochoo.com.

If sleeping in a vintage railroad car sounds romantic to you, here's an opportunity to give it a shot! The 48 sleeper cars offer a nice nostalgic touch to the journey of an off-the-beaten-path road warrior. Several of the cars overlook a formal garden area, which offers a nice selection of plants and shrubs. In early summer the roses are wonderful! A bandstand in the garden features free live entertainment several nights of the week during the summer months. This is a huge complex. In addition to the sleeper cars, the hotel consists of three buildings of hotel rooms, plus one indoor and two outdoor swimming pools.

The hotel's lobby, the original railroad terminal, was built in 1909 and is considered an architectural wonder. The 85-foot-tall freestanding brick dome is the largest of its type in the world.

The city was one of the country's earliest and largest railroad centers, and this station was the hub of that activity. On the top floor of one of the terminal buildings, one of the world's largest model railroad layouts showing the area as it was during its heyday has been created by a local model railroad club. During the week it can be seen running under automated control, but on weekends members of the club come out and "play" with their creation.

The entire display is 174 feet long and contains more than 3,000 square feet of space. The HO-gauge layout has about 100 locomotives and several hundred passenger and freight cars on about 100 miles of track. Admission is charged but is usually included in the various hotel packages.

Several stores sell copies of Glenn Miller's version of the "Chattanooga Choo Choo" song. The phrase itself was coined in 1880 when a reporter took the first train ride out of Cincinnati on the new Cincinnati-Southern Line. Since the tracks went only as far as this city, he called the train the "Chattanooga Choo Choo." The original recording is framed and hanging in the old terminal, now the hotel lobby.

Climb aboard a train at the **Tennessee Valley Railroad Museum** and see what all the choo-choo excitement is about. Located at 4119 Cromwell Road, the museum helps relive the golden age of railroading. The museum offers a wide variety of trips, such as the 55-minute Missionary Ride Local. It's quick but it packs in all sorts of entertainment, from a ride through a Civil War–era tunnel to a guided tour of the restoration shop, as well as a chance to witness how a locomotive is turned around using a turntable. Looking for something a little longer? Try the Chickamauga Turn, a five-and-a-half-hour round-trip journey to historic Chickamauga. For true rail enthusiasts, multiple Dixie Land Excursions are offered throughout the year. Among the most popular of the Dixie Land trips is the Autumn Leaf Special that covers a 100-mile round-trip ride to Summerville, Georgia, to enjoy the splendor of autumn foliage. Get more information by calling (423) 894–8028 or visiting www.tvrail.com.

In downtown Chattanooga the historic **Sheraton Read House Hotel** has undergone a $2 million renovation and now has much of the same charm it possessed through the years when five U.S. presidents, Winston Churchill, and Eleanor Roosevelt were numbered among its guests. The building is listed on the National Register of Historic Places.

What makes the historic hotel unique today is that each of its 13 floors is dedicated to a different battle of the Civil War. As you walk off the elevator, you'll see a 40-by-60-inch framed print that depicts the battle; a framed parchment next to it explains the skirmish. There are at least 19 additional prints, which show many of the generals who took part in that particular battle, along the corridors.

You don't need to be a guest to enjoy the exhibits. Stop by the front desk and you'll receive a brochure explaining what you'll see on each of the floors. The Sheraton Read House is at the corner of Martin Luther King Boulevard and Broad Street. Call (423) 266–4121.

Bessie Smith, the First Lady of Blues, was born in Chattanooga in 1894 and is today immortalized in the city's **African American Museum.** There the **Bessie Smith Performance Hall** features concerts, lectures, and seminars. There are several exhibits about her life and plenty of samples of her music. Her death certificate and piano are on display and among the museum's permanent collection. Elsewhere in the museum, there's a fun, interactive wall map of Africa before there was an America and several exhibits of local African-American history. There's a nice display of African art as well. Located at 200 East Martin Luther King Boulevard. Open Monday through Friday 10:00 a.m. to 5:00 p.m. and Saturday noon to 4:00 p.m. Admission is $5 for adults, $2 for children. Call (423) 266–8658 or visit online at www.caamhistory.com.

Do any of your kids have a passion for dragons? Well Barbara Newton turned her special love for the critters into a dragon museum called **Dragon Dreams.** Her collection of more than 2,000 dragons spans eight rooms. The dragons are awake and ready to greet you Wednesday through Sunday except for major holidays. "Even the dragons need a day now and then to visit their friends and family," Barbara told us. At 6724-A East Brainerd Road. Admission for adults is $6, children 14 and under, $3; no charge to enter the dragon-filled gift shop. More questions? Call (423) 892–2384 or visit www .dragondreams.com.

Leave Chattanooga via US 41/64/72, also known as Will Cummings Highway, and you'll be in the Raccoon Mountain area, on the "other" side of the city. Follow the signs to the **Raccoon Mountain Caverns & Campground,** quite a fun complex tucked away in the mountains.

Outside the entrance to the Raccoon Mountain Caverns, you can pan for your own gemstones just like the old-timers did. Entrance to the caves is through the gift shop. During the 45-minute guided tour, you'll meander past many beautiful formations and squeeze and duck through many small passages.

Don't miss the unique shield formation toward the end of the tour. There are only 20 such formations known to exist throughout the world, our guide told us. A map of Tennessee can also be seen outlined by formations on the ceiling in one of the rooms. On a hot day, the wonderfully cool cave can be a fun treat. Admission charge; open daily. The campground has a full-service RV camp as well as tent camping sites. Located 1.25 miles north from I–24 at exit 174. Call (800) 823–2267 or go to www.raccoonmountain.com.

Pickers and singers have been gathering together each Friday night since 1979 in the old schoolhouse at the top of Signal Mountain, just north of Chattanooga. "We call it the **Mountain Opry,** and we play from 8:00 to 11:00 p.m.," said Ken Holloway. He won't take credit for starting the weekly event but will say he was with the group that did get it going. "We were looking for a reason to get together and play some music," he told us.

Specializing in acoustic Appalachian-style bluegrass and country music, the Opry features a half dozen or so different groups each Friday night. "Whoever shows up usually gets to play," he said. It's free to get in, but the 325 seats usually fill up, so get there a bit early if you can. The schoolhouse is located just off US 127 on Fairmount Parkway, at the top of the mountain in the little village of Walden. Free admission, but they'd appreciate a donation to help pay the rent and utilities. Pay as you please. Call for more information (423) 886–3252.

In **Dunlap** there's a developing historic site that most overlook mainly because it was the illegal town dump for decades. Through the dedication of volunteers, headed up by Carson Camp, history is being uncovered on the 62-acre **Coke Ovens Historic Site.**

A huge coal industry was present in this area at the turn of the 20th century, and in this Dunlap industrial complex, coal was turned into coke for use in the iron and steel foundries in nearby Chattanooga.

When the company went out of business in 1917, there were 268 beehive-shaped coke ovens in operation. Through the years, the ovens were forgotten, covered up, and neglected. During the past few years, Camp and members of the Sequatchie Valley Historical Association have uncovered a lot of the area's heritage that had almost been forgotten.

During 2001, Camp discovered that the land upon which the ovens were built was the site of an overnight encampment of the Cherokee Indians during their Trail of Tears trek to Oklahoma. Camp figures the Indians stayed here for the same reason the ovens were built: flat land and closeness to a spring.

The 77-acre park has been listed on the National Register of Historic Places, and a replica of the original coal company store commissary has been built on the original foundation of the old structure. That building now serves as a museum, which houses the largest collection of regional historic coal mining photographs in the state. Hundreds of donated mining artifacts are on display in the museum, and one room has been set aside as a local history museum for Sequatchie County and Dunlap.

Outside, the excavation is continuing by Camp and historical association volunteers. The museum is open Sunday through Wednesday year-round. During peak summer months, it's also open on Saturday. Call (423) 949–2156 or (423) 949–3483. Their Web site can be accessed through www.bledsoe.net—a great site that has links to just about everything you could think of, including photos of the solar system.

Dunlap is 50 miles north of Chattanooga on US 127, and the Historic Coke Ovens Park is 0.75 mile west of downtown, just off US 127 on Walnut Street. A Bluegrass Festival takes place on the grounds the first Friday and Saturday in June, and a Fall Fest is held on the first Saturday in October.

If all the excitement of white-water rafting and canoeing is too much for you, stop by **Canoe the Sequatchie** and experience a few gentle thrills. The Sequatchie River is mostly placid, and the water is only about waist deep in most places, according to Scott Pilkington, who owns and operates the livery with his family.

"I've canoed the 113 miles of the Sequatchie River many times in my days," he told us. "I know, love, and live on this river. There are few surprises out there. It's a great river for families and beginners."

Scott offers three different trips, which run from 90 minutes to four hours in length. There are plenty of spots to stop and picnic, swim, and play along the way. Canoes start at $50 for two people. Open weekends from April through October, daily from Memorial Day to Labor Day.

In his home across the street, Scott has quite a model railroad collection that he would be more than happy to show off if he isn't too busy at the livery. He has a 6-by-20-foot operating layout, with hundreds of train cars, automobiles, people, and buildings, mostly in O/O-27 gauge. He's been collecting for more than 50 years and still has a few pieces he got when he graduated from kindergarten. Get on US 127 South, at the river, south of Dunlap. Look for the big bright yellow canoe sign that reads CANOE THE SEQUATCHIE. Call Scott at (423) 949–4400 or go to www.sequatchie.com/canoe.htm.

The *Dunlap Drive-In Theater* is one of fewer than 1,000 drive-ins left in America. The people around here do their best to support this one so that it won't be a part of history as well. The theater opened in 1950, and the current owner, Lavaughn Boston, purchased it in 1963 when admission was 50 cents and hamburgers were a quarter. It's open most of the year on weekends, with double features. Located near the intersection of US 127 South and Highway 28 in Dunlap; call (423) 949–3759. Their Web site, www.dunlapdrivein.com, has some great links to other drive-in and movie sites.

Farther up US 41, just across the county line, you'll see the sign for the TVA's *Raccoon Mountain Pumped Storage Facility* on your right. It is the most unusual of all the Tennessee Valley Authority's operations. This hydro-electric plant uses more power than it generates. The safety officers on duty will usually agree with that arguable fact, but they will quickly tell you that the plant is very cost-effective.

The visitor center is located at the top of the mountain, about 9 miles from the front entrance, and what a view of the Tennessee River Valley it offers! Also at the top is a 528-acre lake. Deep inside the mountain is the mammoth power plant, totally protected from the elements and enemy attack.

At night, during off-peak hours, the extra energy produced at TVA coal-burning plants is used here to pump water from the Tennessee River up a 1,100-foot pipeline to fill the reservoir above. This is cheaper than shutting down and restarting those plants, and the electricity that would have been wasted is now used to stockpile water that will, in turn, create more power.

During the day, when the demand for electricity is greatest, the water is released from the reservoir and tumbles down the 35-foot-diameter intake tunnels to turn the four large generators, thereby producing electricity.

There are fewer than two dozen pumped storage facilities in the United States, and this is the only one that is completely underground. There are several scenic pull-offs on the drive to the top and quite a few picnic areas. At the foot of the mountain, there are fishing areas along the river, all courtesy of the federal government. Admission is free. You can phone them at (423) 825–3100.

When it comes to Southern cooking, few meals can be complete without fresh corn bread, dripping with real butter! The folks in South Pittsburg loved their corn bread so much that they created another reason to eat more of it. The annual *National Cornbread Festival & World Championship Cornbread Cook-off* is held in late April, with a two-day party to remember.

Main Street is closed off and lined with food vendors and exhibits, a carnival comes to town, and a juried show for artisans and crafters takes place. Usually there will be 50 or so crafters working, showing, and selling their wares. South Pittsburg is located a few miles west of I–24. Take exit 152 to US 72 West. Don't miss this festive event. Call (423) 837–0022 or go to www .nationalcornbread.com.

Places to Stay in Plateaus and Valleys

ATHENS

Majestic Mansion B&B
202 East Washington Avenue
Roomy B&B with unusual choices of decor, from Japanese to country
(423) 746–9041
www.themansionbnb.com

CELINA

Horse Creek Resort
1150 Horse Creek Road
4 miles from Celina on Dale Hollow Lake
Cabins, houseboats, motel
(931) 243–2125
www.horsecreek-resort .com

CHATTANOOGA

Bluff View Inn Bed and Breakfast
412 East Second Street
Spectacular view of river from restored homes
(423) 265–5033
www.bluffviewartdistrict .com

Sheraton Read House Hotel & Suites
At corner of Martin Luther King Boulevard and Broad Street
Each of 13 floors dedicated to a Civil War battle
(423) 266–4121

Shipp's RV Park
6728 Ringgold Road
200 sites, fishing, showers, grocery, pool
Open year-round
(423) 892–8275

Sky Harbor Bavarian Inn
2159 Old Wauhatchie Pike
Great views of Tennessee River from private balconies; whirlpool tubs, kitchens, cable TV, hardwood floors
(423) 821–8619
www.skyharborbavarianinn .com

CLEVELAND

Hampton Inn
185 James Asbury Drive
Close to Ocoee whitewater rafting; continental breakfast buffet
(423) 559–1001

Holiday Inn— Mountain View
2400 Executive Park Drive
I–75, exit 25
Exercise room, valet laundry, outdoor pool
(423) 472–1500

CRAB ORCHARD

Renegade Mountain Resort
US 70E
Kitchen, pool, tennis, golf
(931) 484–5285

DUCKTOWN

Company House Bed & Breakfast
125 Main Street
On National Register of Historic Places
(423) 496–5634
www.companyhousebandb .com

MCMINNVILLE

Falcon Manor
At end of Faulkner Springs Road
Bed-and-breakfast in Queen Anne–Victorian mansion
(931) 668–4444
www.falconrest.com

MONTEAGLE

Edgeworth Inn
On Assembly grounds
Victorian bed-and-breakfast
(931) 924–4000
www.edgeworthinn.com

Jim Oliver's Smokehouse
US 64/41A
Motel with swimming pool
in shape of a ham
(931) 924–2268
www.thesmokehouse.com

MONTEREY

The Garden Inn
1400 Bee Rock Road
An atmosphere of relaxed
elegance; mountain and
garden views
(931) 839–1400

RACCOON MOUNTAIN

Raccoon Mountain Caverns & Campground
1.25 miles north from I–24
at exit 174
Full-service RV camp and
tent camping sites
(800) 823–2267
www.raccoonmountain
.com

RED BOILING SPRINGS

Armour's Red Boiling Springs Hotel
321 East Main Street
Mineral baths, steam baths,
and massages available
(615) 699–2180
www.armourshotel.com

SMITHVILLE

Evins Mill
Evins Mill Road
Lodge and rustic cabins
serve as a bed-and-
breakfast
(800) 383–2349
www.evinsmill.com

WATERTOWN

Watertown Bed & Breakfast
116 Depot Avenue
Restored 19th-
century railroad hotel; private baths, nonsmoking,
breakfast
(615) 237–9999

Places to Eat in Plateaus and Valleys

CHATTANOOGA

Big River Grille & Brewing Works
222 Broad Street
Microbrewery, sandwiches,
snacks
Open daily at 11:00 a.m.
(423) 267–BREW
www.bigrivergrille.com

Rib & Loin
5946 Brainerd Road
Considered the city's best
rib restaurant
Open daily at 10:30 a.m.
(423) 499–6465
www.ribandloin.com

212 Market Restaurant
212 Market Street
Grilled salmon, chicken,
steaks
(423) 265–1212
www.212market.com

CLEVELAND

The Gondolier
3300 Keith Street
Greek and Italian cuisine
Open daily for lunch and
dinner
(423) 472–4998

DECATUR

Lee's Restaurant
Highway 58
Fish in a light batter
Thursday and Friday 4:00
to 9:00 p.m., Saturday
noon to 9:00 p.m., Sunday
noon to 8:00 p.m.
(423) 334–5695

LIVINGSTON

The Apple Dish
116 North Court Square,
inside the Antique Market
Great home cooking and
desserts
Hours vary, call first
(931) 823–3222

MCMINNVILLE

Eckert Drug Store
201 East Main Street
old-time soda fountain,
hamburgers, fries
Open daily 8:00 a.m. to
4:00 p.m.
(931) 473–2234

MONTEAGLE

Jim Oliver's Smokehouse

US 64/41A
Pit barbecue and hickory-
smoked meats
Sunday through Thursday
6:00 a.m. to 9:00 p.m.,
Friday and Saturday 6:00
a.m. to 10:00 p.m.
(931) 924–2268
www.thesmokehouse.com

MONTEREY

Cup & Saucer Restaurant

118 East Commercial
Avenue
Homestyle cooking
Open Monday through
Saturday
(931) 839–6149

Heart of the Heartland

Nashville. It very well could be the smallest city with the biggest reputation in the world. Anyone who has ever listened to a radio knows that Nashville is the country music capital of the world.

What a lot of people *don't* realize, however, is that the city's nickname is Music City, not *Country* Music City. It has some of the best recording studios in the world and absolutely the best studio musicians in the business. Everyone from Paul McCartney to Pearl Jam to Garth Brooks has recorded in Nashville. They come for the quality of the city as much as for the state-of-the-art studios.

There is an active jazz and blues culture, as well as rock and rap cultures. Clubs all over town offer a wide variety of music. The Tennessee Performing Arts Center in downtown Nashville has a Broadway Series that's second to none, and the Gaylord Entertainment Center, home of the Nashville Predators NHL club, hosts some of the world's biggest stars, from Luciano Pavarotti to Shania Twain to the Rolling Stones.

The National Football League's Tennessee Titans play in

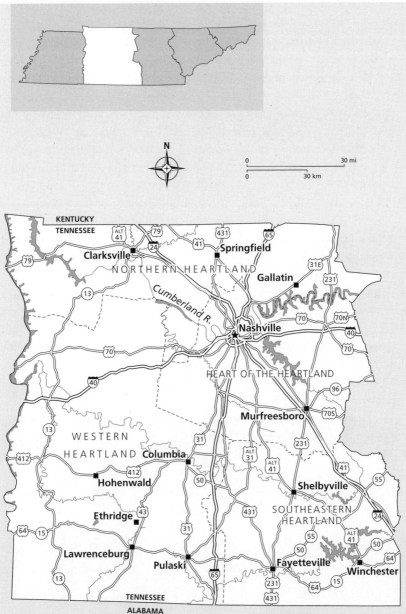

KENTUCKY
TENNESSEE

NORTHERN HEARTLAND

Clarksville

Springfield

Gallatin

Cumberland R.

Nashville

HEART OF THE HEARTLAND

Murfreesboro

WESTERN
HEARTLAND

Columbia

Hohenwald

Ethridge

SOUTHEASTERN
HEARTLAND

Shelbyville

Lawrenceburg

Pulaski

Fayetteville

Winchester

TENNESSEE
ALABAMA

N

0   30 mi
0   30 km

the Coliseum across the Cumberland River from downtown, and on Football Sundays the action is definitely in the various downtown districts.

Nashville is far from a mainstream city. It's one of those unique areas where the unbeaten path crosses the well-traveled path and merges for a few miles and dozens of experiences. The city's maternal relationship to country music has created quite a few one-of-a-kind attractions and events.

Music City (aka **Twangtown**) is not only a place where musicians record, it's also the place they call home. While you won't find George Jones or Wynona Judd listed in the phone book, it's not hard to find their homes. It's also not unusual to see the stars at the local supermarket, or at a gas station or musical event.

With all that Nashville has going for it, the majority of the visitors to the city still come to see the music-associated attractions—and that's good news for those who *don't* visit those attractions. The crowds are smaller (and sometimes nonexistent) at the doors of many of the city's other fun experiences.

The city of Nashville and the county of Davidson are one and the same, with a metropolitan government running the place. The 2000 census showed the area with a population of 569,891, a growth of nearly 12 percent over 1990.

There's plenty to do in downtown Nashville, but let's start our journey in the northwest quadrant of the city, where you'll find the mammoth Gaylord Opryland Resort & Convention Center approximately 13 miles from downtown.

Across from the Opryland complex and the world-famous WSM-AM radio station, the broadcast station of the Grand Ole Opry for more than 60 years, is the **Music Valley Area** and its complex of shops and activities. That's where you'll find the **Nashville Palace.** The Palace is where country superstar Randy Travis was discovered while working as a dishwasher. Live music nightly and a

AUTHOR'S TOP TEN PICKS

Hatch Show Print	Jack Daniel Distillery
Schermerhorn Symphony Center	Elephant Sanctuary
Nash Trash Tour	Bell Witch Cave
Ernest Tubb Record Shop	Nashville Cowboy Church
Cannonsburgh Pioneer Village	Mule Day Festival & Parade

OTHER ATTRACTIONS WORTH SEEING

Adventure Science Center,
Sudekum Planetarium,
800 Fort Negley Boulevard, Nashville,
(615) 862–5160
www.adventuresci.com

Cheekwood Gardens & Art Museum,
1200 Forrest Park Drive, Nashville,
(615) 356–8000
www.cheekwood.org

Elliston Place Soda Shop,
Original soda shop dating back to 1939,
2111 Elliston Place, Nashville,
(615) 327–1090

Frist Center for the Visual Arts,
919 Broadway, Nashville,
(615) 244–3340
www.fristcenter.org

The Hermitage,
Home of Andrew Jackson,
4580 Rachel's Lane, Hermitage,
(615) 889–2941
www.thehermitage.com

Ryman Auditorium,
Home to Grand Ole Opry for 31 years,
116 Fifth Avenue North, Nashville,
(615) 889–3060
www.ryman.com

Smith-Trahern Mansion,
Restored 1851 mansion,
First and McClure Streets, Clarksville,
(931) 648–9998
www.smith-trahernmansion.com

Tootsie's Orchid Lounge,
Famed country music honky-tonk next
to Ryman Auditorium, 422 Broadway,
Nashville,
(615) 726–0463
www.tootsies.net

delicious menu that includes "the best catfish in town" are featured. Give them a call at (615) 889–1540 or www.nashvillepalace.net.

The *Ernest Tubb Midnight Jamboree,* the second-oldest live country music radio show in America, is broadcast live each Saturday night from the Texas Troubadour Theater, 2416 Music Valley Drive, a few blocks behind the Nashville Palace. The show is broadcast on WSM-AM 650 and features top-name country talent, many of whom may have played the Grand Ole Opry earlier that night across the street at the Opryland complex. Be there by 11:30 to get a good seat. Free; call (615) 889–2474 late in the week to see who's booked for the Saturday show. If you're looking for vintage country music, the *Ernest Tubb Record Shop* next door is the place to search.

The Texas Troubadour Theater is also the site of the famous *Nashville Cowboy Church.* It's a unique Nashville experience. Where else can you hear top-shelf Southern gospel music while a genuine Stetson hat is passed for the offering? Services are held each Sunday at 10:00 a.m. Call (615) 889–2474.

The *Gaylord Opryland Resort & Convention Center,* formerly known as Opryland Hotel, is a huge, amazing place. With 2,881 guest rooms, 165 suites, 12 restaurants, 10 lounges, and 30 retail stores, *all inside,* you can start to realize why this place is so amazing. Add to that five ballrooms, 85 meeting rooms, and nearly one million square feet of exhibit space, and you have one of the unique hotels in the world. It's worth a visit, but make sure you wear your tennies; you'll be doing a lot of walking!

The fun thing to see and do here is to visit the three different atrium areas, which are under nearly nine acres of skylights. The Conservatory and the Cascades are each two-acre atriums featuring tropical gardens, running streams, and multilevel viewing areas. The newest area, the Delta, is a four-and-a-half-acre interiorscape with a flowing river and 25-passenger flatboats that take guests on a voyage through the area.

Christmas at the hotel is especially fun. Nearly two million lights decorate the exterior of the hotel, and inside there are holiday-themed dinner shows, an arts and antiques show, and other seasonal activities. Their number is (615) 889–1000 or visit www.gaylordopryland.com. The new concept of "shoppertainment" has come to Nashville. The 1.2-million-square-foot *Opry Mills* is located next to the resort. The 200-plus retailers offer up a bevy of fun experiences, shopping opportunities, and dining facilities. Among the tenants: Gibson Bluegrass Showcase, Rainforest Cafe, and an IMAX Theater.

Outside Opry Mills, in the plaza of the nearby Grand Ole Opry House, the *Grand Ole Opry Museum* offers an extensive salute to the stars who have walked the Opry stage. Interactive exhibits, artifacts and costumes, photos, and

TOP ANNUAL EVENTS

Main Street Festival,
Crafts, food, entertainment,
late April, Franklin,
(615) 591–8500

Old Timer's Day,
Crafts, flea market, quilt show, first
weekend in May, Dickson,
(615) 446–2349

Annual Irish Picnic,
St. Patrick's Church,
last weekend in July, McEwen,
(931) 582–3417

African Street Festival,
American Cultural Alliance,
mid-September, Nashville,
(615) 329–3540

Polly Crockett Arts & Crafts Show,
mid-September, Winchester,
(931) 967–6788

Yulefest: A 1780s Christmas,
at Mansker's Station Frontier Life
Center,
December, Goodlettsville,
(615) 859–FORT

The Performing Arts Are Alive!!!

The **Tennessee Performing Arts Center** (TPAC) is an oasis of the arts in downtown Nashville. Its three separate theaters are home to the Nashville Ballet, Tennessee Repertory Theatre, Nashville Opera, and the Nashville Symphony. The building also houses the Tennessee State Museum. In addition to the resident groups' activities, the management of TPAC promotes a quality Broadway series each year, as well as other special shows and attractions. They're at 505 Deaderick Street; call (615) 782–4000, or go to www.tpac.org. Most tickets are available through Ticketmaster, (615) 255–ARTS.

Other performing arts venues in Middle Tennessee include Darkhorse Theatre, 4610 Charlotte Avenue, Nashville (615–297–7113); Austin Peay University, Clarksville (931–221–7876); Roxy Community Theatre, 100 Franklin Street, Clarksville (931–645–7699); and Chaffin's Barn Theatre, 8204 Highway 100, Nashville (615–646–9977).

plenty of music provide tribute to the likes of Minnie Pearl, Marty Robbins, and Roy Acuff. The gift shop has some fun and funky country music souvenirs. Admission is free. Their number is (615) 871–OPRY.

In downtown Nashville, an area called **_The District_** is centered on Second Avenue, running north off Broadway to the county courthouse. It's where you'll find the typical tourist traps, but it's also where you'll find some great restaurants and drinking emporiums. All the businesses are located in restored turn-of-the-20th-century buildings and warehouses.

Country music wasn't always as slick as it is today, and that wonderful old-time sound is still alive and well and being played daily in the honky-tonks of Lower Broadway, just around the corner from The District.

There's a big difference between a honky-tonk and a country music club. First of all, honky-tonks are real beer joints with small, crowded dance floors and live music from great musicians you've probably never heard of—and if you order a glass of wine or a fancy drink, you'll probably be laughed right out the back door!

Lower Broadway's honky-tonk neighbors are the genuine articles, left virtually untouched through the years. Most keep their doors open so that you can hear the music from the sidewalk, and most have the bands up front so that you can watch the performers through the large windows.

Hillbilly heaven is anchored by the grandmother of all Nashville honky-tonks, Tootsie's Orchid Lounge, at 422 Broadway; call (615) 726–0463; www .tootsies.net. The back door of Tootsie's is across the alley from the back door of the Ryman Auditorium, where the Grand Ole Opry took place for years.

Hattie Louise "Tootsie" Bess ran the joint from 1960 to 1978 and during that time welcomed some of the greatest Opry performers through the back door while they waited for their turn to perform on the stage. When Tootsie bought the club, she hired a painter who mistakenly painted the exterior purple. She kept the color, and today the purple facade stands out from the rest.

While Tootsie's has the history, it also attracts more of a tourist crowd; it's the place many locals take visitors from out of town. Try a few of the others that will probably be less crowded: **Roberts Western World,** at 416 Broadway (615–244–9552); **Layla's Bluegrass Inn,** at 418 Broadway (615–726–2799); and the **Second Fiddle,** at 420 Broadway (615–248–4818).

Across Broadway from these honky-tonks is the funkiest of the three **Ernest Tubb Record Shops** we have in town. This one was opened by the country star himself in 1950 and was the location of the Midnite Jamboree, now held at the Music Valley location, every Saturday night for many years. During those years, Tubb featured many of the top Opry stars on his stage. Today the shop's walls are lined with autographed pictures and album covers. While the shop doesn't carry vinyl records anymore, it's still a good place to find a huge selection of bluegrass and country music. They specialize in the

Immaculate Confection

The Bongo Java Coffeehouse is home to the world-famous NunBun. Baker Ryan Finney decided to eat one of the rolls he was baking one morning, and he caught a divine image just before taking a bite. The roll possessed an uncanny likeness to Mother Teresa. It was indeed the immaculate confection, Finney said. "I was horrified because I almost ate this religious piece of dough," he was heard to say. It was stored in a freezer for a week and then became the center of a nine-minute video documentary titled *A Music City Miracle: The Story of the NunBun.* Local papers and television stations ran stories, and before long it appeared on David Letterman, Paul Harvey, Hard Copy, in the *Calcutta Times*, on the BBC, and other media worldwide.

Properly preserved, the NunBun was on display at the coffeehouse so the masses could take a look for themselves. On Christmas Day 2005, the unthinkable happened. The NunBun was stolen and has never been seen since. A NunBun replica, however, now graces the same spot where the original used to hold a place of honor. Go online to read the saga for yourself at www.bongojava.com. Located at 2007 Belmont Boulevard, across from Belmont University; call them at (615) 385–5282.

P.S. Don't forget to eat while you're there; they have some great nontraditional food items. But take a look before you bite and you may discover something cool. Open daily for all three meals.

older, harder-to-find artists on CDs and tapes. Located at 417 Broadway; call (615) 255–7503 or visit www.etrecord shop.com.

If it's vinyl records (remember those?) you are looking for, visit *Lawrence Record Shop,* at 409 Broadway, a few doors down from Tubb's establishment. You'll find a huge selection of country and bluegrass and some early rock and roll on LP vinyl, and it's all factory sealed and in original condition! In business since 1954, the owners have amassed a great selection. Open Tuesday through Saturday 10:00 a.m. to 6:00 p.m. Call (615) 256–9240 or www.lawrencerecordshop.com.

Situated among the honky-tonks and shops is *Hatch Show Print* at 316 Broadway. Open to the public, this is one of America's oldest surviving show poster printers. Founded in 1879 by two brothers, the business printed posters for the circus, sporting events, and vaudeville shows. It won the Grand Ole Opry account and printed not only the Opry's posters but the show posters for most of country music's greatest legends. Thousands of posters printed from the original cuts are available for purchase. Admission is free; call (615) 256–2805 or www.countrymusichallof fame.com.

abitofnashville trivia

The world's first nighttime airplane flight took off from Cumberland Park on June 22, 1910.

President Theodore Roosevelt coined the phrase "good to the last drop" while drinking coffee at the old Maxwell House Hotel.

The Grand Ole Opry House is the world's largest broadcast studio.

Iroquois, a Nashville horse, was the first American horse to win the English Derby. The Iroquois Steeplechase race held here each May is named for him.

While visiting the Belle Meade Plantation, President William Howard Taft got stuck in the bathtub. The owners then installed a stand-up shower for his next visit.

With more than 800 churches, synagogues, and temples, the city is known as the "buckle of the Bible belt."

The driveway at the Hermitage, home of President Andrew Jackson, is shaped like a guitar.

Elvis Presley recorded more than 200 songs at RCA's Studio B.

The *Country Music Hall of Fame and Museum* opened in 2001 to much ballyhoo in Nashville and the world's country music circles. The place is a classy celebration of the musical genre that made Nashville famous worldwide.

The building takes up an entire block at the corner of Fifth and Demonbreun Avenues and houses an extensive collection of memorabilia, gold records, the Hall of Fame, and Elvis's 1960 solid gold Cadillac. Even if you're not into country music, this is a fun and quite educational place to visit. In the rotunda there's a plaque depicting country great Kitty Wells. You might notice that her nose is smudged on the plaque. It's now a ritual that if you rub her nose as you walk by, you'll have good luck. Don't know who started it or if it's true, but it's probably worth a rub, just in case.

The **SoBro Grill** and **SoBro2Go** are located in the conservatory and does not require an admission to visit. Live performances are a part of the museum experience and Country Music Television broadcasts a live daily show from the conservatory. Everyone is invited to be a part of the live audience!

The design of the building sets this place apart from all other buildings in Nashville. The symbolism is amazing. Here is a short narrative, direct from the building's architects, Tuck-Hinton:

"Note the dark windows on the face of the building meant to resemble piano keys. Can you see the hint of a '50s Cadillac fin in the sweeping arch of the structure? And yes, that's a radio tower rising from the silolike rotunda honoring the WSM tower, so instrumental in the rise of country music."

Look for the suggestion of a drum kit in the rotunda's exterior, while the four disc tiers of its room trace the evolution of recording, from 78 to 45, the vinyl LP, and the CD of today (all in proportion). The stones that ring the top of the rotunda wall are more than an ornamental arrangement; they're also a musical arrangement. Each stone represents a note in the classic Carter Family song, "Will the Circle Be Unbroken." Great stuff!

The museum opens daily at 9:00 a.m. and closes at 5:00 p.m. Admission is charged. Call (615) 416–2001 or (800) 852–6437; also check out their Web site at www.countrymusichalloffame.com.

"Come see what you've heard" is the slogan of the **Musicians Hall of Fame and Museum.** Opened in 2006, the attraction honors the people who provide the sounds behind the songs. Located on the corner of Clark Place and

More than a Candy Cane

Howell Campbell, a Nashville candy maker, invented the King Leo peppermint stick in 1901 for the Standard Candy Company, the makers of the popular Goo Goo Cluster. King Leo differs from the traditional candy cane in that it is lighter and crunchier, and as it dissolves in your mouth, it releases its flavor. It's also porous to use as a straw, which in turn adds flavor to your glass of milk as you sip it! Once strictly a Southern treat, King Leo, now owned by the Quality Candy Company, is available nationally and has been featured in high-level shops such as Restoration Hardware. It also now comes in several other flavors, such as Key lime and chocolate.

within sight of the Country Music Hall of Fame and Museum, the attraction honors the players—whether stars, session pickers, or sidemen—from all genres of music. The multimillion-dollar museum is the brainchild of Joe Chambers, a guitar store owner, who said the idea had been brewing for about a decade. Chambers's extensive collection includes a restored stage, where a young Jimi Hendrix once performed; Pete Drake's steel guitar, played on Bob Dylan's "Lay Lady Lay"; a snare drum of the Red Hot Chili Peppers; Marshall Grant's basses from Johnny Cash's "Walk the Line"; and Eddie Willis's guitars, used in countless Motown sessions. Call the museum at (612) 244–3263 or visit www.musicians halloffame.com.

topchoice

Nashville was named the number one "Smart Place to Live" by *Kiplinger's Personal Finance* magazine in their May 2006 cover story. Reasons included Nashville's Southern hospitality, comfortable climate, hilly landscape, large and affordable homes, and a "phenomenal entertainment scene" that includes much more than just country.

Nashville has a new landmark, comparable to the greatest music halls in the world. Opened in 2006, the $120-million **Schermerhorn Symphony Center** was designed to be an acoustic masterpiece. Located at One Symphony Place, the center is home to the Nashville Symphony Orchestra. Designed by architect David M. Schwarz, the 197,000-square-foot center has 30 soundproof windows above the hall, making it one of the only major concert halls in North America with natural light. Named in honor of the late orchestra conductor Kenneth Schermerhorn, the center is a sophisticated modern building that is neoclassically inspired, with a classic limestone exterior and columns. A garden is open to the public throughout the day and during concerts. For more information call the center at (615) 687–6400 or www.nashvillesymphony.org.

Songwriting is a revered occupation in Nashville. No other city pays attention to its writers the way **Music City** does, and radio announcers are just as apt to say who wrote a song as who performed it. Writers' nights are held in various locations on a regular basis and are great places to get right down to the basics of country music. Hearing a popular writer singing his or her list of hits that others made into million-sellers is like listening to an oldies jukebox.

Perhaps the best-known cafe in the city, the **Bluebird Cafe,** is also one of the best places to attend a writers' night. The food is good, the talent is excellent, and chances are good that you might be sitting next to a country superstar. They hang out here a lot, especially during writers' shows. Several of today's superstars were regulars here on their way up the ladder, including Garth Brooks and Kathy Mattea. The Bluebird is located in the Green Hills area

Wackiest Tour in Town

The Jugg Sisters, Sheri Lynn and Brenda Kay, wear boots and tight pants and have some of the biggest hair around. They also promise to take you on a country music tour of Nashville you'll never forget. In fact, you probably won't even pay attention to what the girls are talking about outside the bright pink bus you'll be riding on because there's so much going on inside the bus.

The *Nash Trash Tour* is the wackiest tour in the state, no doubt. It's truly tacky and tasteless, and if you're into political correctness, stay off their bus! A journey with the Juggs is comedy kitsch at its best. They point out the underbelly of the city's music industry. They dig up the dirt on such notables as George Jones, Tammy Wynette, and Tanya Tucker. Bubba, or Bubbette, depending on who's available to drive the bus, takes you past the county jail, and the girls roll off a roster of famous names who have slept there. The sisters sing original songs about the seamier side of Music City, and they even have a bit of choreography to go with it. They point out the pool where Elvis went skinny-dipping and the bar where Tanya Tucker took off her shirt for a national reporter.

Other highlights of the tour include celebrity sightings. You might see Garth Brooks, Burt Reynolds, Dolly Parton, Willie Nelson, or George Jones. "Of course the stars all look different without their hair and makeup on," the girls are quick to point out.

The Juggs offer makeup and styling tips, casserole recipes, and fancy cracker-and-cheese hors d'oeuvres. They make sure all their passengers are aware that the major tour operators in the city don't have snacks aboard. "No cheese, no crackers," they sing.

This is a fun and very, very entertaining 90 minutes, and it's cheaper than a ticket to a comedy club. The bus loads at the north end of the Farmers' Market, next to the Bicentennial Mall, downtown. Get there at least 30 minutes early, because the fun and jokes begin as soon as you arrive. Guests are encouraged to bring coolers with anything they want inside. Tours leave at 10:30 a.m. on Thursday and Friday and at 11:00 a.m. and 2:00 p.m. on Saturday and Sunday. Rates are $29.50 per person; there's a tips bucket if you are so inclined. Find out more by calling (615) 226–7300 or (800) 342–2132 or go online at www.nashtrash.com.

of the city, about 15 minutes from downtown at 4104 Hillsboro Pike; call (615) 383–1461 or go to www.bluebirdcafe.com.

Bagel shops are everywhere, but there's only one Bruggers Bagels & Brews. Located in the Vanderbilt University area at 422 21st Avenue South, this is one funky and fun place. The perfect bagel was discovered by Marc, Jeff, and Chris, who, in their hopes of finding clarity and the meaning of life, meditated and contemplated for several days. The only thing they discovered, however, was that they were famished.

Inspired by their enlightening experience and motivated by their savage hunger, they set out to create the Zen of snack. From deep within they found the answer, but it was more than just a bagel—it was a way of life, the Alpine way of life.

The bagel boys not only created a great bagel, but they also developed 12 of the smoothest, creamiest, most delicious bagel toppings on the planet! Costa Rican and Colombian coffees are ground and brewed fresh all day. A wild bunch of bagelwiches is offered for lunch and dinner, including the Hootie & the Tuna Fish Sammy, the Hummus Is Among Us, the Pilgrim's Pride, and the Presidential Pardon.

With the slogan that their bagels are "so fresh they should be slapped," the eatery is open Monday through Friday 6:30 a.m. to 6:00 p.m. and Saturday and Sunday 8:00 a.m. to 5:00 p.m. They have a tendency to change closing hours often, so check first by calling (615) 327–0055.

Remember when coffee was just another cuppa joe? Those days are now gone forever. Less than a mile south on 21st Avenue, down in Hillsboro Village, the Bongo Java Roasting Co. shares the old Jones Pet Shop with **Fido,** a cafe named for the dog who discovered coffee. The cafe opened when the pet shop closed in 1996, after 50 years in business. The funky neon pet shop sign has been restored and sits upon the roof.

Fido features a breakfast menu until 11:00 a.m., with such items as Spuds McFido, Egg McFido, and, if you're real hungry, the Bubba Breakfast Burrito. During the rest of the day, there's a full menu of sandwiches, soups, snacks, bagels, and full meals, including a veggie paella, homemade ratatouille, and a veggie lasagna. A popular sandwich is the Yummy Hummy Pita, a mixture of roasted vegetables and hummus stuffed in a pita.

There are plenty of specialty coffee drinks, and the desserts are great, especially the Dog Bowl—a pint of Ben & Jerry's ice cream cut in half and topped with homemade mocha sauce, whipped cream, and other sweet stuff. They are open daily until 11:00 p.m.; opens Monday through Friday at 7:00 a.m. and on Saturday and Sunday at 8:00 a.m. Their address is 1812 21st Avenue South; call (615) 777–3436.

When a country music record company executive or a group of songwriters want to meet for a "power breakfast," there is usually no discussion of where that meeting will take place.

The **Pancake Pantry** has served the Music Row area for more than four decades now, and it's a great place for breakfast at any time of the day, even if you aren't into the music business. The wild blueberry pancakes, sweet potato cakes, buttermilk stacks, and myriad other choices are all quickly served by waitresses who have been here so long, they probably have seen it all. But they don't usually have time to tell it all because they are busy taking care of the constant crowds that frequent the pancake fixture at 1796 21st Avenue South in Hillsboro Village, a few doors down from Fido's. Open daily for breakfast and lunch. Call (615) 383–9333 for hours orgo to www.pancakepantry.com.

The state of Tennessee turned 200 years old in 1996, and as a present to itself, officials created the **Bicentennial Capitol Mall State Park,** down the steps and across James Robertson Parkway from the state capitol. In addition to being a nicely appointed park and gathering place, the mall has permanent state historical exhibits and a great view of Capitol Hill.

The 19-acre state park and outdoor history museum feature an amphitheater, a 200-foot-long granite map depicting every city in the state, 31 fountains representing each of the state's rivers, a botanical garden, and a 1,400-foot wall engraved with images of Tennessee's historic events. Free; open 6:00 a.m. to 10:00 p.m. daily.

The more than 360,000 Tennesseans who served their country in World War II are honored here in the Bicentennial Mall at the **World War II Memorial,** located on the west side of the mall. We've all seen war memorials before, but we think this one is quite impressive and well worth a visit. There are ten granite pylons, which feature interesting information about the major events that took place during the war.

The prominent single landmark of the memorial is an eight-ton solid granite globe, the largest of its type ever made. The 1940s-world globe pinpoints major battle sites to illustrate how far Tennesseans traveled during the global conflict. The sphere rotates on a thin cushion of water and can be turned by hand. Take time to study, learn, and appreciate. The mall is open daily, year-round. Call (615) 741–5280 or www.tennessee.gov/environment/parks/bicentennial.

Adjacent to the Bicentennial Mall is the **Farmers' Market.** Here, you'll find fresh Tennessee-grown produce, from apples to zucchini, plants, flowers, and trees. On the inside are two restaurants, an international market, a hot sauce vendor, and fresh fish and meat peddlers. Early-morning crowds consist mostly of buyers from local restaurants coming in for their fresh-picked produce. Open year-round, with peak operating hours during the summer growing season from 5:00 a.m. to 9:00 p.m., but with shorter hours during the winter months. A flea and crafts market takes place here each weekend, year-round, and there are various festivals on the grounds every second Saturday of the month, from May through November. Located on Eighth Avenue North, just off James Robertson Parkway. For more information phone (615) 880–2001.

Also in the heart of downtown Nashville lies the **Tennessee State Capitol.** Finished in 1859, it was designed by **William Strickland,** who also helped design the U.S. Capitol. The beautiful building was recently renovated and should not be undervalued by tourists. Strickland loved the place so much that he requested to be interred in its walls. President James K. Polk is also buried there. Admission is free. For tour information call (615) 741–2692 or www.tnmuseum.org.

The city has its own *Arcade,* and it has been restored to its finest. It was built in 1903 as a two-tiered shopping mall, an identical copy of the Galleria Vittorio Emmanuele II arcade in Milan, Italy. Today it is occupied by specialty shops, including several restaurants and the mandatory roasted-nut store, whose aroma pervades the entire complex. The arcade runs 350 feet long to connect Fourth and Fifth Avenues, between Church and Union Streets. Check out their great Web site for a history of the Arcade as well as a listing of its current tenants. Visit them online at www.onepaper.com/nashvillearcade, or call (615) 244–8060.

Across the street and down a few storefronts from the Arcade's Fifth Avenue entrance is Nashville's funkiest art gallery, the *Arts Company.* Headed up by one of the city's great arts cheerleaders, Anne Brown, the full-service art gallery represents regional, national, and international artists in photography, painting, sculpture, and contemporary folk art. The latter category is what sets this fun place apart from the rest of the great galleries in the city. If you're looking for eclectic art, from fine Parisian art to rusted tin monkeys, this is the place! Located at 215 Fifth Avenue North. Open Monday through Saturday 10:00 a.m. to 5:30 p.m. and on an occasional Sunday. The gallery's Web site, www.theartscompany.com, offers links and calendars for other cultural events in Nashville as well as a photographic inventory of their own offerings. Call the gallery at (615) 254–2040 or (877) 694–2040.

civilwarfacts

More battles were fought in Tennessee than in any other state except Virginia.

Tennessee was the last state to secede from the Union and the first state to be readmitted after the war.

East Tennesseans were strongly pro-Union, while west and middle Tennesseans were primarily on the side of the Confederacy.

The free booklet *A Path Divided: Tennessee's Civil War Years* provides a thumbnail history of the war and a list of related events and attractions throughout the state.

LOOK! UP IN THE SKY! At 632 feet, the Bell South Building, fondly known locally as the *Batman Building* because of its uncanny resemblance to the caped crusader, is the tallest building in the state. It has 27 floors of office space and above that several other storage, mechanical, and open floors. At the very top, two spirals go heavenward from either side, hinting of Batman's pointed ears. The behemoth makes quite a statement.

"That's what the architect wanted to do," said a Bell South official. "The design philosophy was to be unique, be distinctive in the Nashville skyline, and avoid being another boxy skyscraper." He noted that while not planning to make it look like Batman, the design "does evoke that image, and others as well. Many people think it looks like a phone receiver and handset at the top," he said, adding that he has been told the nine-level underground parking garage was the largest building construction excavation ever in the state.

When the ***Hermitage Hotel*** was built in 1910, it was the city's first million-dollar hotel, and it became a symbol of Nashville's emergence as a major Southern city. It flourished for more than 50 years, only to start deteriorating with the rest of the downtown area in the 1960s. Now, as the downtown area has gained a new life, so has the Hermitage Hotel. From its Beaux Arts design, the only commercial example of it in Tennessee, to its magnificently ornate lobby, the hotel is once again a symbol of pride for downtown Nashville.

Make sure you check out the men's room, next to the Capitol Grille on the lower level. It is the coolest restroom in the city. A bronze plaque mounted next to the door reads "Once the site of many business transactions, this unique Art Deco bathroom has been the selected location of several interviews, music videos, and fashion photography. It has been said that more women have toured this men's room than any other in the country." Ladies, make sure you announce yourself before entering.

The Hermitage, owned by Historic Hotels, received a $15 million renovation in late 2002 and early 2003, and within a short time of reopening on Valentine's Day 2003, it received a five-diamond ranking, followed by a five-star listing as well. It is now the only five-diamond, five-star hotel within a nine-state area.

Located across from the Tennessee Performing Arts Center, across from the State Capitol, at Sixth Avenue and Union Street, it's a comfortable, classy place to call home while exploring Music City. For more information call (615) 244–3121 or www.hermitagehotel.com.

Several decades before the city was known for its music, it had a reputation as a regional center of culture and education. Numerous colleges advanced the learning of the classics, and it wasn't long before the city was known as the Athens of the South. In 1896 it was only natural for planners of the state's centennial celebrations to elaborate on this classic theme.

An exact replica of the ***Greek Parthenon,*** with a tolerance of less than one-tenth of an inch, was built for the huge exposition, held in what is now known as Centennial Park, just a few miles out West End Avenue from downtown. Now fully restored and still the world's only full-size replica, the Parthenon houses art exhibits and serves as a backdrop for various cultural events in the park. A 42-foot replica of Athena Parthenos has been sculpted and is on display in the main hall. Open Tuesday through Saturday 9:00 a.m. to 4:30 p.m. Admission is charged. You can reach them at (615) 862–8431 or www.nashville.gov.

Next to the Parthenon, the neatest structure in the park is the concrete ship's prow, near the 25th Avenue North entrance. Now about 100 years old, the reinforced concrete replica of the front end of a ship has an ornate metal figurehead, the original cast that was used to make the one on the *Tennessee,* a U.S. cruiser that plied the waters during the 1898 Spanish-American War. The decorative metalwork was exhibited at the 1909 Seattle Exposition, and when that event was over, the metalwork was shipped here by request of Nashville-raised Navy admiral Albert Gleaves. The concrete prow was built

The Plant That's Eatin' Tennessee

That's **kudzu** (pronounced *cud-zoo*) you see growing all over the roadsides through-out Tennessee. The large hairy-leafed, bright green invasive vine is also known as the mile-a-minute vine and the vine that ate the South. It grows as much as a foot a day or 60 feet a summer in good weather and can take up to a decade to kill. It is said that Southerners keep their windows shut at night to keep out the kudzu.

Kudzu was introduced to the United States in 1876 at the Centennial Exposition in Philadelphia by the Japanese. During the Great Depression of the 1930s, the Soil Conservation Service promoted kudzu for erosion control, and hundreds of men planted it on roadsides throughout the south. Farmers were paid by the government to plant fields of the vines in the 1940s.

It does control erosion, but it also runs rampant and kills virtually everything in its path and climbs anything it contacts, including telephone poles and trees. Where it grows, kudzu has the ability to out-compete and eliminate native plant species and upset the natural diversity of plant and animal communities.

The vine has been known to kill entire forests by preventing the trees from getting light. During warm weather, the plant, classified a weed by the government in 1970, bears 6- to 10-inch spikes of small, fragrant purple flowers. The state has been hav-ing some success eradicating the vine by using various tools available. Methods include mechanical treatment (usually brush-hogs and shredder mulchers), pre-scribed burning, herbicides, and biological control. The emphasis is on persistent and consistent attempts to eradicate kudzu.

Don't be tempted to dig up any of the plants to take home with you. They will soon become a nuisance, and you'll spend the rest of your life trying to get rid of them.

and the metalwork mounted, making the structure look like "a ship that had been driven ashore in the shrubbery," as one Nashville journalist described it at the time.

Centennial Park is the site of many events during the year, including three quality arts and crafts fairs that I wouldn't miss for anything. In May the Tennessee Association of Craft Artists (TACA) produces a juried crafts festival that is one of the largest marketplaces for quality crafts anywhere in the state. Nearly 200 Tennessee craftspeople show up to peddle their wares. Phone (615) 385–1904.

In June the *American Artisan Festival* takes place during Father's Day weekend. More than 150 craftspeople from 35 states show up for the weekend. The food at this particular festival could be considered the best of any food at any festival in the state. It's eclectic, with an emphasis on the unusual and the healthy. This show is sponsored by the American Artisan Crafts Gallery, just down the road from Centennial Park. Get more details at (615) 298–4691.

Held in late September the *TACA Fall Crafts Fair* is a juried show for all craftspeople, not just those from Tennessee (as is the May festival). Again, quality crafts are abundant, and the show comes at a perfect time to start Christmas shopping. Call (615) 385–1904.

There are notables buried in just about every cemetery in the world, and Nashville is no exception—except that we have more than our share of country crooners interred.

At the huge *Woodlawn Memorial Park,* on Thompson Lane between Interstate 65 and Nolensville Road just south of downtown, several country and music legends are buried, including Roy Orbison, Webb Pierce, Marty Robbins, Red Sovine, and Tammy Wynette. To find exact locations, go to the office; someone there will provide you with a map. Phone them at (615) 383–4754.

Roy Acuff, Floyd Cramer, and Hank Snow are among the country notables buried at the *Spring Hill Cemetery,* 5110 Gallatin Road. Also there is *Beth Slater Whitson,* who wrote the lyrics to "Let Me Call You Sweetheart." Get more information at (615) 865–1101.

Nashville City Cemetery is the oldest public cemetery in the city, and with 23,000 graves dating back to 1822, you can imagine the scope of the historical figures buried here, including three Civil War generals—Bushrod Johnson, Richard Ewell, and Felix Zollicoffer; William Carroll, who served as Tennessee governor from 1788 to 1844; and James Robertson, the founder of Nashville. Also here is Captain William Driver, who first called the American Flag "Old Glory."

The cemetery is run by the Metro Historical Commission and is listed on the National Register of Historic Places. Historical markers are placed throughout with specific information. Located at 1001 Fourth Avenue South, at Oak Street, this historic site is open daily until dusk and can be reached at (615) 862–7970.

Over at the Tennessee State Fairgrounds, on Nolensville Road near downtown Nashville, the ***state's largest flea market*** takes place the fourth weekend of each month. There are nearly 2,200 vendors on any particular weekend, with 600 of them located indoors. They are open from 6:00 a.m. to 6:00 p.m. on Saturday and 7:00 a.m. to 4:00 p.m. on Sunday. *Hint:* Vendors can set up any time after 3:00 p.m. on Friday, and most will sell to you if you drop by as they set up their booths. That's when they all wheel and deal with one another, and it's when you'll definitely get the best choice. Admission is free, but there is a $2 parking charge. Call (615) 862–5016 or go to www.tennesseestatefair.org.

The ***Tennessee State Fair*** is held on these same grounds the second week of September. Lots of carnival rides, great-tasting (albeit fatty) foods, and plenty of farm animals are on hand for the entertainment and the education of guests. There's usually a circus and a major country concert held during the event. A village with log cabins and working craftsmen provides a glimpse into the early days of the state. Call (615) 862–8980 or visit www .tennesseestatefair.org.

Adjacent to the west entrance to the fairgrounds is the ***White Trash Cafe,*** a fun little eatery that specializes in all kinds of comfort foods. Located in a tacky blue building with a huge EVERYONE WELCOME sign out front, the lineup of menu items is probably a replication of your weekly meals as you were growing up. The menu is different each day. Baked chicken, meat loaf, fried chicken, liver and onions, BBQ chicken, BBQ pork, chicken and dressing, and broiled pork chops are all featured sometime during the week. Lots of side dishes are available, including pinto beans, mashed "taters," steamed cabbage, white beans, corn, turnip greens, sweet "taters," beets, okra, and "mac and cheese."

Two desserts are offered daily, and if Aunt Polly Ester's Nanner Puddin' is available, try it! Open Monday through Friday and on the Saturday when the flea market is in operation. Located at 1914 Bransford Avenue. Call (615) 383–0109.

Two additional close-by, fun, and delicious places to eat can be found on Elliston Place. ***Rotier's*** is located just east of Centennial Park, behind Eckerd's Drugs at 2413 Elliston Place. Year in and year out, "Mama" Rotier's comes in at the top, or very close to the top, in the best hamburger in town competition. Served on French bread, the burgers and all the fixings are held together with a toothpick when they reach you. It seems like everyone comes here, and at times it seems like all the waitresses know everyone! I've seen some of country music's top stars here enjoying a burger and a chocolate milk shake. The popular spot also has daily luncheon specials, including some very good meat loaf, and a big variety of bottled beers. Phone (615) 327–9892 for daily specials or www.rotiers.com.

Continue east on Elliston to find the **Elliston Place Soda Shop** on your right, just before you get to the Krispy Kreme, the doughnut den of heaven. Virtually unchanged from when it opened in the 1940s, the shop has turned into much more than a funky soda shop. The milk shakes are the best in town, and it's fun sitting there sipping your shake in your own booth, choosing music on your personal jukebox. Country ham, fresh biscuits, a bevy of vegetables including black-eyed peas, and plenty of other "meat-and-three" offerings can be found on the menu. Breakfast is served daily. Call (615) 327–1090.

Another classic blast from the past is **Bobbie's Dairy Dip** at 5301 Charlotte, at the corner of 53rd Street. It's an old-fashioned, walk-up ice-cream stand, which also serves a great burger and fries. They sell soft serve and real, premium ice cream and are great at piling it together to create some wonderful concoctions, including the Everyday is Sundae, which sells for $3.50. For $3.50 you get a giant, handmade Shiverin' Shake, very possibly the biggest shake in town. Call (615) 292–2112.

On Charlotte, between Bobbie's and 49th Street, there are a bunch of other notable places to spend a bit of your time. The **Southern Thrift Store,** at 5010 Charlotte, is the best-stocked thrift shop in Nashville. It is constantly getting new (old) stuff, and it has some of the best deals. If you're looking for a country star T-shirt, you'll find a huge selection here, hung neatly on hangers, for as little as 99 cents (Alabama) and as high as $3.59 (Garth Brooks). There is also plenty of furniture and other thrift-shop couture. For more information call (615) 292–1807.

Every town has its used-CD stores where one can pick up CDs, cassettes, and videotapes at cheaper than new prices. Well, Nashville has gone one better. We have the **Great Escape Half-Price-or-Less Store,** at 1907 Broadway on the Music Row side of the Vanderbilt area. Open only on Friday and Saturday afternoon and early evening, the store sells used CDs, vinyl records, cassettes, videos, and comic books for 50 cents and up, with few if any prices more than $4 in the entire store! Located up the street less than a block (at 1925 Broadway) is the original **The Great Escape,** which has been around for years and is known for its large selection of CDs, vinyl records, and tapes, as well as comics, books, and collectors items. Open daily; its number is (615) 327–0646.

For a truly amazing site visit the **Upper Room Chapel and Museum.** The stars of this establishment are an 8-by-17-foot wood carving of da Vinci's

The Last Supper and an 8-by-20-foot stained-glass window with a Pentecost theme. Beautiful!

The museum features religious paintings and art objects dating back to the 1300s as well as religious artifacts from throughout the world. At Christmastime the museum displays its collection of Ukrainian eggs and more than 100 nativity scenes. Open Monday through Friday; free, but donations are graciously accepted. 1908 Grand Avenue. Call (615) 340–7207 or go to www.upperroom.org.

The Nashville Convention and Visitors Bureau has a helpful Web site: www.visitmusiccity.com. There are streaming headlines and plenty of quick links to more than 50 area attractions, upcoming events, tours, and shopping. The CVB can be reached by phone at (800) 657–6910, or you can stop by the Nashville Visitors Center in the Gaylord Entertainment Center, downtown at Broadway and Fifth Avenue.

If you plan to visit several of the paid attractions in the Nashville area, stop by the visitor center to buy tickets for those attractions at great savings. In addition to the admissions, you'll get complimentary VIP coupon books and a free admission to the Tennessee Sports Hall of Fame. Learn more by calling (800) 657–6910.

Next to the **Loveless Cafe,** the Natchez Trace Shell gas station about 15 miles from downtown out West End Avenue (which becomes Highway 100), could really be called Last Chance Gas & Food. It's located at the entrance to the Natchez Trace Parkway, where you won't find any food, gas, or lodging for your entire 450-mile trip to Natchez, Mississippi.

If you're going to travel the wonderful Natchez Trace for more than a couple of days, you'll probably want to stay overnight close to the trace, and a bed-and-breakfast inn is definitely your best choice. The trace itself is very noncommercial, with no buildings and no billboard or lodging signs, so it's a good idea to plan ahead and have reservations. The Natchez Trace Bed and Breakfast Reservation Service is a good way to get access and get information to the nearly 40 inns close to the trace. Phone (931) 285–2777 or visit www .bbonline.com/natcheztrace.

Just west of the entrance to the Natchez Trace, you'll find some of the best fresh produce in middle Tennessee. **McNeil's Fresh Produce Stand** is open from April through October, and the open-air stand is known widely for carrying the best of whatever is in season. The corn is the best I've found in this area, and the locally grown vine-ripened tomatoes are huge and plump. It's a good place to load up on some healthy snacks before you hit the trace. Located at 8750 Highway 100. Call (615) 673–1016.

About 30 miles east of Nashville, the downtown square of **Lebanon** is antiques heaven! Within a 2-block area there are more than a dozen antiques

The Loveless Gets a Face-lift!

The "new" Loveless Cafe has the same food and the same ambience but new owners. Nashville's own Tom Morales, owner of the noted movie-location catering business, TomKats, purchased the business and closed it for three months to make major renovations, including expanded seating, new restrooms, and a new kitchen. In addition to work on the restaurant itself, he created a retail deli and store in one of the old motel rooms where the famous jams and jellies are now made and sold. You can watch them being made from a special viewing room while buying your country ham and other delicacies.

Other motel rooms adjacent to the restaurant now house a bicycle shop, an art shop, a canoe shop, and other "outdoorsy" retail. The little complex is less than one-tenth of a mile from the northern terminus of the famed Natchez Trace Parkway, which follows one of the oldest pioneer trails of the South.

Fifty years of serving thousands of people the best country ham breakfasts in the South had put quite a stress on the little house in the country. The house needed repairs, and its dining room needed to be expanded to keep up with the demand. The old kitchen had trouble keeping up with the orders. Donna McCabe, one of the owners, was ready to retire, and her son George, the other owner, decided to sell—but not to just anyone. Both the McCabes were very selective about whom they allowed to buy the business. They were looking for someone who would keep the name, the menu, and the ambience while investing in the business to guarantee that it would be around for another 50 years.

Through the years, anyone who is (or was) anyone has eaten here. Country stars, national TV celebrities, and politicians from all over are spotted here almost on a daily basis. ABC–TV called the Loveless "the best country restaurant in America," and Martha Stewart told her audience once that the best breakfast she ever had was served at the Loveless Cafe.

The trademark neon sign still marks the spot on Highway 100 in the little community of Pasquo. Open 7:00 a.m. to 9:00 p.m. seven days a week. Check it out at (615) 646–9700 or www.lovelesscafe.com.

stores and antiques malls. Most are open daily. The largest, and probably the most packed with the biggest selection, is Cuz's Antiques, in the corner on the square. There's plenty of parking, and there's always plenty of action in the downtown area.

The award-winning **Wilson County Fair,** voted the state's best county fair several times, is held each August, and it truly is small-town Americana at its finest. Former Vice President Al Gore showed animals here as a child, and thousands of kids before and after him prepare for the fair all year long. The carnival is colorful and fun, the exhibits are great, and the entertainment is top-notch. Call (615) 443–2626.

The fair takes place at the James E. Ward Agricultural Center, where picturesque *Fiddlers Grove* is also located. The grove consists of more than 30 original and replicated log cabins moved to the fairgrounds, creating a compound of what a Wilson county community would have looked like in the 1800s.

There are such frontier staples as a jail, post office, blacksmith shop, and general store, and it's still growing year by year. Here is a low-key, out-of-the-way community where the early life of Tennessee is preserved and presented. It's a lot of fun, and the workers here are well versed in this particular era of the state's history. It's open during the fair and from 10:00 a.m. to 3:00 p.m. Tuesday through Saturday from May through mid-October. Free admission; phone them at (615) 443–2626.

If you like wildflowers, make sure you visit the *Wildflower Pilgrimage* each year in mid-April at the Cedars of Lebanon State Park, just outside Lebanon. The two-day event is structured to dazzle the experts and to create an interest in those just learning to appreciate one of nature's best gifts. Call Sandy Suddarth for more information at (615) 443–2769.

The country stars and the top bankers and businesspeople of the state might make their millions in Nashville, but when it comes to investing in their lifestyles and families, many come south to Williamson County. It consistently has the state's highest per capita income and the lowest unemployment rate.

Maps that show where many of the stars live are available at most bookstores. Dolly Parton, Gary Morris, the Judds, and Tom T. Hall are among the inhabitants of the area. If you want to see them, though, you probably have a better chance hanging out at the local Kroger store than in front of their houses.

At www.visitwilliamson.com, the official Web site of the Williamson County Convention and Visitors Bureau, you'll be able to find out a great deal more about the county. Or you can call (615) 794–1225 or (800) 356–3445.

Franklin, the county seat, is 17 miles and "100 years" south of Nashville and is associated with old, restored homes and businesses, antiques shopping, and the Civil War. The entire downtown section is on the National Register of Historic Places.

The *Carter House,* south of downtown on Columbia Avenue, was caught in the middle of the fight aptly known as the *Battle of Franklin* on November 30, 1864. Bullet holes are still evident in the main structure and various outbuildings. One of the outbuildings has 203 bullet holes in it, making it the most battle-damaged building from the Civil War still standing anywhere.

The property is one of the 11 historic sites in the state owned and operated by the Association for the Preservation of Tennessee Antiquities. Open daily; admission is charged. Call (615) 791–1861 or www.carterhouse1864.com.

The Blue Moon Is Looking Good!

One of the classiest, most distinctive bed-and-breakfast operations in the state is just outside Franklin. The *Blue Moon Farm, a Private Cottage Bed & Breakfast,* offers one three-room cottage, complete with kitchen, dining room, living room with fireplace, and a huge master bedroom with amazing countryside views. A spa-quality bathroom with an ultra-tub and a huge rain shower opens up into the master bedroom. A wraparound deck offers great views, and there's a private deck off the bedroom. The cottage is connected to the main house, where the owners live, and is adjacent to a huge covered dining area. Everywhere you look you'll see rolling hills and cows, and in the morning a very healthy rooster will likely greet you with a song.

It's quite the romantic getaway, and being the only guests, you can be sure you'll get all the attention of innkeepers Susan and Bob Eidam. They can be quite flexible and create just about any ambience you want, whether it's a candlelight gourmet dinner or a rose petal-covered bed in the boudoir. A TV with a VCR and a large selection of films are available, as is a CD player.

And maybe the biggest surprise of all is the stocked cupboards and the stocked refrigerator and freezer. If anything is made with Blue Moon written on it (including beer), you'll find it in the kitchen. The place can be yours for a night or longer, for $250 per night, including a full breakfast. Stays longer than a couple of days can be negotiated.

This place offers first-class big-city hospitality in a rural area of the state. It's a great combination. I won't go into directions here, as I'm sure I'll get you lost. Call Susan or Bob and they'll get you there; (800) 493–4518 or www.bluemoonfarmbb.com.

About 5 miles away, the *Carnton Mansion* also played an important role in the Battle of Franklin. On the rear lines of the Confederate forces, the elegant estate witnessed a steady stream of dying and wounded during the battle. At one time the bodies of five slain Confederate generals were laid out on the back porch. Within view of that historic porch rests the only privately owned *Confederate cemetery* in the United States. Open daily; admission is charged to the house; the cemetery is free. Phone (615) 794–0903 for hours; www.carn.org.

A few blocks east of Franklin's town square, where the Confederate monument (circa 1899) rests, is the *Hiram Masonic Lodge.* When the three-story building was built in 1823, it was said to be the tallest structure in Tennessee. It was constructed to house the first Masonic Lodge in the state, which was chartered in 1803; later, in 1827, the first Protestant Episcopal Church in Tennessee was founded here.

The historic downtown area of Franklin is quickly becoming known as the newest "antiques capital of Tennessee." There are nearly three dozen antiques and craft stores within the downtown area, all within walking distance of one another. **Franklin Antique Mall** is the city's oldest and largest antiques mall. Used as a flour mill in the 1800s, the handmade-brick structure was the county's icehouse at the turn of the 20th century. Today it houses the goods of more than 50 different antiques dealers spread out over 12,000 square feet of space. At Second Avenue South and South Margin Street; open daily. Call the antiques mall at (615) 790–8593.

On US 31 is the **Rippavilla Plantation.** Built in 1852, the home has been restored and is the headquarters for the Tennessee Antebellum Trails organization and houses the **Armies of Tennessee Civil War Museum,** which chronicles the effects of the war on the family, the plantation, and the community.

The Confederate army spent the night on the property before they moved north to join the Battle of Franklin, one of the last major battles of the Civil War. Legend has it that all five of the Confederate generals who were killed in that battle had slept at Rippavilla and had breakfast together before heading off to battle.

Today the beautifully restored home features many of the original family's heirlooms and furnishings and is open to the public Tuesday through Saturday. There is an admission fee to enter the home, but you can walk the grounds and visit the welcome center for no charge. For more details call (931) 486–5000 or go to www.rippavilla.org.

Columbia is the center of commerce for Maury County. In addition to its reputation as the Antebellum Homes Capital of Tennessee, Columbia claims James K. Polk, one of the three presidents from the state, as a former resident. His ancestral home is open to the public at 301 West Seventh Avenue. Built by his parents in 1816, this is the house where Polk began his legal and political career. There are plenty of one-of-a-kind memorabilia housed here, and the gift shop has more books written about Polk than you could have ever imagined. Contact them (931) 388–2354.

A unique structure among Tennessee's antebellum homes is the **Athenaeum Rectory,** built in 1837 in a Moorish-Gothic architectural design. In 1852 it became the home to the Columbia Athenaeum School for Young Ladies. Today the building is owned by the Association for the Preservation of Tennessee Antiquities and is operated as a historic house museum.

Among things to look for as you tour the house is the chandelier in the reception room. It is made of seven metals and is original to the house. The front door side panels are flashed glass containing gold leaf from Europe, and the walnut and oak floors throughout are in a design known as wood carpeting.

Open for guided tours Tuesday through Saturday from 10:00 a.m. to 4:00 p.m., the house is located at 808 Athenaeum Street. Call (931) 381–4822 or go to www.athenaeumrectory.com.

The Polks were quite the building family here in Columbia. In addition to the James K. Polk Home, *Rattle and Snap Plantation,* and the Athenaeum Rectory, the family built two other historic structures—the Hamilton Place and St. John's Episcopal Church. All five were built within a 30-year period and only a few miles from one another. Special tours have been developed to visit all Polk structures. Call (931) 388–2354.

The James K. Polk Home and Rattle and Snap Plantation are two of the 60-plus homes along the *Tennessee Antebellum Trail.* Within a 30-mile radius of Nashville lies the highest concentration of antebellum homes in the South today. Eight of the houses are open to the public. A splendid tour map that lists and describes each house is available at area attractions or by calling the Middle Tennessee Convention and Visitors Bureau at (931) 381–7176 or www.rattleandsnapplantation.com.

If you think you have stubborn friends, they are probably nothing compared with the critters that gather here each year during the first week of April! That's when the *Mule Day Festival* and parade take place to celebrate Columbia's proud heritage as the mule-raising capital of the state. The parade

Oh, to Be a 19th-Century Lady Again

Columbia's Athenaeum Rectory was a well-respected girls' school for more than 50 years, teaching a wide range of quality courses, including mathematics, physics, science, and business—studies that were normally reserved only for young men. The school flourished from 1852 to 1904.

Today the Association for the Preservation of Tennessee Antiquities, owners and operators of the restored structure, conducts the 1861 Athenaeum Girls' School each summer. For one full week each July, young ladies ages 14 to 18 from all over the country dress in authentic 19th-century costumes and study the same courses in etiquette, penmanship, art, music, dance, and social graces as did the young ladies of 150 years ago. The week is highlighted on Friday evening with graduation ceremonies, followed by a formal ball.

All is not lost for you older ladies, age 19 and over. A condensed two-day version of the school is offered each May just for you. And you get to dress up, too! For more information call (931) 381–4822.

features mules pulling just about everything down the highway, and the festival is loaded with arts and crafts booths, all kinds of food (no mule meat, they assure us), a liar's contest, square dancing, and a mule show. Need more information? Call (931) 381–9557.

On Highway 50W about 8 miles from downtown Columbia, you'll find a good example of how industry and nature can live together. From 1937 to 1986, the Monsanto company had a plant here that produced elemental phosphorus. Through the years, as the company finished up strip mining an area of 5,345 acres, it planted trees and created lakes. Wildlife began moving in, and when the plant closed in 1986, the company worked with the Tennessee Wildlife Resources Agency to turn the entire area into a wildlife enhancement zone.

Out U.S. Highway 43 from Columbia is ***Mount Pleasant,*** a small community that calls itself the Best-Kept Secret in Middle Tennessee. Their other slogan, which might be a bit more appropriate for this sleepy little burg, is Stop, Shop, Eat, and Tour.

The town witnessed a great deal of troop movement during the Civil War, and after discovery of high-grade phosphate in 1896, the village of 400 residents became a boomtown of more than 2,000 when workers from 25 states and ten countries came to toil in the local phosphate mines. By the early 1900s there were more than a dozen companies operating here, and it was known as the "phosphate capital of the world."

Today the phosphate heritage and hundreds of other historical artifacts are preserved in the ***Phosphate Museum,*** downtown at 108 Public Square. Open weekdays and Saturday 9:30 a.m. to 4:30 p.m. Closed Wednesday and Sunday. Admission is $1 per adult or $3 for the entire family. Any questions? Phone them at (931) 379–9511.

One mile from downtown Murfreesboro is an obelisk marking the geographic center of the state. The ***Dimple of the Universe,*** as it is called locally, is on Old Lascassas Pike. Turn left off Greenland Drive opposite the football fields at Middle Tennessee State University. Call (615) 893–6565.

In the early days ***Murfreesboro*** was a little village known as ***Cannonsburgh.*** Today ***Cannonsburgh Pioneer Village*** is a living museum depicting 125 years of Southern life amid the hustle and bustle of the metropolitan area the city has become. Among its collections are a log house, blacksmith shop, general store, gristmill, one-room schoolhouse, and museum.

But the real star here is the ***World's Largest Red Cedar Bucket,*** manufactured locally by a bucket factory that toured the oddity as an advertising gimmick. It was built in 1887, is 6 feet tall and 24 feet around the top, and holds nearly 2,000 gallons of water. The museum here also holds what officials feel is the **World's Largest Spinning Wheel.** It stands 8 feet tall and was made by a local mortician.

Cannonsburgh is the site of the popular **Uncle Dave Macon Days** early every July. There's plenty of music, food, games, and activities for the kids. There is a juried arts and crafts show and a special gospel music celebration on Sunday morning. Cannonsburgh is open May through October, Tuesday through Sunday, at 312 South Front Street. Grounds open year-round; admission is free. Call (800) 716–7560 or www.uncledavemaconday.com.

More information on Murfreesboro, Smyrna, and the rest of Rutherford County can be found on the Web at www.rutherfordchamber.org. Call the Tourism Council at (800) 716–7560.

One of the most interesting factory tours in the state is located north of Murfreesboro, just off U.S. Highway 41. The **Nissan Motor Manufacturing Corporation** Truck/Auto Plant offers tours on Tuesday and Thursday. During the hourlong tram ride through the modern plant, you'll see men and women working side by side with hundreds of robots to produce more than 1,000 vehicles a day.

The complex covers about 800 acres and employs more than 6,000 local workers. To be safe, it's best to call ahead and make a reservation for your tour, because times change depending on production. Admission is free, and of course they don't give samples. No children under five are permitted on this tour. Call (615) 459–1444 for your reservation.

Mr. Miller ran Christiana's only grocery store for 75 years, and in that funky old building today is **Miller's Country Cafe.** It's a "meat and three" during the week, a bluegrass music and catfish eatery on Friday night, and fine dining and jazz room on Saturday night. It's also the tiny town's only restaurant.

Two meats and an array of veggies are available as a blue-plate lunch Tuesday through Saturday from 11:00 a.m. to 2:00 p.m., and the dinners are served Friday and Saturday nights from 5:00 to 9:00 p.m. A Sunday buffet is served from 11:00 a.m. to 2:00 p.m. There's a lot of old-time flavor in this old building: oilcloth-covered tables, wood floors, and all kinds of antiques and memorabilia that line the walls. Live bluegrass music is performed every Friday night, and live music of other genres is performed on Saturday night. Located about 8 miles from Murfreesboro and 7 miles south of Interstate 24 off U.S. Highway 231. Head south, and when you see the Christiana signs, turn left onto Highway 269. Cross the railroad tracks, make an immediate left, and you're in the neighborhood. Call (615) 893–1878 or visit the Web site at www .millersgrocery.com.

The little crossroads community of **Triune,** 25 miles south of Nashville at the corner of Highway 96 and US 31A/41A, has two claims to fame—the weekly *Triune Flea Market* and the annual Tennessee Renaissance Festival at Castle Gywnn.

The flea market is of the small-town, let's-dig-deep-for-a-bargain type of event. Cars pull up, open their trunks, throw out a few blankets full of stuff, and start selling. If it rains, you'll get wet and plenty muddy. As in any type of flea market, there's a lot of junk out there; but if you are patient, you'll probably find some good things. Prices seem a bit high on the true antiques and popular collectibles, but the dealers will usually come down, especially on Sunday afternoon. It's open every Saturday and Sunday 7:00 a.m. to 5:00 p.m.

The 16th century is celebrated at the *Tennessee Renaissance Festival,* held every weekend in May each year at Castle Gywnn, a wonderfully eclectic 20th-century castle. This is the time of King Henry VIII, and he's joined in the festivities by plenty of court jesters, street entertainers, musicians, Shakespearean actors, period games, combat chess, and full-armor jousts. Hundreds of craftspeople are open for business in the medieval marketplace, and there's a whole lot of great, unusual food and beverages. Located 25 miles south of Nashville on Highway 96, about halfway between I–24 and I–65 in Triune. Call for details at (615) 395–9950 or visit their Web site at www.tennessee renaissancefestival.com.

Southeastern Heartland

If you happen to be in *Manchester* during late August, be sure to visit the *Old Timer's Day celebration.* The city fathers shut down the streets around the square for a Saturday and fill it with fun things to do, including a bluegrass music concert, arts and crafts, kiddie rides and games, and a whole lot of food. Call (931) 728–7635 for date and time or go to www.cityofmanchester.com.

Foothill Crafts in Manchester may be the ultimate quality crafts store. Run entirely by volunteer members of the Coffee County Crafts Association, the shop has an amazing array of handcrafted items for sale. It's a hard process to get your crafts represented here, but that process ensures that only the highest-quality items will be represented. Currently more than 400 different artisans are selling their items out of this old-time grocery store; it's open daily year-round. Give them a call at (931) 728–9236.

On Highway 55, just before you reach Tullahoma, be on the lookout for the *Coca-Cola Bottling Company* plant. Next to it is the Company Store, a retail outlet open to the public. You'll be amazed at how many things are made with the Coke and Dr Pepper logos on them. It's a virtual plethora of red-and-white merchandise, from clothes to antique reproductions to glasses.

Open Monday through Friday 9:00 a.m. to 5:00 p.m., Saturday 10:00 a.m. to 5:00 p.m.; closed Sunday. Call (931) 454–1030.

The *Tullahoma Fine Arts Center* and the *Regional Museum of Art* share space in the city's oldest brick house, at 401 Jackson Street. The arts center features work of local and regional artists, including crafts as well as the fine arts. All items on display may be purchased. The Regional Museum of Art features traveling exhibits and the museum's private collection. Open Monday through Friday; admission is free. Phone (931) 455–1234 or visit www .tullahomafinearts.org.

When George Dickel first discovered tranquil Cascade Hollow outside Tullahoma, he knew he had found a gold mine. It was the water from a nearby spring that Dickel considered so valuable. The ancient limestone shelf of the plateau provided water that ran fresh and clear, without mineral deposits. That iron-free water was the perfect ingredient for smooth sippin' whisky. Dickel also made another important discovery—the batch of whisky he had made in the winter with that water was far smoother than the whisky he had produced in the summer. Dickel used the traditional Scottish spelling of "whisky" (as opposed to "whiskey") because he believed his product to be as high in quality as the best Scotch whiskies.

First produced in 1877, George Dickel whisky is still handcrafted. After a four-year shutdown, the *George Dickel Distillery* reopened in October 2003 and is now going stronger than ever. The distillery offers tours of this isolated spot surrounded by true hill beauty. Visitors also can watch a George Dickel video in the visitor center, which is filled with antiques and photos. The George Dickel General Store is a nice place to shop and look. On site is a U.S. Post Office—the only working post office at any distillery in the United States. Visitors can also see Oscar, a 1910 replica of the George Dickel Whisky delivery truck with the old-fashioned Dickel sign painted on the side. Call the distillery at (931) 857–3124 or check out www.dickel.com.

If your taste in bed-and-breakfasts is more rustic and rural than froufrou and finery, here's a place for you! *Ledford Mill Bed & Breakfast* is located inside an 1884 gristmill and is on the National Register of Historic Places. John Spear purchased the inn during June 2002. The previous owners, who turned the mill into a bed-and-breakfast, decided not to remove the equipment but instead created a bed-and-breakfast around all the milling apparatus.

In the Loft Room, the corn-cleaning machine separates the sleeping and sitting areas. The Creek Room has an entire wall of stone, an old-time tub, and a large private deck with a view of the falls and wooded hillside. The Falls Room, with a wall of Chattanooga shale, is the closest to the falls and has a large bathroom that showcases the main wheel—the "heart" of the mill. Plank flooring is throughout.

Located in a "holler" at the spring-fed headwaters of Shipman's Creek, the mill sits over the water; that same spring water is what comes through the taps to drink.

Rooms run from $95 to $125, and the facilities are pretty well booked up in advance, so you'll probably need to do some planning if you want to stay here. Turn onto Ledford Mill Road at the Lowe's Superstore on US 41A, and go 3 miles to the mill. Call (931) 455–2546 for reservations.

Shelbyville, the Bedford County seat, is also the center of Tennessee's horse country. It plays host each year to the ***Tennessee Walking Horse Celebration,*** an event during which the World Grand Champion is named.

This special breed of horse, developed during 150 years of selective breeding, is promoted today as the world's greatest show and pleasure horse. The horse has an unusual rhythmic, gliding gait in which each hoof strikes the ground separately in an odd one-two-three-four beat.

The Celebration Grounds are located on Madison Avenue, which is US 41A, east of downtown Shelbyville. For more information call (931) 684–5915.

The breed emerged from the plantations around here during the later part of the 19th century but today can be found across the country. The area around Shelbyville is still known for its farms, and most of the owners are happy to show off their facilities. Many have signs out welcoming you, but you might want to call the Breeders Association in advance. There may be a special event or training session at one of the farms that you'd find interesting; reach them at (800) 359–1574.

Nobody seems to know exactly how ***Rover*** got its name, but the most accepted story is that a bunch of bickering regulars at a local drinking establishment decided to name their community. After hours of arguing over a name, one of them piped out, "Why don't we just call it Rover—we all fight like dogs anyway." So be it.

Along Highway 269 in the northern corner of the county lies the quaint little village of ***Bell Buckle.*** The little downtown area, located along Railroad Square facing the active railroad, is a trip back in time. A covered wooden sidewalk leads you from one store to another. All the benches, rocking chairs, flowers, and store displays have a tendency to slow down pedestrian traffic a bit, but it gives you more time to look in the window or watch a train go by.

Ten little antiques and craft shops make up the downtown lineup. Margaret Britton Vaughn (friends call her Maggi), the state's official poet laureate, runs the ***Bell Buckle Press.*** Take time to drop in and chat with her for a few minutes; she's a true Southern lady. Contact the press at (931) 389–6878.

Featured prominently a few shops down is J. Gregry's **Bell Buckle Cafe and Music Parlour.** In addition to some great hickory-smoked barbecue and the world's greatest hand-squeezed lemonade, the cafe features live music three nights a week and is the site of a Saturday-afternoon live broadcast on WLIJ Radio 1580 AM from 1:00 to 3:00 p.m. You'll hear a lot of new and old country and bluegrass coming from the back room here. Thursdays are writers' nights, and there are at least a couple shows each Friday and Saturday night. Food is served seven days a week. Find out more at (931) 389–9693 or www .bellbucklecafe.com.

Phillips General Store has an amazing assortment of cool things. Of course beauty is in the eye of the beholder, but this shop has it all. From architectural items to folk art to garden art, the place is heaven. Open daily, the store's number is (931) 389–6547.

The roads to Bell Buckle are lined with daffodils, and the city founders felt those flowers were a good reason for a party. **Daffodil Day** is held on a Saturday in mid-March each year, and the town celebrates with a bake sale, Easter egg hunt, old-fashioned menu at the Bell Buckle Cafe, and people dressed up like it's the 1800s all over again.

For a bit of the true South, be here during the third weekend of June to help celebrate the **Moon Pie Festival.** That's when you'll get to join in the celebration of one of the area's finest traditions, Moon Pies and RC Cola. Yum yum!

The village is also the home of **Webb School,** a preparatory school that has produced ten Rhodes Scholars and the governors of three states. The Junior Room, the original wood-shingled one-room schoolhouse built in 1870, has been preserved as it was then, complete with potbellied stove and teaching paraphernalia. It's open for visitors daily and is free. The school hosts a well-respected art and craft festival the third weekend of each October. Call (931) 389–6003.

The area west of Shelbyville on Highway 64 is loaded with horse stables and horse farms. A drive along this corridor into the city of **Lewisburg** definitely reminds you that you're smack-dab in the middle of Tennessee Horse Country. If you see training sessions taking place, chances are the owners won't mind if you stop and watch, but of course it's always polite to ask first.

If you'd like to learn a little history while you're in the Lewisburg area, drive south on US 31A from downtown and you'll run into the **Abner Houston home,** across from the Lone Oak Cemetery. The log cabin was the site of the first court of Marshall County in October 1836. It was moved to this site in 1957.

Hi-Way 50 Drive-in movie theater in Lewisburg is the state's oldest, continuously operated drive-in. There are now 14 drive-ins operating in the state, and only 401 in the United States. Most are operated seasonally. Hi-Way 50 has been around since 1947, and its current owners, Gary and June Douglas, have had it since 1995. Located in Marshall County, just outside Lewisburg on Fayetteville Highway 431. Reach them at (931) 270–1591 or http://hiway 50drivein.net. For a history of America's drive-in theaters and a listing of those still in business, not only in Tennessee but across the country, check out www .driveintheater.com.

Deep in dry Moore County you'll find a famous distillery known for its Tennessee sour mash whiskey. *Jack Daniel Distillery* put Lynchburg, a community of 360 residents, on the map. Mister Jack (as he is locally known) founded his business in 1866 and received the first federal license ever issued for a distillery.

If you want to take a tour, make sure you wear comfortable shoes: There's a lot of walking and hill climbing. This is true history and Americana at its finest.

One of the highlights of the tour is the visit to Daniel's office, left virtually the way it was when he died. Make sure you ask the guide to show you where Mister Jack lost his temper one day, eventually causing him to experience a slow, painful death.

Start your tour at the visitor center, located in the hollow. It's a huge stone building with a magnificent front porch; you can't miss it. Inside, you'll learn just about everything you'd ever want to know about Mister Jack, plus you'll see some great exhibits of rare bottles and jugs and a reproduction of his first-ever still. Tours leave from 9:00 a.m. to 4:30 p.m. daily and last for approximately 75 minutes. New tours leave every 15 minutes or so. Call (931) 759–6180 or go to www.jackdaniels.com.

There's a great deal of charm in the nearby village of *Lynchburg,* where Daniel lived his entire life. Today, surrounding the 1855 redbrick courthouse, the square is chock-full of gift shops, general stores, arts and crafts outlets, and stores selling Jack Daniel merchandise. Among the shops that are fun to visit is the *Lynchburg Ladies Handiwork,* on the north side of the square. The shop features handmade items, mostly needlework, by people in Moore County. The ladies working the shop spend their time quilting, sewing, and crocheting. Contact them at (931) 759–7919.

Used whiskey barrels, Jack Daniel memorabilia, and antique reproductions can be found at the *Lynchburg Hardware and General Store,* on the east side of the square. Tommy Sullenger is the proprietor here, and the friendly guy knows just about everything there is to know about the community. Also, as a professional bass fisherman, he may be able to point out a good local fishin' hole for you. Call (931) 759–4200.

The best-known place to eat in these parts is ***Miss Mary Bobo's Boarding House*** in the southwest corner of downtown. Miss Mary began serving meals in 1908 and served many of them to Mister Jack, who had lunch here quite often. Of course both Mister Jack and Miss Mary are gone now, but the tradition lives on. Specializing in Southern traditional foods, they serve their meals family style.

Each meal is different, and the usual offerings include your choice of two meats, six vegetables, bread, beverage, and a totally awesome dessert. Reservations are a must, since the popular eatery seats only 65 people. During most of the year, seatings are at 11:00 a.m. and 1:00 p.m., Monday through Saturday. They are closed on Sunday. During the slower periods, especially on Monday, there may be only one seating. It's best to be flexible when you call for reservations, and if you're looking for a Saturday seating, you'll probably have to call several months in advance! Meals for adults are $16; $8 for children under ten.

Lynne Tolley, Mister Jack's great-grandniece, is now the proprietress of Miss Mary Bobo's and can be found in the kitchen daily preparing the noontime meal. However, on Friday afternoon she runs off to her part-time job—as an official taster at her great-uncle's distillery, where each week she tastes the latest aged batch of the famous whiskey. Try a visit! Call (931) 759–7394.

Tennessee Table is a virtual Southern cooking cookbook and recipe-sharing Web site that tells you more about Miss Mary Bobo's menu. In fact, the recipes of many of the most-requested meals at the restaurant are listed, as well as recipes from all over the world that people have created using "the spirits" of Jack Daniel. A great site! Visit them at www.jackdaniels.com/tennes seetable/main.htm.

If you're hungry for the best barbecue in the country, make plans to come to Lynchburg in late October. That's when the ***Jack Daniel's World Championship Cook-off*** takes place. Participation is by invitation and qualification only. In order to compete here, your team must have won a championship cook-off of 50 or more participants or be the designated champion of a state competition. There are also international teams involved. Of course there are a lot of food booths for sampling, as well as games and music. Call (931) 759–6180 for dates and times.

The ***Tennessee Walking Horse Museum*** is located along the square, about a block from Miss Mary Bobo's. Among the fun things in here are photos of all the world champion Tennessee Walking Horses from 1939 to the present. In addition, there are hundreds of other photos, memorabilia, and tools of the trade. Owned by the Tennessee Walking Horse Celebration in nearby Shelbyville, the museum is open 10:00 a.m. to noon, 1:00 to 4:00 p.m. Tuesday

Claim to Fame for Miss Mary

Miss Mary Bobo, a close personal friend of Jack Daniel's and the proprietress of Miss Mary Bobo's Boarding House in Lynchburg for many years, holds the distinction of being the oldest woman to ever appear in the pages of *Playboy* magazine.

A Jack Daniel Distillery advertisement ran in the magazine in June 1980, congratulating Miss Mary on her 99th birthday. The ad ran a photo of her and encouraged everyone to send her a card. As a result of that ad, she received thousands of cards, 36 cakes, and numerous gifts.

Miss Mary ran her boarding business for another three years, dying in 1983—just shy of her 102nd birthday.

through Saturday. Call for more information at (931) 759–5747 or www.twh bea.com.

As you head west across the mountain from Monteagle on US 41A/64, you'll pass the beautiful ***University of the South*** in ***Sewanee.*** Founded in the late 1850s, the 10,000-acre mountaintop campus is known for its shady lawns and Gothic sandstone buildings patterned after Oxford University in England.

Farther down the mountain you'll enter the village of ***Cowan,*** where you'll find the ***Cowan Railroad Museum*** along the still-busy railroad tracks. The museum is housed in the large circa 1904 depot that once served as the busy passenger station.

People would come from all over the South to visit the Sewanee area and the ***Monteagle Assembly.*** They would disembark from the passenger train in Cowan and take the Mountain Goat, a smaller train, up the mountain to their destinations. The mountain goat track, built in 1853, is no longer in use as a railroad track. It has been converted to a mountain bike trail.

Today the museum is full of railroad antiques and memorabilia of those early days. Outside there's a steam engine, a flatcar, and a caboose. Run by volunteers, the facility is open from May through October on Thursday through Saturday from 10:00 a.m. to 4:00 p.m. and on Sunday from 1:00 to 4:00 p.m. The museum's phone number is (931) 967–3078 or www.cowanrailroadmuseum.org.

Hang on, we're really going off the beaten path on this one. The ***Cumberland Tunnel*** is the longest and steepest railroad tunnel in the United States. Built in 1852, it's 2,200 feet long, 21 feet high, and 15 feet wide. It's still used today and is listed on the National Register of Historic Places.

To get there is a somewhat tedious, albeit fun and adventurous trek. Across the track and the small park from the museum is Tennessee Avenue.

Take it south to the first right possible and go over the tracks. Make an immediate left turn onto a gravel road located next to the track. The tunnel is nearly 2 miles up that road. Go slowly, and if you have a low-rider, forget it. The road is bumpy, uneven, and when it rains, a bit muddy in spots, but it's worth the trip once you're there.

The gravel road crosses about 25 feet above the track, just 50 feet from the tunnel entrance. Before you come up, get a train schedule and plan on watching a few trains go through—it's quite fun. Pack a lunch, and between trains take a hike into the raw mountains that surround you. The working rail yard in Cowan has a pusher locomotive working 24 hours a day to help trains climb up to the tunnel and then help them through it.

Remember when you could buy a house from Sears & Roebuck? The company sold a great many for several years, and a few are still standing, including the one at 518 West Cumberland Street (US 41) here in Cowan. The house was ordered from the catalog in the early 1900s and is now owned by Leland Farmer.

Do not pass through **Winchester** without first going to visit the **Old Jail Museum.** Built in 1897, the structure is now open only to those who really want to be here. After having served as the county jail for more than 75 years, the museum now preserves the various elements of the jail, including the cell area and maximum-security block. Six additional rooms have exhibits highlighting the county's history, from the frontier days through the Civil War to the present. The Old Jail Museum is located on Dinah Shore Boulevard at Bluff Street, a few blocks from the Winchester Courthouse. Open mid-March through mid-December, Tuesday through Saturday 10:00 a.m. to 4:00 p.m. Admission for adults, $1; children, 50 cents. Call (931) 967–0524.

In 1987 a group of Mennonite families migrated to mid-south Tennessee in search of farmland and a desire to start a Mennonite church in an area that had none. Among those in the group was the Miller family, who saw the demand for homemade breads and pastries. The **Swiss Pantry** had its beginning in the kitchen of Mrs. Miller, who sold her products to friends and neighbors. In 1989 Mrs. Miller was joined by her three sisters, and they moved the business into the present building, located along U.S. Highway 64 just west of Belvidere. In 1999 Mrs. Miller's brother, Enos Miller, and his family purchased the store from the ladies and now run the business.

Not only will you find ten different types of fresh-baked breads but also rolls, cookies, pastries, homemade salad dressings and relishes, a large selection of fresh herbs and spices, more than 30 different cheeses, smoked bacon and sausages, nuts, snacks, dried fruits, homemade candies, and a selection of baking and cooking supplies. Outside, a small garden center has been established. Open Tuesday through Friday 8:00 a.m. to 5:30 p.m. and Saturday 8:00 a.m. to 4:00 p.m.; their number is (931) 962–0567 or www .swisspantry.com.

When you leave the Swiss Pantry, continue west on US 64 and head into Davy Crockett country. You'll be going by a roadside marker designating Kentuck, the homestead that he left in 1812 to go off to the Creek War. He and his first wife, Polly, and their children settled near here when he came back from the war. She died in 1815 and is buried in an old cemetery overlooking nearby Bean's Creek.

If you want further information on Davy Crockett's ties with this part of Tennessee, stop by **Falls Mill** near Belvidere and talk with owner Janie Lovett. In addition to her duties at the mill she owns with her husband, John, she's active in the local historical association and seems to know everyone in the area.

The Lovetts bought the mill in 1984 and have been busy restoring it ever since. Built in 1873, the mill has operated as a cotton-spinning and wool-carding factory, a cotton gin, a woodworking shop, and a grist and flour mill through the years. Since 1970 it has also served as a sort of museum. But it wasn't until the Lovetts bought it that it started realizing its true potential.

Make sure you take a walk down to the river behind the mill to get a good view of the falls and the 32-foot overshot waterwheel, which is the largest still in operation in the country.

Grain is still ground and is available at the mill store, along with other local items. There's a weaving exhibit upstairs in the mill. An 1895 log cabin was moved here and reassembled and serves as a bed-and-breakfast for up to five persons. Rates are $90 per night for two people, $5 for each additional body. The mill and picnic grounds are open every day but Wednesday. Admission is charged; call (931) 469–7161 or visit www.fallsmill.com.

Farther south on U.S. Highway 231 is **Fayetteville,** the seat of Lincoln County. The downtown area around the county courthouse is probably one of the busiest in the state. There's nary a building vacancy on the square, and it can be hard to find a parking spot at times.

Start your visit at the chamber of commerce welcome center at 208 South Elk Avenue, where you'll be able to pick up a walking-tour map of the historic downtown area, use their restroom facilities, and obtain a welcome package containing coupons and free gifts. That's what I call Southern hospitality. Find out for yourself! Call (931) 433–1234 or go to www.vallnet.com/ chamberofcommerce.

While downtown, visit the **Lincoln County Museum** at 521 Main Avenue South. Located inside the old Borden Milk Plant, numerous displays and exhibits highlight the town's past. There's a great agricultural exhibit and an amazing display of arrowheads. Call (931) 433–2921 or (931) 438–0339; www .flcmuseum.com

During the second weekend of November, the town features a Christmas celebration and festival. There are trolley rides, strolling musicians, a candle-light walking tour, and an old-fashioned high tea.

One block off the square on Market Street, you can have lunch or dinner at *Caboots,* located in an old firehouse and city jail. Sit out front or in back in one of the rugged limestone cells. Built in 1867, the building was the city's jailhouse until the 1970s. Menu items include burgers, chicken, a variety of sandwiches, and Mexican, seafood, and pasta dishes. For dessert try the French silk pie. Yum! Open Monday through Saturday. Hours vary. They'd love to hear from you at (931) 433–1173.

Western Heartland

The bell that was cast in 1858 and hangs in the *Giles County Courthouse* on the public square in Pulaski still strikes on the hour, each hour, every day. The sound coming from the cupola is just one of the beautiful elements of this neoclassic building built in 1909. Outside, tall Corinthian columns mark the architecture. Inside, a balcony encircles the third floor and 16 caryatids (female figures) hold up the arched vault of the rotunda, with its stained-glass skylights. The courthouse is open Monday through Friday during business hours. Call (931) 363–5300.

Out in front of the courthouse, on the south side of the public square, is a statue of Sam Davis, the young Confederate scout who was captured and executed in Pulaski. He was captured behind enemy lines with damag-ing information in his possession, and instead of betraying the source of that information, he chose to be hanged. The *Sam Davis Museum* now stands on the spot where the "Boy Hero of the Confederacy" was executed on November 27, 1863. The museum contains Civil War memorabilia as well as the leg irons worn by Davis. Located on Sam Davis Avenue, the hours are sporadic, so call the chamber of commerce first if you want to visit. Contact the museum at (931) 363–3789.

The chamber of commerce publishes a driving-tour guide map of Giles County's top antiques, crafts, and collectible shops. Pick up a copy at the chamber's office, 100 South Second Street. Contact them at (931) 363–3789, or log on at www.gilescountychamber.com.

While there are few, if any, physical reminders, there's one part of local history most residents would like to forget—the Ku Klux Klan was founded in

Pulaski. Resentment against the move toward black equality fueled the creation of white supremacist groups throughout the South. The most enduring of those, the KKK, was founded in 1866 by six Confederate officers.

Historic **Lynnville,** population 408, has quite the history as a railroad town, and to help preserve that grand heritage, a reproduction of the circa 1877 depot was built in 1997 to house a local museum of railroad artifacts and vintage railroad equipment. The town's history as a railroad town is unique in that the city was originally located 1 mile away from where it is now.

After the Civil War the city fathers decided to move everything to make it more convenient to the railroad. Today the entire town of 59 buildings is listed on the National Register of Historic Places. Contributing to the quaint factor of the downtown business district are several craft and antiques shops and **Soda Pop Junction,** an old-fashioned soda shop inside the old Lynnville Pharmacy building, built in 1860. You'll find much more than ice cream here, though. A few years ago, their hamburger was voted best in the state and their milk shakes, second best. "I think they cheated when they counted the votes for the shakes; we're definitely the best," kidded the owner. It's open Monday through Friday 10:00 a.m. to 7:00 p.m. and Sunday 7:00 a.m. to 6:00 p.m. Call (931) 527–0007.

The railroad museum is open May through October, Thursday through Sunday until 5:00 p.m. Lynnville is located on Highway 129, 7 miles from exit 27 off I–65. Reach them at (931) 363–3789 or (931) 527–0564.

Although his legacy is divided among several areas in the state, David (aka Davy) Crockett only helped in the organization of one of the counties in which he lived, Lawrence County. He was working as a justice of the peace in the area in 1817 when it was ceded by the Chickasaw Indians to the United States. He helped get things organized and was instrumental in getting Lawrenceburg named as the county seat of government.

In 1922, during the dedication of a large monument that still stands on the south side of the square in Lawrenceburg, officials gave Crockett the title of Father of Lawrence County.

onestop graveyard

The Old Graveyard Memorial Park in Pulaski is a city park, cemetery, and historic monument all rolled into one. It's a great example of how an old, neglected cemetery can once again be useful while preserving the respect due those buried there. It's a well-lit area where one can stroll and truly absorb the area's history. The monuments have all been restored, with inscriptions dating back to 1753. Located at the corner of Cemetery Street and U.S. Highway 31. Call the mayor's office for more information at (931) 363–3789.

Treasures and More on Route 64

If some can get their kicks on Route 66, Tennesseans surely can see more on Route 64. Running from I–24 in the Heartland into the Memphis area, this U.S. highway skirts the bottom of the state through ten counties. Five of those counties have gotten together to create a map of the attractions, accommodations, and events that can be found along the route in their counties. Call (931) 967–6788 or 433–1234 for a copy.

Davy Crockett was truly a Tennessean. He was born in the eastern part of the state, ran a gristmill, was elected to Congress in 1821 from Lawrenceburg, and went off to fight in the *Alamo* from the west. Over his lifetime, Crockett was a pioneer, soldier, politician, and industrialist.

While serving as justice of the peace, Crockett established a diversified water-powered industry consisting of a powder mill, a gristmill, and a distillery. His entire complex and his financial security were washed away in a flood in 1821, causing him to move farther west a few years later.

Today, on the site along the river where Crockett lived and worked, Tennessee has created *David Crockett State Park.* The 1,100-acre park has an interpretive center, which is staffed during the summer months and has exhibits depicting Crockett's life here and a replica of the gristmill he once owned. Other facilities in the park include a swimming pool, 107 campsites, and the David Crockett Restaurant at (931) 762–9541, one of the best eateries in this part of the state. Located on US 64, just west of Lawrenceburg. Call them at (931) 762–9408 or visit www.lawrenceburg.com/crockettpark.

During the second full weekend of August, the park hosts *David Crockett Days,* a fun and educational festival featuring a bevy of frontier-type activities, from tomahawk throwing to long rifle gun making. There's a Crockett film festival, snake shows, and bluegrass music concerts. An arts and crafts festival takes place the first weekend in September each year, featuring a wide variety of exhibitors. Additional unusual events run throughout the year. If you need more information, call (931) 762–9408 or (931) 762–8047.

By the way, the county was named in honor of Captain James Lawrence, who commanded a ship in the War of 1812. Mortally wounded, it was he who shouted out the famous command: "Don't give up the ship."

The pace in the *Ethridge* area, just north of Lawrenceburg, is definitely life in the slow lane. More than 200 Amish families call this community their home. The Amish, known as the Plain Folk, have a reputation for being productive farmers and expert craftspeople. Many families sell their wares from their front porches, but the best place to start your shopping is the ***Amish Country Galleries,*** a five-room antiques store/gallery featuring the works of nearly 200 local craftspeople. Call (931) 829–2126.

Among the locally produced items you'll find here is the hickory bent rocking chair, a wonderfully comfortable rocker made and used by the Amish in their homes. There is also a great selection of Amish baskets. Located 5 miles north of Lawrenceburg on U.S. Highway 43, the shop is open Monday through Saturday 9:00 a.m. to 5:00 p.m.

The ***Natchez Trace*** is truly a road trip back in time. The 450-mile road has been a major highway between Nashville and Natchez, Mississippi, since the late 1700s. It is preserved today as a scenic two-lane parkway with few intersections, no commercial activities of any kind, and numerous pull-offs at historic stands (resting areas usually placed one day's travel from the other). The parkway ends on Highway 100, across from the Loveless Motel and Cafe, in Davidson County.

One of the early travelers on the trace was ***Meriwether Lewis,*** the famed leader of the Lewis and Clark expedition. In 1809 he met a violent and mysterious death at ***Grinder's Stand.*** His grave is marked by a broken column, symbolic of his broken career. The monument is located near the intersection with Highway 20 here in Lewis County, east of Hohenwald.

The trace is overlooked by those in a hurry because the speed limit (50 mph or less) is monitored quite closely. Make sure you have a lot of gas before you set out. For a map and other details, call (800) 305–7417.

Just east of the Natchez Trace Parkway on U.S. Highway 412 is the little village of Gordonsburg, founded in 1806 by early white settlers traveling the original Natchez Trace. The community became the seat of the county's first government in 1843, and in the early 1900s it was a bustling village of 1,600

The Candy Bar Farm

Frank Mars, the founder of Mars Candy Company, may have made his millions elsewhere, but he came to the rolling hills of Tennessee in 1922 to build his dream mansion and farm. Milky Way Farm is nestled among one of the most stately stands of grand magnolias in the South, and the Tudor mansion has 21 bedrooms and 15 baths.

During its heyday, the Milky Way Farm consisted of 2,800 acres, 38 barns, numerous houses, the grand mansion, and its own railroad. The farm produced prizewinning cattle and horses, including a Kentucky Derby winner. The mansion is listed on the National Register of Historic Places.

inhabitants, thanks to the phosphate mines in the area. The mines closed in 1937, and most of the population has since moved on.

Today parts of that original village are preserved on the grounds of the **Historic Blackburn House and Museum,** on US 412, 2 miles east of the Natchez Trace Parkway. Ambrose Blackburn cleared the land in 1806 and built his homestead, one of the few original traceside farms still extant. Open to the public on weekends, the house was the site of the first Lewis County Post Office, and the circa 1806 corncrib in which the first Lewis County jury deliberated; both are listed on the National Register of Historic Places.

The Blackburn site also contains the cemetery where Blackburn, a Revolutionary War captain, is buried. Numerous displays feature farming tools, antique lights, axes, broadaxes, froes, an herb garden, and an American-Indian exhibit. Open weekends April through November, 10:00 a.m. to 4:00 p.m. Call (931) 964–3478 or go to www.blackburn-farmstead.com.

The village of **Hohenwald** is a junker's paradise. The downtown streets are lined with junk and secondhand clothing shops, and people come from miles away to do their bargain hunting. Used clothing is brought in from the Midwest and Northeast in bales and dumped on the floors of the shops. The bales are broken open at most of the shops each Wednesday, Saturday, and Sunday, the days to be there for the best selection. If you're knowledgeable about brands and clothing quality, some real bargains await you here. There are tales about people finding money and even diamond rings in the old clothes.

German immigrants created Hohenwald (which means "high forest") in 1878 as they developed a lumber industry in the area. With the help of the railroad, an organized colony of Swiss immigrants settled in 1894 and built New Switzerland, just south of Hohenwald, and the two towns later merged. A great deal of the German architecture is still evident throughout the community.

The **Lewis County Museum of Natural and Local History,** located at 108 East Main Street, houses one of the largest collections of exotic animal mounts in the United States, including one example of each species of North American sheep. There are also skins of lions, Bengal tigers, and tundra grizzlies. The museum serves as the local history museum and has several displays on the county's past. Open Tuesday through Saturday 10:00 a.m. to 4:00 p.m., Sunday 1:00 p.m. to 4:00 p.m. Admission for adults is $4; $2 for ages 13–17 and $1 for children under 13. Phone (931) 796–1550 or www.lewiscounty museum.com.

Carol Buckley and her elephant, Tara, traveled and performed with circuses for years, and then Carol decided Tara would be a lot happier away from show business and in an environment more natural and more fitting for elephants. She moved the two of them to Hickman County, where she set up the **Elephant Sanctuary,** the country's first official elephant retirement home. "It's for the old, sick, and needy," she said, "There are many elephants out there that need a place like this. I have a strong feeling that we're going to be the first of many such homes." Through donations, special events, and a lot of help from concerned friends, Carol has been able to raise the money to build the necessary facilities. The sanctuary is not open to the public, but if you'd like to see Tara, Carol, and any other residents who may be living here, sign on to www.elephants.com and you can watch them on the ELECAM. All you elephant lovers, call (800) 98–TRUNK.

There's not a single traffic light in the entire 613 square miles of Hickman County. "We used to have one, but some kid kept shooting it out, and they finally took it down," said one county resident. While many of the communities in the state have groups who sit around outside near the courthouse and spit and whittle their days away, you'll find the old-timers in **Centerville,** the county seat, playing checkers while they spit.

In Hickman County, nicknamed the Keg County, there's still a lot of moonshine made in these hills. If you're interested in sampling some, just put out the word. It has a way of finding you.

And speaking of tasty things, make sure you stop by **Breece's Cafe,** on the square in Centerville. In business since the 1940s, it offers country cooking at its finest. A different plate lunch is offered each weekday, and they always have a selection of home-baked pies on hand. Ask for the blackberry; it's especially good. Open Wednesday through Saturday 5:00 a.m. to 8:00 p.m. and Sunday 6:00 a.m. to 8:00 p.m. Call (931) 729–3481.

Head out Highway 100 toward Nashville, and as soon as you cross the Duck River, look to your right and you'll find the hottest spot in town for a catfish dinner. The **Fish Camp Restaurant,** located next to two ponds, features Tennessee River catfish, and people come from all over to sample it. In addition to the fish, they have a full menu, including some great barbecue they smoke right on-site. No alcohol is served or allowed due to city regulations. Open seven days a week for lunch and dinner. You can reach them at (931) 729–4401.

The strangest name of any community in the state is probably located here in Hickman County. Out on Highway 50 south of Centerville is the small community of **Who'd A Thought It.** Story goes that a schoolhouse was being built out in the middle of nowhere, and a man pulled up in his buggy and asked what they were building. They told him, and he was last seen shaking his head and mumbling "Who'd a thought it" as he pulled away.

Other interesting names in the county are Defeated Creek, Little Lot, Only, Pretty Creek, Ugly Creek, Spot, and Grinders Switch. The chamber of commerce in Centerville has a book for sale that explains how more than 64 communities got their names and where to find each one. At 117 North Central Avenue; the number there is (931) 729–5774.

Up in Nunnelly, behind the Church of Christ where Highways 48 and 230 split, you'll find a monument marking the birthplace of *Beth Slater Whitson,* the writer of poems, songs, and short stories. Her best-known song lyrics were "Let Me Call You Sweetheart" and "Meet Me Tonight in Dreamland." She lived here from her birth in 1879 to 1913, when she moved to Nashville. She died there in 1930.

There's a nifty piece of the 1950s alive and well just 3 miles out of Centerville on Highway 100. The *Pink Cadillac Drive-in Theater* is one of the few existing drive-in movie theaters still operating in the state. The ticket office is lined with pink neon, rock and roll scenes are painted on the front fence, and the smell of fresh popcorn permeates the air. Open during the summer months, Friday, Saturday, and Sunday night at dark. After you explain to your kids what a drive-in theater is, call (931) 729–2386.

The coal miner's daughter not only lives in *Hurricane Mills,* she owns it. When country music's most-awarded female vocalist, Loretta Lynn, and her husband, Mooney, were house shopping back in 1966, she was searching for a big old "haunted looking" place. When she saw this century-old mansion, she knew this was her dream. She wanted it immediately, not knowing the entire town and old mill came with it. The *Loretta Lynn Ranch,* on Highway 13 in Hurricane Mills, is her home as well as her museum and special place to welcome fans.

In 1975 a campground was developed, and since then numerous other attractions have been added to the ranch, including Loretta's personal museum, a replica of the coal mine her father worked in, a replica of her Butcher Holler house, a western store, and a gift shop.

Tours of the first floor of her antebellum plantation mansion are given daily. Make sure you ask the guide about the haunted aspects of the building. There is no charge to enter the ranch, but there is for the tours, museum, and other activities, including miniature golf and canoeing. There are dances every Saturday night during the summer, and Loretta schedules a few concerts during that time also. When she's home she enjoys walking around meeting people and signing autographs. Located 7 miles north of I–40; open April through October. Call (931) 296–7700 or visit www.lorettalynn.com.

Along the Tennessee River at US 70 is the Johnsonville *Tennessee Valley Authority* (TVA) facility. Built in 1950 it was the TVA's first major coal-fired power plant. Tours are given "when someone shows up who wants one." The length of tour and how long you might have to wait for one to start can vary depending on the workload of the staff at that particular time. It's most likely they'll find time for you Monday through Friday between 8:00 a.m. and 3:00 p.m.

One of the things to look for during the tour is the coal-unloading facilities. If you're lucky enough to be there on the day the coal is being unloaded from a barge, you'll see a huge crane in operation that is capable of unloading coal at a net rate of 700 tons an hour. The coal then goes by conveyer to the crusher building, which is a sight in itself. After you leave here, you'll have a real appreciation for electricity and the work that goes into producing it. Call (931) 535–8212.

Charlotte, the seat of Dickson County, looks much as it did in the mid-1800s. The circa 1834 courthouse is considered the oldest such building still in use in the state. Pre-Civil War buildings line the downtown square, and the old-timers still gather at the drugstore on the square to solve the world's problems.

But it could have been so different! The now quaint and quiet town was two votes short of becoming the capital of Tennessee. Only Nashville received more votes.

Northern Heartland

The 170,000-acre peninsula between ***Kentucky Lake*** and Lake Barkley is owned and operated by the Tennessee Valley Authority and is aptly called the ***Land Between the Lakes,*** or LBL, as locals refer to it. About a third of it lies in Tennessee and the rest in Kentucky.

The area is an awesome display of nature. The Trace, the main north-south road, is 60 miles long, with southern entry just west of Dover off U.S. Highway 79. There's plenty to do here, and according to the rangers, most of the area is underutilized.

In addition to all the hiking trails and water activities, there are more than 100 miles of paved roads for biking. The ***Homeplace*** is a 19th-century living-history museum with 16 restored structures that were moved from other LBL locations and rebuilt. Costumed personnel work the farm, and most will take time from their chores to talk history with you.

Homeplace employees eat here, with all food prepared over the open fires and in the kitchens of the restored buildings. While walking through the kitchens, talk with the cooks. They have some great stories to tell about their past cooking experiences. The Homeplace is open March through November.

One of the unique events held here each year is the Habitat Helpers Weekend, which usually takes place in mid-June. The program was named one of the American Horticultural Society's Top 75 Events in 1997 and is based on how individuals can improve backyard habitats. Bird feeders, bat boxes, and wildlife gardens are explained, as are butterfly gardens and ways to attract the great mosquito conqueror, the purple martin. The program takes place at the Nature Station.

There is a fee for many of the attractions, and there are several other special events during the year that the LBL newsletter covers in detail. Call (800) LBL–7077 for a free copy or go to www.lbl.org.

Although it has to share honors with Kentucky, Montgomery County is the home of the famed 101st Airborne Division—Air Assault of the U.S. Army. *The Fort Campbell Military Reservation* covers more than 100,000 acres on the state line and is the county's largest employer.

The base is open, which means visitors are welcome as long as they pick up a pass at Gate 4 on US 41A. Located near the gate is the visitor center and the *Don F. Pratt Memorial Museum.* Named for Brigadier General Don Pratt, who was killed while leading the 101st Airborne's legendary glider assault into Normandy during World War II, the museum traces the history of the division from World War I through the present. Exhibits also depict the history of Fort Campbell and the land it occupies.

Probably the most interesting exhibit in the place is the replica of the fragile-looking glider that the members of the 101st Division used in France during the D-day invasion of 1944. More than 14,000 of the canvas-covered cargo gliders were built during the war, with such unlikely businesses as the Steinway Piano and Heinz Pickle companies contributing to the effort.

Across the street from the large indoor portion of the museum is a lot with a large collection of tanks, artillery field pieces, and airplanes. Open every day but Sunday 9:30 a.m. to 4:30 p.m.; free admission. Get more information at (270) 798–3215.

Clarksville is the state's fifth-largest city, with a population of about 104,000, but it probably has the largest selection of architectural marvels of any one city in the state. "Anyone interested in architecture will have a field day in Clarksville," maintains the curator of the *Customs House Museum & Cultural Center.*

Any tour through the city should start at the Customs House, at the corner of Commerce and Second Streets. Originally constructed as a U.S. Post Office and Customs House in 1898, its eclectic architecture consists of Italianate ornamentation, a Far East-influenced slate roof, Romanesque arches, and Gothic copper eagles perched at each of the four corners.

Olympic star **Wilma Rudolph** is a Clarksville native. A bronze life-size statue of her is now on display inside the Customs House. It's a great tribute to the late, three-time Olympic gold medal champion.

Attached to the post office, the museum has a 53,000-square-foot cultural center complete with a 200-seat auditorium, several different art galleries, classrooms, exhibit halls, and the state's best artisan gift shops. If you can't find something here, maybe you're too picky!

Exhibits include one on the local tobacco industry and a salute to the local firefighters. This is one of the finest local museums in the state. Area tour maps can be picked up here. Open Tuesday through Sunday free admission on Sunday. Phone (931) 648–5780 or www.customshousemuseum.org.

There are two self-guided tours of the city and county—a 2-mile (25-site) walking tour of the downtown architectural area and a 14-mile (50-site) driving tour.

Clarksville has a proud river heritage, and to celebrate the relationship between the city and the mighty Cumberland River, the city fathers have created the **Cumberland RiverWalk,** a meandering riverfront promenade. Along the path you'll experience river overlooks, a playground, picnic areas, and a wharf. During the winter holidays, Christmas on the Cumberland, with dozens of colorful displays, takes place along the RiverWalk.

As The River Flows is the name of an exhibit in the **RiverCenter,** located along the RiverWalk. The center offers a great view of the river, and among its exhibits is a 12-panel chronological history of the Cumberland River and its significance to the development of Clarksville. The entire RiverWalk area is open daily. Call (931) 645–7476 or go online at www.clarksville.tn.us.

McGregor Park, located along the RiverWalk, is home to the annual Riverfest, a three-day arts, music, and food celebration in early September. There is a visual fine arts competition, which means you'll find some great, original regional art for sale. There are four stages with continuous musical performances and performing arts presentations. Plenty of food, ethnic culture, and youth activities can also be found. This is one of the more fun festivals in this part of the state! Call (931) 645–7476.

Remember the Monkees's big hit "The Last Train To Clarksville"? Some say it was inspired by the **L&N Train Station** here in Clarksville. Built in 1890, the once-busy depot is now open as a museum and art gallery. Located at Commerce and Tenth Streets. Open Tuesday, Thursday, and Saturday 9:00 a.m. to 1:00 p.m. Call them at (931) 553–2486.

There are several buildings high on the hill on the public square where advertising painted on their river-facing exterior walls years ago is still visible. Originally painted to be seen by river traffic, most of the ads have faded during

Big Art in Public Places

Tennessee artist Al Keim has some big art in the Tennessee Welcome Center on I-24 at the Kentucky border, just north of Clarksville. Entitled *The Man in the Wind and the West Moon,* the bright blue-and-yellow abstract sculpture could possibly be imagined as phases of the moon. The artist notes that the branching off of colorful lines in space on the sculpture as being similar to the improvisations in jazz music.

Keim's artwork is one of 11 large outdoor sculptures in Tennessee Welcome Centers, thanks to a public arts program created by the Tennessee Arts Commission in 1982. These works of art stand as visual ambassadors for the state and are quite cool to look at while stretching your bones and picking up a few maps and information. A brochure showing each of the 11 pieces of large artwork is available by writing the Tennessee Arts Commission, 401 Charlotte Avenue, Nashville 37243. For additional information call (615) 741-1701.

the years. However, the ad on the circa 1842 Poston Building on the square can still be seen and appreciated. It was painted back when the Uneeda Biscuit Company was selling their product for a nickel a package.

For fun entertainment, the local professional theater group, the **Roxy Regional Theatre,** offers up ten productions a year, all staged in the renovated Roxy theater at 100 Franklin Street. Call (931) 645–7699.

Annually judged as one of the Top 20 March Events in the Southeast, the Old-Time Fiddlers' Championships is a great time to visit for some authentic old-time music. It takes place at the Northeast High School and, with a large cash purse for the winners, attracts some great nationally known entertainers. One nice thing about this contest is that it takes place before the myriad outdoor music festivals are held during the summer throughout the state. It's like a warm-up to get you excited about great Tennessee music. Categories include Dancing 30 and Under, Harmonica, Dobro, Bluegrass Banjo, Mandolin, and Beginner Fiddler. Fiddle on up to your phone and call (931) 647–2331.

More information about Clarksville and Montgomery County can be found by calling (800) 530–2487 or at www.clarksville.tn.us.

Just outside Clarksville is **Historic Collinsville,** an authentically restored 19th-century log pioneer settlement that's a lot of fun to visit. It's a great glimpse into what it was like living in this area of the state 200 years ago. The buildings have all been saved and moved to the village and lovingly restored by JoAnn and Glenn Weakley. There are now 15 buildings, including a dog-trot house and several outbuildings. Annual events range from a quilt show to a Civil War encampment. Located off Highway 48 South on Weakley Road.

Admission is charged. Open mid-May through mid-October, Thursday through Sunday 1:00 to 5:00 p.m.; don't miss it! Call (931) 648–9141 or go to www .historiccollinsville.com.

Montgomery County's answer to California's Napa Valley can be found at the *Beachaven Vineyards & Winery,* a few miles off I–24's exit 4. Co-owner Ed Cooke thinks his winery can offer as good a tasting tour as do his counterparts in California. "We offer the same thing, but we add Southern hospitality," he said.

Beachaven's tasting concept is a great plus for those needing a little education before buying a wine. Ed or one of the employees will be glad to give you a taste of all their varieties. Tours are given year-round for those who would like to see how the fruit of the vine becomes so divine. And these wines are really divine. Wine judges across the country think so, too. Look at all those ribbons awarded to the various products of Ed and his family lining the walls. Their champagne is of "world renown," having been written up in the major wine books.

The most exciting (and aromatic) time to visit is in the fall while the crushing is taking place, but there is always something going on. During the summer, special concerts are presented in the vineyard's picnic area. They can't sell by the glass, but they would be glad to sell you a chilled bottle to enjoy with your cheese during a concert. Call (931) 645–8867 or visit www .beachavenwinery.com.

The *Dunbar Cave State Natural Area* is 110 scenic acres of true history and legend. The activities on this site range from when the local Native Americans inhabited the cave entrance 10,000 years ago to when country music legend and Grand Ole Opry star Roy Acuff owned the property and held weekly country music shows in the cave entrance.

A stately old bathhouse now serves as a visitor center and museum. If you want to take a cave tour, you have to call ahead and see when the group tours are being held. Even if you don't take the tour, the museum and the nature trails make this a fun place to visit. Fishing is permitted on the lake. Located on Dunbar Cave Road just off US 79, 4 miles from I–24 (exit 4). Open seven days a week; call for hours and events at (931) 648–5526 or www.dunbarcave.org.

While new 1950s-style eateries currently are being built across the country, *Stratton's Restaurant and Soda Shop,* in Ashland City, continues quietly to serve up ice cream and hamburgers as it has since 1954. The interior of this neat little place is truly a blast from the past.

"Everything you see in here is authentic; I guarantee it," said Steve Stratton, the founder's son and the current owner. From a 1954 Seeburg jukebox to original Coca-Cola posters on the wall, Stratton takes great pride in preserving the past in his popular establishment.

The soda shop was built by his father in 1954 as the Dairy Dip, Steve has been running it since 1972. Originally a carryout that sat 12 people inside, Steve remodeled in 1985, expanding the eat-in capacity to 50. After another expansion it's now up to 75.

Traditional platters are served with house-made coleslaw or hush puppies. Besides the tasty burgers, menu items also include grilled chicken sandwiches, chopped steak, and charbroiled chicken breast.

But save room for dessert! Twenty-ounce malts are made with Carnation powdered malt, and other tasty concoctions can be made from soft-serve or hand-dipped ice cream. They also make their own pies and cobblers.

You'll find Steve here every day except Sunday. Make sure you say "Hi" to him; he'll be happy to share some of the history of the place with you. Located at 201 South Main Street; open 361 days a year. For additional information call (615) 792–9177.

There have been ghosts and there have been legends, but the ***Bell Witch of Adams*** is probably the most documented story of the supernatural in all of American history. This witch is unique because of the large number of people who have had direct experience with it.

John Bell was a well-respected and influential member of the Adams community. He and his family lived on a 1,000-acre plantation along the Red River. The trouble started in 1817 when bumping and scratching sounds were first noticed in the house, but the Bells passed them off as being caused by the wind. The big problems started in 1818, when continuous gnawing sounds were heard on each member of the family's bedposts each night. When someone would get up to investigate, the sound would stop. The sound would go from room to room until everyone was awake. Then it would stop until the candles were blown out and everyone went back to bed, when it would start all over again.

Things grew from there. People came to town to witness the occurrences and weren't disappointed. Gen. Andrew Jackson came up to Adams from his Nashville home to investigate the matter but turned around when the wheels on his carriage mysteriously locked.

This has gone on through the decades. A few years ago, several reporters came to Adams with plans to stay in the Bell cave, where many of the experiences have occurred. They lasted a few hours before fleeing.

Today the ***Bell Witch Cave*** is open to those who think they are brave enough to possibly face the witch herself. Many have. Located off US 41 on Keysburg Road, the cave is open daily May through October but is closed during rainy periods due to possible flooding. Admission is $10 per person. To try to face the witch, call (615) 696–3055 or www.bellwitchcave.com.

All the Bell buildings are gone now, except for a small, log slave building. It has been moved to the grounds of the old elementary schoolhouse and is open for viewing. You can't miss the graves of the Bell family at the Bellwood cemetery. There's a magnificent tower marking the graves—and a stone fence keeping the Bell Witch out.

The historic Red River is an easy river to experience by canoe. Where US 41 crosses the river in Adams, you'll find *Red River Valley,* where you can both rent a canoe and get river information. Open weekends April through October, daily from Memorial Day to Labor Day. Call (615) 696–2768.

Springfield is the county seat of Robertson County, and its past is told nicely in the restored circa 1915 U.S. Post Office, now the *Robertson County History Museum.* It's located just off Court Square on Sixth Avenue West. One of the exhibits points out a facet of the county that few people realize today: At one time it was home to 75 whiskey distilleries. That's a lot of booze, especially for the state that's considered the buckle of the Bible Belt!

The Catholics of Tennessee

The state's oldest Catholic church still in use is St. Michael's, located in the Flewellyn community near Cedar Hill. The church was built in 1842, and in the late 1890s a structure from the nearby Glen Raven Estate was moved and attached to the original church to make it larger. Today the white-clapboard church sits serenely among the trees in this rural area, surrounded by a cemetery.

St. Michael's is a mission church, which means it doesn't have a resident priest. Father Joseph Desmond of Our Lady of Lourdes in nearby Springfield administers to the congregation of approximately 70 families and makes the drive out from town every Sunday morning to say the 8:00 a.m. Mass.

As you walk in the front door, look immediately to the right and you'll see a cutaway that shows what the original construction looks like behind the walls. Also of interest is the outdoor altar, built at the bottom of the cemetery. It was built with the stones from the original foundation of St. Michael's Academy for Boys, a long-defunct educational adjunct of the church.

To get to Flewellyn, take Highway 49 South from Springfield for 4 miles. At the Highway 49 Market, turn right (west) onto Highway 257. Go another 4 miles to Catholic Church Road, which is the first paved road to the left. Turn left and go another 4 miles until you reach the fork in the road; go right and you'll soon see the church. It's locked up during the week, but you are invited to enjoy the grounds and the exterior of the church and to join the congregation for Mass on Sunday. Call for their schedule at (615) 384–6200.

Since 1820 the county has been known for its tobacco crops and is widely acknowledged as the dark-fired tobacco capital of the world. An exhibit chronicles those 180 years of agricultural significance. Open Wednesday through Saturday. A unique site! Call (615) 382–7173 or go to www.rchsonline.com.

The county courthouse on the Springfield square dates back to 1879. Along Main Street you'll find several interesting stores and shops located in the old distillery warehouses, dating back to the early 1900s.

Cross Plains was the first settlement in Robertson County when it was founded in 1779. Today there's a great deal of charm in the community of 1,353 people. The houses that line Main Street and the side streets are beautifully framed by big, mature trees, and there are plenty of friendly shops to keep you busy.

Pharmacist Dan Green is now caretaker of a bit of history in Cross Plains. He and his wife, Debbie, are the owners of *Thomas Drugs* and its historic black-and-chrome antique soda fountain. While Green tends to the business of pharmacy, his soda jerk mixes up his own concoctions, from milk shakes to vanilla Cokes to ice-cream sundaes. Lunch is served Monday through Friday from 10:00 a.m. to 2:00 p.m. and includes an array of fresh sandwiches and soups.

In addition to the "regular" drugstore stuff, the store features antique reproduction toys and books, and local crafts including quilts and coverlets. Located at the corner of Main and Cedar Streets at the four-way stop sign. Open Monday through Saturday; admission is free. Call (615) 654–3877 or visit www.thomasdrugs.com.

Head back toward I–65, and you'll find the large Red River Antique Mall at the interchange with Highway 25. The mall has more than 60 dealers spread out in a 10,000-square-foot building. Open daily. Find out more at (615) 654–7799.

In the *White House,* on Highway 76, 1 mile east of I–65 at exit 108, next to the firehouse, is one of the most distinctive library and museum buildings you'll find anywhere in the state. It's a reproduction of the original White House Inn, which gave the area its name. The inn was a major stopover between Nashville and Louisville during the horse and buggy days.

The community library is on the first floor, the museum is on the second, and the chamber of commerce is out back in the bachelor's quarters. For a small community, they've done a splendid job in presenting a local history museum. Make sure you take a look at the firehouse next door, and don't miss the fun statue of a Dalmatian out front. Nice touch! Open daily except Sunday. Enjoy this unique site—call (615) 672–0239 or see www.cityofwhitehouse.com.

Up in northern Sumner County, **Portland** has a long history and today has one of the longest-running commodity festivals in the state. Strawberries became an important crop for the area in the 1920s and soon became a major export item. Today the **Middle Tennessee Strawberry Festival** is a salute to both the present and the past strawberry business. The festival has been held each mid-May since 1941, and the weeklong roster of activities ends on a Saturday with a Rotary Pancake Breakfast, a parade, and the Lion's Club Bluegrass Festival.

There's plenty of food, crafts, entertainment, and of course strawberry delicacies. Check out the Web site (www.portlandtn.com) for more details on the festival as well as a list of local farms where you can pick your own berries, or call (615) 325–9032.

If you're into the quaintness of one-room schoolhouses, check out the **Cold Springs School.** Built in 1857, the building is now a museum of local history with a great deal of Civil War memorabilia. It was moved into Richland Park in Portland in 1975 and restored. Originally built in an area of the city that was a military training camp for Civil War soldiers, the little school was used as an infirmary during the war. It's run by the Highland Rim Historical Society.

The **Old Country Store** is a gem in Westmoreland, in northern Sumner County. It's really several stores wrapped into one in a great old-time environment. It's a fun candy store. It's an antiques and collectibles store; and it's an old-fashioned, 1880s-era ice-cream parlor that specializes in shakes, malts, sundaes, and the best banana splits this side of the Cumberland.

Located at 1043 Park Street, the Old General Store is open Monday through Saturday 10:00 a.m. to 5:00 p.m. and on Sunday, if they decide to open, 11:00 a.m. to 5:00 p.m. Call (615) 644–4244 first on Sunday before visiting.

The annual **Old Westmoreland Days** celebration is held the first weekend in May and features arts and crafts, food, games, an antiques show, and music competition. It's a fun festival! Find out more by calling (615) 644–4244.

Another crop that is making a name for itself since the mid-1990s is the grape. That's when the **Sumner Crest Winery** was founded by two brothers on Old Highway 52 at exit 117 off I–65. Tours and tastings are available, and there's a nice little antiques gallery. Some of the wines they specialize in are Tennessee blackberry, Merlot, Cabernet, and Summer Queen.

Open daily at 9:00 a.m. and on Sunday at noon. Closes at 5:00 p.m. on Sunday, the rest of the week at 6:00 p.m. during the summer months, 5:00 p.m. during winter. During the summer, evening concerts are held on the grounds. Call (615) 325–4086 or go to www.sumnercrestwinery.com.

The downtown commercial area of **Gallatin** is quite the historic area. With more than 25 restored buildings, many of which predate the Civil War, the area has been listed on the National Register of Historic Places. Occupying some of those buildings are antiques shops and restaurants.

A block off the main square area, you'll find the **Sumner County Museum,** located behind the historic Trousdale Place. The museum, at 183 West Main Street, is the keeper of nearly a quarter million artifacts that tell the history of the county. Included in that collection are 475-million-year-old fossils and several displays featuring Native American and African-American life in the area. Open seasonally and by appointment. Go back in time at this historic site: Call (615) 451–3738 or go to www.sumnercountymuseum.org.

Trousdale Place was home to Tennessee governor William Trousdale, who served the state from 1849 to 1851. The home has been restored and contains period antiques as well as a small Confederate library. Open by appointment. Admission is charged. Call (615) 452–5648 or www.sumner countytourism.com/trousdaleplace.

In **Castalian Springs,** what may be the largest log structure ever erected in Tennessee still stands. **Wynnewood** was built in 1828 as a stagecoach inn and mineral springs resort, and by 1840 a row of cottages adjoining the inn had been built, as well as a horse racetrack.

The main house is 142 feet long with a dogtrot through the middle. Some of the logs, mostly oak and walnut, are 32 feet long. All the rooms have outside doors and are entered from a gallery that extends 110 feet across the back of the building. A stairway in the dogtrot goes to the second-story rooms.

Owned by the state, Wynnewood is located 45 miles northeast of Nashville, 8 miles east of Gallatin on Highway 25. It's open daily April through November. Admission is charged. Phone them at (615) 452–5463.

About 100 yards east of the entrance to Wynnewood is a stone monument marking the location of a giant, 9-foot-diameter sycamore tree in which Thomas Sharp Spencer lived during the winter of 1778-79. Spencer, the first white settler in middle Tennessee, called the tree home while he was building a cabin nearby.

Also located along Highway 25, about 5 miles from Gallatin, is **Cragfront,** one of the finest examples of Federal architecture in the state. Built between 1798 and 1802 by **General James Winchester** of Revolutionary War fame, the limestone house has been restored and is open to the public. Open daily except Monday, mid-April through October. Admission is charged. Call (615) 452–7070.

More information on Gallatin and the rest of Sumner County can be found at www.sumnertn.org. You can call Sumner County Tourism at (615) 230–8474 or (888) 301–7866 or visit www.sumnercvb.com.

Places to Stay in the Heartland

CLARKSVILLE

Hachland Hall B&B
1601 Madison Street
Rooms in 200-year-old log
guest houses furnished
with antiques
(931) 647–4084

DICKSON

East Hills Bed & Breakfast
U.S. Highway 70
Quiet country inn, close to
the city;
bountiful Southern
breakfast
(615) 441–9428
www.easthillsbb.com

LAWRENCEBURG

Davy Crockett State Park (camping)
Highway 64
Swimming, restaurant, boat
rentals, fishing
(931) 762–9408
www.lawrenceburg.com/
crockettpark

MANCHESTER

Tim's Ford State Park
Off Highway 50
Cabins and campsites;
waterskiing, boat rentals,
swimming, hiking
(931) 962–1183

MURFREESBORO

Country Inn & Suites
2262 Armory Drive
Indoor pool, exercise room,
continental breakfast
(615) 890–5951
www.countryinns.com

NASHVILLE

Hermitage Hotel
At Sixth Avenue
and Union Street
Beaux Arts design
(615) 244–3121
www.hermitagehotel.com

Nashville KOA
2626 Music Valley Drive
435 sites, 25 cabins
Free country music shows
(615) 889–0282

Union Station Hotel
1001 Broadway
Vintage Nashville train station; gold-leaf mirrors,
Tiffany windows
(615) 726–1001
www.unionstationhotel
nashville.com

TULLAHOMA

Ledford Mill B&B
1195 Shipman's Creek
Road Rural setting next
to natural spring waterfall;
1884 gristmill is on historic
registers
(931) 455–2546

Places to Eat in the Heartland

ADAMS

Thomas Drugs
On corner of Main
and Cedar Streets
Soda fountain serving
lunch; vanilla Cokes
Lunch Monday through
Friday 10:00 a.m. to
2:00 p.m.
(615) 654–3877
www.thomasdrugs.net

ASHLAND CITY

Stratton's Restaurant and Soda Shop
201 South Main Street
Hamburgers, hush pup-
pies, malts, and pies
Sunday through Thursday
10:30 a.m. to 9:00 p.m.,
Friday and Saturday
10:30 a.m. to 10:00 p.m.
(615) 792–9177

BELL BUCKLE

Bell Buckle Cafe and Music Parlour
Hickory-smoked barbecue,
hand-squeezed lemonade
Food served seven days
a week, live music three
nights a week
(931) 389–9693
www.bellbucklecafe.net

CENTERVILLE

Breece's Cafe
On the square
Country cooking, home-made pies
Wednesday through Saturday 5:00 to 8:00 p.m.,
Sunday 6:00 a.m. to
8:00 p.m.
(931) 729–3481

CHRISTIANA

Miller's Country Cafe
Meat and vegetables,
bluegrass music Friday
Blue plate lunch Tuesday
through Friday 11:00 a.m.
to 2:00 p.m., dinner Friday
and Saturday 5:00 to 9:00
p.m., Sunday 11:00 a.m. to
2:00 p.m.
(615) 893–1878
www.millersgrocery.com

FAYETTEVILLE

Cahoots
Market Street
In old firehouse and city jail;
eat in a limestone cell
Monday through Saturday 10:30 a.m. to 9:00 or
10:00 p.m.
(931) 433–1173

FRANKLIN

Dotson's Restaurant
99 East Main Street
Popular local eatery; family
owned; Southern cooking,
bountiful breakfasts
Open daily at 7:00 a.m. for
breakfast; also serves lunch
and dinner
(615) 794–2805

LYNCHBURG

Iron Kettle Restaurant
On the square
Plate lunches daily, home
cooking
Monday through Sunday,
6:00 a.m. to 4:00 p.m.
(931) 759–4274
www.ironkettle.net

Miss Mary Bobo's Boarding House
Southern traditional foods
served family style
Two seatings Monday
through Saturday, at 11:00
a.m. and 1:00 p.m.
For reservations, a must,
call (931) 759–7394

NASHVILLE

Bruggers Bagels
422 21st Avenue South
Great bagels, toppings,
and bagelwiches
Monday through Friday
6:30 a.m. to 6:00 p.m.,
Saturday 8:00 a.m. to 5:00
p.m., Sunday 8:00 a.m. to
5:00 p.m.
(615) 327–0055
www.bruggers.com

The Bluebird Cafe
4104 Hillsboro Pike
Country superstar hangout
Hours vary
(615) 383–1461
www.bluebirdcafe.com

Bongo Java Coffeehouse
2007 Belmont Boulevard
Great nontraditional food,
home of the NunBun
Open daily for all three
meal times
(615) 385–5282
www.bongojava.com

Boscos Nashville Brewing Co.
1805 21st Avenue South
Brewpub known for its
pizza, sandwiches
Open daily for lunch and
dinner
(615) 385–0050
www.boscosbeer.com

Cheeseburger Charley's
400 21st Avenue South
Healthy fast food
Veggie, turkey, black bean
burgers
Open daily, 11:00 a.m. to
8:00 p.m.
(615) 327–0220
www.cheeseburgercharleys
.com

Nashville Farmers' Market
Eighth Avenue North,
adjacent to Bicentennial
Mall
Two restaurants inside as
well as the market. Open
9:00 a.m. to 5:00 or
6:00 p.m.
(615) 880–2001
www.nashvillefarmers
market.org

Fido
1821 21st Avenue South
Veggie paella, homemade
ratatouille, veggie lasagna
Monday through Friday
7:00 a.m. to 11:00 p.m.,
Saturday and Sunday 8:00
a.m. to 11:00 p.m.
(615) 777–3436
www.bongojava.com

Jack's World Famous BBQ
416 Broadway
"A Nashville Institution"
Tennessee pork shoulder,
Texas beef brisket,
St. Louis–style ribs
Open 10:30 a.m. Monday
through Sunday; open for
dinner Thursday through
Saturday till 8:00 p.m.;
Sunday till 6:00 p.m.
(615) 254–5715
www.jacksonbarbecue
.com

Loveless Motel and Cafe
Highway 100
Fried chicken, country
ham, fresh biscuits
Open daily 7:00 a.m. to
9:00 p.m.
(615) 646–9700
www.lovelesscafe.com

Monell's
1235 Sixth Avenue North
In historic Germantown
Southern home cooking
Lunch Monday through
Friday; dinner Tuesday
through Saturday; country
breakfast Saturday, 8:30
a.m. to 1:00 p.m.; and
Sunday brunch, 10:30 a.m.
to 3:00 p.m.
(615) 248–4747

Nashville Palace
Music Valley Drive, across
from Opryland Hotel
Live music nightly with
delicious menu
Open daily 3:00 p.m. to
3:00 a.m. (Food service
5:00 to 11:00 p.m.)
(615) 855–1540
www.musicvalleyattractions
.com

Sole Mio
94 Peabody Street
Italian cuisine with best
view of Nashville skyline
Open Monday through
Sunday for lunch and
dinner.
(615) 256–4013
www.solemionash.com

NORMANDY

Cortner Mill Restaurant
1100 Cortner Mill
In historic mill,
part of Paris Patch Farm
Steak, ham, chicken, quail,
ribs, trout, beefalo
Open Tuesday through
Saturday 5:30 to 9:00
p.m., Sunday buffet 11:30
a.m. to 1:30 p.m.
(931) 857–3017
www.parispatch.com

THE WESTERN PLAINS

→

History on the Plains

Nathan Bedford Forrest, the notorious hard-riding Confederate cavalry officer known for his unexpected and often offbeat tactics, pulled off one of the Civil War's most interesting victories along the Tennessee River here in the fall of 1864. It was probably the first time in military history that a cavalry force attacked and defeated a naval force. High atop *Pilot Knob,* the highest point in this part of the state, Forrest secretly assembled his troops. He had his eye on the Union army's massive supply depot, directly across the river.

At the time the depot had more than 30 vessels, most fully loaded and waiting to head out to Union forces. Stacks of supplies lined the wharf. Forrest attacked and caught the Yanks off guard. Within minutes all 30 vessels and the various warehouse buildings were on fire, and within two hours everything was destroyed. By nightfall Forrest's troops had vanished into the dense woods.

The land surrounding Pilot Knob is now known as the *Nathan Bedford Forrest State Park.* Atop the hill is a monument to Forrest. Also at the top is the *Tennessee River*

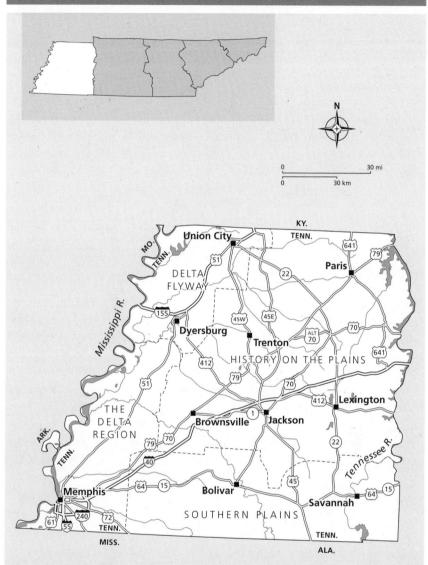

Folklife Center, "designed to explore the relationship between the river and the people who use it."

Most of the exhibits incorporate segments of oral histories taken from the locals who "lived the life." Separate accounts recall the early industries and the music, religion, and community events of the area.

The most colorful audio presentation highlights the days when folks would gather at the river to welcome the big showboats to their landing. The biggest exhibit is *Old Betsy,* an entire workboat from the early musseling industry along the river. The most visual representation of early river life is from the Brownie camera of Maggie Sayre. She lived on a houseboat for more than 50 years and photographed everyday life around her.

lotsoffish,too

With more than 2,300 miles of shoreline, Kentucky Lake is the second-largest man-made lake in the world.

Most rural areas throughout the South have their own version of the liar's bench and the spit and whittle club. The view from the porch or from under the tree may be different from town to town, but the plot is the same. A story is told, then retold, then exaggerated to the point where it becomes a modern-day myth. A typical riverfront liar's bench has been reconstructed here at the center, with a breathtaking view of the Tennessee River far below. Walk up, push a button, and sit down and relax. The series of taped stories (from original spit and whittlers) will keep you in stitches.

The center is open every day 8:00 a.m. to 4:30 p.m. Admission is free. For more information and details, call (731) 584–6356. As you enter the park, the visitor center is to your right. Inside are several exhibits, including artwork and tanks containing local fish. Check here to see if the folklife center is open; if

AUTHOR'S TOP TEN PICKS

Tennessee River Folklife Center	Danny Thomas Grave & Gardens
World's Largest Fish Fry	Mindfield Outdoor Sculpture
West Tennessee Strawberry Festival	Saltillo Ferry
Buford Pusser Home & Museum	Dixie Gun Works
Sun Studio	Flippens Hillbilly Barn

not, ask and they will probably send someone up with you. The historical park area offers camping, hiking trails, and picnic areas. Both areas are located at the end of Route 191, about 10 miles out of Camden.

It has been found that the Tennessee River and Kentucky Lake provide the perfect environment in which to grow freshwater pearls. It is warm year-round, nonpolluted, and high in lime content.

That's what John and Chessy Lantendresse discovered when they were perfecting the process of growing freshwater pearls that are today worn by the likes of Hillary Rodham Clinton, Tipper Gore, and Kathleen O'Brien.

The ***Tennessee River Freshwater Pearl Farm and Museum*** is located at the Birdsong Resort and Marina, along the river just outside Camden. There are pontoon boat tours of the operation and a jewelry shop inside the marina that features the cultured pearls. The story behind the procedure—how river mussels are implanted with pieces of shell and how those pieces grow into pearls inside the mussels through a "secret process"—is explained by the experts. Call (731) 584–7880 for details or go to www.birdsongresort.com.

Tennessee ranks twelfth in the nation in sorghum production, and Benton County is one of the largest producers in the state. Madison and Donice Furr run the ***Tennessee Sorghum Company,*** one of the largest operations in the county.

Sorghum is used mainly as a sweetener and is rich in vitamins. It's used in gingerbread and is poured over hot biscuits and butter. "It's very good and very healthy for you," claims Donice. "We sell a lot of it to health food stores."

The Furrs grow about 30 acres of sorghum cane and produce their own syrup. They also buy from other Benton County sorghum producers and market the product under the Tennessee Sorghum Company moniker. Locally produced honey is also available.

The most aromatic time to visit the Furrs' operation is in the fall when the sorghum cane is being stripped of its juices and cooked down to the right consistency. The cooking is done down at the Furrs' farm, and the marketing and packaging takes place at their warehouse in ***Camden.***

Donice welcomes visitors to the farm and promises to let them stick a finger in the cooking sorghum for a once-in-a-lifetime taste treat. The farm is located off Highway 192 about 5 miles north of Holladay. Call her and see if anything is happening on the day you want to go out, and she'll give you specific directions. Contact her at (731) 584–6742.

Talented country music star ***Patsy Cline*** was killed on March 5, 1963, when her airplane crashed about 2.5 miles northwest of Camden. Today there's a small monument marking the spot, way off the main road, down a gravel path. The monument was set up to honor Cline and those killed with her: Cowboy Copas, Hawkshaw Hawkins, and Randy Hughes. Next to the monument is a mailbox where fans can drop off fan letters. There's also a gazebo with newspaper articles describing the careers of the stars and the monument itself.

The monument is located deep in the woods 12 miles north of Interstate 40, off U.S. Highway 641. Just north of U.S. Highway 70, turn west on Mt. Carmel Road at the Shell gas station; go 3 miles, and turn right onto a gravel road. Be careful and don't go too far—there's a big dropoff at the end of the path. Country music fans, call (731) 584–8395 or visit www.bentoncounty camden.com.

There's no place better than an organized wildlife refuge to observe that area's wildlife population, and the **_Tennessee Wildlife Refuge_** is no exception. Nature trails, paved roads, and observation points are plentiful in this 80-mile-long area along the Tennessee River. The area is an important resting and feeding place for migrating waterfowl each winter.

Beginning about mid-October, up to 100,000 Canada geese and 250,000 ducks start their annual fall trek to the refuge, where they will spend the winter safe and warmer—and well fed. The major attraction here for the animals is the farming program, which provides them with a great deal of food all winter long.

In addition to the waterfowl, the refuge is home for more than 200 species of birds, a fact that brings in serious bird-watchers from all over the country. Maps, brochures, and specific wildlife information are available. Open Monday through Friday year-round. Don't miss this refuge—call (731) 642–2091.

OTHER ATTRACTIONS WORTH SEEING

Britton Lane Battlefield,
Jackson,
(731) 935–2209

Chucalissa Archaeological Museum,
Memphis,
(901) 785–3160

Fire Museum of Memphis,
(901) 320–5650
www.firemuseum.com

Memphis Botanic Garden,
Memphis,
(901) 576–4100
www.memphisbotanicgarden.com

Oaklawn Gardens,
Germantown,
(901) 757–7200

For more information on Camden, Holladay, and the rest of Benton County, call (731) 584–8395 or log on to www.bentoncountycamden.com.

In nearby **Paris** the self-proclaimed ***world's largest fish fry*** is held at the end of each April. Since the early 1950s the city has hosted the event at the fairgrounds and has achieved a well-deserved reputation for the quality of its catfish dinners and the traditional Tennessee way of preparing them.

Each year more than 10,000 pounds of fish are cooked in black pots containing more than 250 gallons of vegetable oil. The four-day event also includes a rodeo, a carnival, a three-hour parade, and a fishing rodeo.

Here it is, a sugar heaven if ever we tasted one! With more than 100 varieties of freshly made candies, **Sally Lane's Candy Farm** is a stop well worth making in the Paris area. Founded in 1958, the store has customers who regularly drive up to a couple of hours to get here. In addition, people in 48 states use mail order to receive their treats, which range from hand-dipped chocolates to hard candies to the famous Kentucky Lake Frog—a chocolate, caramel, and pecan concoction. Make sure you try the divinity; it's made from scratch and is totally awesome, as are most of the goodies. It's the store's pink and green mints, though, that put them on the map. "We literally make tons of mints each year," said candy makers and store owners Bobby and Shelby Freeman and Pan and Rick Rockwell. The candy is sold locally at Paris Landing State Park and Najie's Gifts 'N Baskets at 112 East Washington Street. Call (731) 642–5801 or order online at www.sallylanes.com.

And what would Paris be without the Eiffel Tower? There's a 65-foot scale model of the famous structure standing at the entrance of Memorial Park on Volunteer Drive, east of downtown between Highway 69A and U.S. Highway 79.

The E. W. Grove–Henry County High School was the first privately funded public high school in the state. Known locally as the school "that came out of a bottle," the building was funded from the proceeds of "Grove's Tasteless Chill Tonic." Today the tower building houses the Henry County Board of Education and is located on Grove Boulevard, at the highest elevation in West Tennessee. Turn off Veterans Drive onto Dunlap Road, just north of US 79. Turn right onto Grove Boulevard and go to the top of the hill.

If you'd like to get a closer look at some of the historic structures in West Tennessee's oldest incorporated community, an audio-taped walking tour is available. Cassette players, tapes, and maps can be had at the chamber of commerce, W. G. Rhea Library, and the Paris–Henry County Heritage Center at no charge. (The maps may be kept but the tape players and cassettes are to be returned at the end of your tour.) The chamber is located at 2508 East Wood Street. Call them at (731) 642–3431 or visit www.paris.tn.org.

TOP ANNUAL EVENTS

Elvis Presley Birthday Celebration,
mid-January, Memphis,
(800) 238–2000
www.elvis.com

Teapot Festival,
late April, Trenton,
(731) 855–2013

Memphis in May International Festival,
weekends in May, Memphis,
(901) 525–4611

West Tennessee Strawberry Festival,
first week of May, Humboldt,
(731) 784–7770

Tennessee Iris Festival,
early May, Dresden,
(731) 364–3787

Shannon Street Blues & Heritage Festival,
Jackson, first week of June,
(731) 427–7573

Savannah Bluegrass Festival,
July, Savannah,
(800) 552–3866

Saltillo River Days,
mid-September, Saltillo,
(731) 687–3889

Gordon Browning's first driver's license is on display at the *Gordon Browning Museum* in the old post office building in downtown *McKenzie* in Carroll County. What makes that license so special is that it is *Tennessee's first driver's license.*

Browning got it because he happened to be governor of the state in 1938, when licenses were first required. In all, Browning served three terms as governor. He was also a U.S. congressman and a chancery court judge, and he served in both world wars. By the looks of the quantity of the memorabilia on display, he never threw anything away. A flag that he brought back from World War I is on display, as are various other patriotic mementos.

The museum is a great small-town collection dedicated to the life of the county's favorite son. It gives a good perspective on the values that he and the curator of the museum deemed important.

The museum is open Monday, Tuesday, Thursday and Friday 9:00 a.m. to 4:00 p.m. Admission is free. The museum is at 640 North Main Street. Call (731) 352–3510.

Actress *Dixie Carter* was born and raised in *McLemoresville,* population 311. Even though she left town and became a successful star, she comes back home each year for several weeks to enjoy Tennessee and her family and friends. Her house is just off the little business section, and just about anyone around can point it out to you.

The ***Billy O. Williams Museum*** is located on Main Street on the square. Run by a spirited group of volunteers, the museum highlights the history of the community, as well as the entire county. The facility is dedicated to the late Billy O. Williams, who was Carroll County's poet laureate and an associate poet laureate of the state. An exhibit honors his literary contributions and displays some of his printed as well as unpublished poetry, according to his sister, Rachel McKinney, who helps run the museum. Open Thursday, Friday, and Saturday 1:00 to 4:00 p.m. If you get there and no one is around, call the phone number posted on the door; someone will come over and let you in. Call (731) 986–4563.

When bare-knuckled pugilism was popular and legal in America during the first half of the 19th century, one area of Gibson County was well known for its unique version of prizefighting sans gloves.

Skullbone and the surrounding ***Kingdom of Skullbonia*** hosted a type of fighting that became known as skullboning. All bare-knuckled punches had to be delivered to the head. Hits below the collar were not permitted and were considered fouls.

To "play," fighters would stand opposite each other and take turns trading blows. Each round lasted until one fell to the ground. The match lasted until one was satisfied that he had had enough.

After bare-knuckled fighting became illegal in America and communities went "underground" for the excitement, matches in Skullbone continued to be held in the open. When adoption of standard rules for prizefighting occurred in 1866, nongloved activities died out just about everywhere except Skullbone, where it continued well into the 20th century.

Today just about all that remains of Skullbone is the general store, built in 1848. It has been owned since 1964 by Landon and Ruby Hampton and is known locally as ***Hampton's General Store,*** widely as the Skullbone Store.

The busy little store serves what is left of the "kingdom." Yellowed newspaper clippings of the area's heyday hang on the wall. Outside, the building is quite a landmark. With a map of the Kingdom of Skullbonia painted on one side and various soft drink signs and paintings on the front, a stranger can't drive by without stopping to investigate.

Across the street a stacked row of directional road and mileage signs points the way to worldly centers such as Singapore 9,981 miles; Anchorage 3,320 miles; and Shades Bridge 1 mile.

In addition to the regular fare of a country store, the Hamptons sell souvenir T-shirts. Skullbone isn't on most maps, but the Hamptons are trying to get Tennessee's governor to put it on the official state map. It's located on Highway 105 about 3 miles from Bradford. Open every day. Call (731) 742–3179.

It's amazing that just 3 miles away from the skullbone capital of the world one can find the ***Doodle Soup Capital*** of that same world.

What is Doodle Soup? It's a spicy, cold-weather dish. It's actually more of a sauce or gravy than it is a real soup. One of the most popular methods of eating it is by pouring it over a plateful of cracker crumbs or homemade biscuits and letting it soak in for a while before eating.

Here is one of the "official" recipes. Be forewarned: There has been a battle going on for years as to which of the myriad recipes floating around should be considered official.

Take a large broiler chicken. Melt butter and run it all over the chicken. Put in broiler pan, split side down; salt to taste. Put in oven at 375 degrees; let cook until brown and tender; take chicken out of the drippings that were cooked in the pan. Add 11 cups of water, one cup vinegar, plenty of hot peppers, and three tablespoons of cornstarch so it won't be just like water and will stay on the biscuits. Let cook until it gets as hot as you want. Taste it along.

Although Doodle Soup is a local tradition, most locals haven't eaten it, saying it sounds too greasy.

Back in the 1930s, country music fans would flock to this area for a day of listening to the stars of the Grand Ole Opry. Reportedly up to 10,000 people would come to the Dowlands Grove Picnics for a musical afternoon. Today Allen Blankenship's ***Skullbone Music Park*** offers entertainment of all sorts several times each spring and summer. Among the fun is the Skullbone Bike Rally, held each April. The weekend offers up live music from top biker bands, camping, field events, and a bike show. It may not be Sturgis, but, hey, it's our own. Call Allen or log on to his Web site for the next show and directions. The phone number is (731) 742–4291; the Web site is www .skullbonepark.com.

At the municipal building in ***Trenton*** you'll find the ***world's largest collection of 18th- and 19th-century night-light teapots*** (*veilleuses-théières*). A New York doctor, originally from Trenton, was going to give his multimillion-dollar collection of 525 pieces to the Metropolitan Museum of Art in New York City, but his brother convinced him to give them to his hometown instead.

Originally displayed in the trophy cases at the local high school, the unique collection found a permanent home when a new city building was built. The teapots now line the walls of the city building's chambers. If you get there during regular business hours, you're welcome to walk around and study this one-of-a-kind collection. If you happen to get there late, a sign on the front door directs you to police headquarters, where a friendly policeman will hand over the key to city hall on the promise that you'll lock up and return the key before you leave town. Admission is free.

The teapot Web site offers great photos of the collection and has information about the well-attended annual **Teapot Festival.** Call them at (731) 855–2013, or visit www.teapotcollection.com.

No one seems to know why it was done in the first place more than ten years ago, but there are no 30 mph signs in Trenton. They are all 31 mph signs. "I have no idea, but I think it's kind of cool. We get a lot of publicity out of it, like in *Off the Beaten Path: Tennessee*," laughed one city official when asked about the signs.

Up U.S. Highway 45W from Trenton is **Rutherford,** where a former home of Davy Crockett is open to the public. David (as residents prefer him to be called) moved to the area in 1823. His original cabin, built 5 miles east of town along the Obion River, was dismantled and stored with the intent of rebuilding it at a later date near where his mother is buried. But before it could be rebuilt, some of the logs were used in fires by campers.

Some of the logs were saved, though, and are now a part of the reproduction of that original cabin. On display are tools, furniture, and utensils from the period, as are letters that Crockett wrote home during his years in Congress. The grave of Rebecca Hawkins Crockett, Davy's mother, is next to the log home.

The cabin is open from the end of May through Labor Day weekend. It's located on the city's grammar school property on US 45N. To learn more about David Crockett and his current-day relatives, sign onto www.goahead.org. It's open daily; admission is charged. Call (731) 665–7253.

For more information on Trenton, Rutherford, and the rest of Gibson County, contact the chamber of commerce at (731) 855–0973 or www.gibson countytn.com.

Farther up US 45W you'll find an amazing colony of **white squirrels,** one of only a few such colonies in the world. As you enter **Kenton,** a town of about 1,500 residents, you'll be greeted by a big proclaiming KENTON: HOME OF THE WHITE SQUIRRELS. Although the exact number is hard to pinpoint, as most white squirrels look alike, the city's official stance is that about 200 of the critters live here. The squirrels are fed by just about everybody, and there's a $50 fine if you kill one.

A wildlife biologist explains that the animals are actually "albino gray squirrels who have survived for so many years because the people have taken such good care of them." They have inbred for so long that the normally recessive albino trait has become predominant.

Exactly how the first such squirrels came to the area about 120 years ago is the subject of a great many speculations. The most common theory is that during the early 1870s a band of Gypsies spent the night on a local farm. The next morning, in appreciation of the farmer's kindness, the leader of the Gypsies presented two white squirrels to the farmer. Thus it began.

The best time to see the flock (bevy? herd?) of white squirrels is in the morning and evening, when they are most apt to be scurrying from tree to tree. Stop by the city hall, which also informally serves as a white squirrel visitor information bureau.

Several cities in the United States sport white squirrels, and Craig Thom has made a hobby of visiting the towns and the squirrels. You can read of his adventures here in Kenton, as well as other white squirrel cities he has visited, at his fun Web site www.thom.org/gallery/set/squirrels.html.

Across Gibson County from Kenton is *Humboldt,* home of the *West Tennessee Strawberry Festival* each May. It features a big parade, which is promoted as the longest nonmotorized parade in the nation; a street dance; a checkers tournament; a strawberry recipe contest; and a carnival with all sorts of family and kiddie amusement rides, plus any kind of strawberry-flavored food you can think of.

A museum for a strawberry festival? Yep, this may be the only one of its kind. The West Tennessee Historical/Strawberry Festival Museum is located on the first floor of the 1912 restored neoclassic building that once served as city hall. The museum salutes local Humboldt history as well as the history of the popular festival, from its beginning in 1934 to its latest event. Open Monday, Wednesday, and Friday 9:00 a.m. to 4:00 p.m. Contact (731) 784–7770.

The *West Tennessee Regional Arts Center* is located on the upper floors, over the strawberry exhibits. It represents works of regional artists throughout Tennessee as well as surrounding states, including Red Grooms, Paul Harmon, Carroll Cloar, and Gilbert Gaul. The valuable collection was owned by a local doctor who donated it in honor of his parents and for the aesthetic education of students of all ages.

The museum and the arts center are open Monday through Friday 9:00 a.m. to 4:30 p.m. at 1200 Main Street. Admission is $2 per adult. For more information call (731) 784–1787 or go to www.wtrac.tn.org.

Crockett County was established in 1871 and named in honor of the famed Tennessee frontiersman Davy Crockett. The county seat of the 14,000 residents of the county is *Alamo,* where the *Crockett Time*s newspaper has been published for more than 120 years. Get more info at (731) 696–4558.

Crockett had already been killed when the county was formed, so when it came to finding a name for it, locals thought naming an entire county for the man would be an appropriate tribute. Cageville was renamed Alamo and became the county's center.

Crockett never lived in the county, and there is no record that he ever visited here, but the people are proud of their living monument to one of the state's best-known sons.

Carl Perkins, Elvis, Roy Orbison, and all the other rockabilly stars are honored in *Jackson's International Rockabilly Hall of Fame.* The history of the genre is told on tape and film by the stars themselves.

The founder of the facility, Henry Harrison, told me that *Jackson* is the only place in the world where this facility should be located. "West Tennessee is the birthplace of rockabilly. It all started here and spread through the world. The roots are right here," he said, adding that the attraction is "located halfway between Graceland [in Memphis] and the Grand Ole Opry [in Nashville]."

Each August the *Rockabilly Fest* is held at the fairgrounds, and entertainers from all over come to show off their rockabilly roots. The festival promotes itself as the "world's largest gathering of rockabilly entertainers and history makers."

If you're into this genre, here's a piece of rockabilly heaven for you. For $55, you can get a three-day ticket to the festival. That includes free RV hookup. During the festival you can meet and talk with the stars. A huge 28-foot-by-66-foot mural outside the Rockabilly Hall of Fame features Carl Perkins and his band members, brothers Jay and Clayton Perkins, and other rockabilly artists. Look closely and you can see Paul McCartney in the painting. The Beatle was a great fan of Carl Perkins, and Harrison said McCartney was honored to be included.

The museum is located at 105 North Church Street in Jackson and is open daily 10:00 a.m. to 4:00 p.m. Visit their Web site, www.rockabillyhall.org, for a great video on the history of rockabilly music. Call (731) 427–6262.

Right off Courthouse Square, the *West Tennessee Farmers' Market* features fresh-from-the-garden produce and flowers during the growing season. Located at New Market Street and North

tennessee's only archeofest

A unique two-day festival takes place each fall deep in the heart of Pinson Mounds State Archaeological Park. *Archeofest* is a celebration of Native American culture and archaeology and features Native American dancers, haywagon tours, storytelling, Native American foods and crafts, wildlife programs, flint knapping, and artifact identification. And it's all free. Pinson Mounds is a 1,086-acre prehistoric Indian ceremonial center containing the second-highest mound in the United States. The fest takes place the third weekend of September. Located off U.S. Highway 45, south of I-40, southeast of Jackson. Call (731) 988–5614.

College, the covered market is open daily except Sunday and features various activities and festivals during the year. Call (731) 425–8308.

Jackson's original Greyhound Bus Terminal is still in operation and is as beautiful as ever in its 1920s Art Deco glory! Several movies have been filmed here, and it's a popular spot for still photographers from all over the mid-South. Located across from city hall at North Cumberland and East Main Streets. Call (731) 427–1573.

A few blocks from downtown Jackson, on the left side of South Royal Street just after you cross the railroad tracks, is the site of the city's first modern waterworks. During its construction in the mid-1880s, one of the area's most prolific underground mineral rivers was discovered. By the early 1900s thousands were visiting and drinking water from this artesian well, searching for a cure for their stomach, liver, and kidney ailments. Today the powerful *Electro Chalybeate Well* still bubbles forth inside a gazebo built adjacent to the city's restored Art Deco water plant. A small park separates the well from the railroad tracks. For information or directions contact the chamber of commerce at (731) 425–8333 or visit online at www.jacksontncvb.com.

On the other side of the tracks is a local railroad museum, created inside the restored century-old railroad depot. The city purchased the depot from the railroad, which had not used it for 20 years and had plans to tear it down. Restoration was completed in 1994, and it was opened as a museum in late 1995. Inside are exhibits, photos, a model railroad, and other memorabilia that tell the story of the five different railroads that serviced Jackson through the years. Known locally as the *N.C. & St. L Railroad Depot,* the museum is open Monday through Saturday 10:00 a.m. to 3:00 p.m. Admission is free. You can reach them at (731) 425–8223.

A very pleasant place to stay while you're in this area is the *Highland Place Bed & Breakfast.* Innkeepers Cindy and Bill Pflaum have created quite an elegant home that is convenient to downtown Jackson. It's a traditional Colonial Revival mansion, circa 1911, with 10-foot-wide hallways, towering ceilings, an elegant center stairway, and a warm, very studious feeling cherry-paneled library. Old French Country pine furniture and comfortable couches dominate the huge living room. The modern rooms have private baths, TV–VCR-stereo jacks, Internet access, and a wide choice of books, tapes, and CDs. No smoking or pets, and no children under 12. Rooms run $145 to $175 per night. Call for more info at (731) 427–1472 or (877) 614–6305 or go to www.highlandplace.com.

"Come all you rounders if you want to hear a story about a brave engineer." That's the beginning of the tale of Casey Jones, an engineer who became a legend after being killed in a much-publicized train crash. The *Casey Jones*

Home and Railroad Museum tells the story of that fateful night. Casey was at the throttle of "Old 382" when it approached a stalled train on the same track near Vaughn, Mississippi, on April 30, 1900. The fireman jumped and yelled to Casey to do the same, but instead he stayed on and valiantly tried to stop the train. He didn't succeed, but he slowed it down enough so that he was the only casualty of the wreck. The engineer immediately became a folk hero, and his story has been recounted for more than a century in story and song.

Casey was living in Jackson at the time of his death. His home has since been moved and now serves as the centerpiece of the museum, located in Jackson's ***Casey Jones Village*** on the US 45 Bypass, just off I–40. Open daily, year-round; admission is charged. Contact (731) 668–1223 or www.caseyjones.com.

In addition to the museum, the village contains specialty shops and the ***Brooks Shaw and Son's Old Country Store,*** a country restaurant complete with an 1890s-style soda fountain and a large gift shop.

The restaurant has become quite famous for its three daily all-you-can-eat buffets. The breakfast buffet costs $6.99 during the week, $7.99 on Saturday and Sunday. The luncheon buffet is $7.99 every day; the dinner selection is $8.99 during the week, $12.99 on Friday and Saturday nights, when they add several seafood selections.

Outside, in addition to the Casey Jones Museum, there's a train store, a well-shaded and well-run miniature golf course, and a bunch of shops, including a tourist information center.

Covering 48,000 acres, the ***Natchez Trace State Resort Park and Forest*** is Tennessee's largest state-run facility. It is cared for by three state agencies. The Division of State Parks cares for the people, the Tennessee Division of Forestry cares for the trees, and the Tennessee Wildlife Resources Agency cares for the animals.

The park is also the home of the ***world's largest pecan tree.*** The tree is 106 feet tall, has a spread of 136 feet, and was planted in 1815. Legend says that one of Gen. Andrew Jackson's men returning home from the Battle of New Orleans gave a pecan to a man named Sukey Morris, who then planted it because he didn't want to eat it. The rangers here are quick to point out they don't know whether the legend is true or not, but they do admit this is one huge tree. Surrounded by a picnic area, 4 miles north of I–40 at the Natchez Trace State Park/Highway 114 exit, the tree has seen better days. It doesn't produce pecans anymore, but it's still a great sight to behold, especially if you believe the legend. It's a fun, substantial link to the past.

The massive park, with its lakes, trails, and heavily forested areas, is a success story for one of President Franklin Roosevelt's New Deal programs. When the U.S. Department of Agriculture acquired the land in the early 1930s, the area was some of the most heavily abused and eroded land in the state. The area's occupants were relocated, and a "Land-Use Area" project was set up to demonstrate how wasteland could again be made productive through proper conservation practices.

This is an interesting place to explore, with its three lakes, miles of hiking and equestrian trails, and plenty of off-the-beaten-path solitude.

There are three active churches within the park's borders. One of them, Mt. Comfort Missionary Baptist Church, was founded in 1846 by the great-grandfather of Gene Autry, the singing cowboy. Tombstones in the adjacent cemetery date back to 1830. In all, there are 25 cemeteries in the park. All are marked and allow visitors.

There are plenty of lodging opportunities here. The **Pin Oak Lodge,** located next to the 700-acre Pin Oak Lake, offers 47 modern rooms. Nearby are ten new two-bedroom villas, offering great views of the lake. There are also 18 rustic cabins, five camping cabins, a new RV campground with full hookups, and plenty of rustic camping throughout the park.

On May 5, 1999, a windstorm leveled 7,200 acres of trees but Mother Nature is slowly reforesting the area. The roads were cleared, but the forest areas are being left alone to reforest themselves. It's going to be interesting to watch how it grows back," said ranger Walter Pope. Walter is another good source for local information. He was raised in the area and after college came to work at the park.

For further information on this great treasure, call the park office at (731) 968–3742 or visit www.tnstateparks.com. For reservations call the Pin Oak Lodge at (800) 250–8616.

Each April coon hunters gather at the Decatur County fairgrounds just south of Parsons on Highway 69 to take part in an event that is billed as the **world's largest coon hunt.** Depending on the year and the weather, about 600 hunters from 35 states come here to hunt for the state's "official" animal, the raccoon.

This is basically a competition for dogs, so no guns are allowed and no coons are hurt. The hunter with the dog who does the best "tracking and tree-ing" goes away as the winner. Since coons are nocturnal, most of the action on this weekend takes place at night. A country band plays until 3:00 a.m., and the local Jaycees keep their concession stands open around the clock for the entire weekend. Contact them at (731) 847–4202.

The event is considered to be the biggest independent fund-raiser for **St. Jude Children's Research Hospital** in Memphis. More than $100,000 is raised and donated each year.

If you're in the area on a Monday, make sure you drop by the **County Courthouse** in Decaturville. That's when the judges come to town for court. The circuit and juvenile courts are held each Monday, and there's usually a crowd gathered to watch the action. "It's a real big and busy day around here, especially if there's a murder trial going on," said one local observer. Call (731) 847–4202 for hours.

Down the road apiece, where Highway 100 meets U.S. Highway 412, is the little riverside community of **Perryville.** In town, up on the very top of Pentecostal Hill, the **Tennessee River Flea Market** does business year-round every Friday through Sunday. Lloyd Privitt has taken over an old church camp that now features more than 50 dealers within their 12,000-square-foot building. There's a big collection of antiques in here as well, including a lot of glassware. What a collector's heaven this is! You'll find some great stuff, and the best part, it's off the beaten path. Follow Pentecostal Camp Road to the top. Phone (731) 847–9383.

Southern Plains

The **Shiloh National Military Park and Cemetery,** 12 miles south of Savannah on Highway 22, is a grim reminder of how bloody the Civil War really was.

On April 6 and 7, 1862, the North and South fought the first major battle in the western theater of the war here, just a few miles north of the Mississippi state line. More than 23,000 soldiers died, about one-fourth of the total forces that fought. The casualties in this one battle exceeded the total American casualties from the nation's three preceding wars: the Revolutionary War, the War of 1812, and the Mexican War.

Known as Bloody Shiloh, the battle went down in the history books as one of the most gruesome in all American warfare. The park was established in 1894 and includes the battlefield and environs. A 9-mile self-guided auto tour highlights the battle and explains the various monuments that have been erected. The visitor center has a library and a museum complete with relics and maps and a movie explaining the battle. Open daily, year-round; admission is charged. Don't miss this historic site; call (731) 689–5275 or www.nps .gov/shil.

For a month prior to the Shiloh battle, the Union forces, under the leadership of Gen. Ulysses S. Grant, used the grounds of **Cherry Mansion,** 101 Main Street in nearby Savannah, as Union headquarters. Tents were set up in the yard, and Grant slept in the house and dined with the Cherry family. He was eating breakfast on April 6 when he got word of the battle of Shiloh.

Built in 1830, the house is the oldest structure in Savannah and is currently a private residence. The owner doesn't mind your taking pictures and looking at the exterior of the house, but please be considerate. There's a monument to General Grant 1 block east of the mansion. Call (731) 925–2364.

South of Shiloh, in the small and peaceful community of Counce, the Packaging Corporation of America has developed an *arboretum* on its corporate property. Pull into the parking lot off Highway 57 and follow the signs directing you to the paved nature trails that will lead you into the woods. There you'll find 70 native tree species from Tennessee, Mississippi, and Alabama. The trees are well marked, and the walk is an easy one and is wheelchair accessible. Brochures are available at the gate. Open daily during daylight hours; admission is free. Phone (731) 689–1274.

The *Tennessee River Museum* in Savannah is a tribute both to the Tennessee River—from Paducah, Kentucky, to Muscle Shoals, Alabama—and to the influences it has had on the people who lived and worked along it. Several exhibit areas include displays on the early steamboats that plied the river, paleontology, archaeology, the Civil War, and a great collection of locally made musical instruments. Several gunboats are on display. Officials say their ceremonial Shiloh Effigy Pipe is world famous. Located in the old post office building at 507 Main Street, the museum is open daily year-round. Contact (800) 552–3866 or go online to www.tourhardincounty.org.

little-knownfacts abouttennessee

One of the toughest-fought elections in the state took place in 1933 during the election to determine which bird should be the Tennessee State Bird. More than 72,000 votes were registered, with the mockingbird edging out the robin by 450 votes.

About 11 miles north of Savannah on Highway 128, take a left turn at the Saltillo Ferry sign and go down to the river. The *Saltillo Ferry* is owned by Hardin County and runs Monday through Saturday 7:00 a.m. to 4:00 p.m. For $1 you can take your car for a ride across the Tennessee River to Saltillo. Blow your horn if the ferry is on the other side.

Both Saltillo and Cerro Gordo were named for Mexican communities by soldiers returning to their Tennessee farmlands following the Mexican War. Homes throughout the area date back to the 1840s and include an eclectic assortment of architecture, from early farmhouse to Greek Revival. Several cemeteries predate the Civil War. A brochure listing 17 points of interest in Saltillo is available from city hall.

The signs along U.S. Highway 64 outside *Adamsville* proclaim the community to be the *biggest little town in Tennessee.* A lot of that obvious pride may come from the fact that the town was home to one of America's most celebrated lawmen, Buford Pusser.

Pusser, who died in an auto accident in 1974, is immortalized in the **Buford Pusser Home and Museum,** located at 342 Pusser Street. He was sheriff of McNairy County from 1964 to 1970 and had the reputation of a no-nonsense, hard-nosed lawman. The exploits of this 6-foot, 6-inch tall, 250-pound "legend" were the basis of the three *Walking Tall* movies.

Today in the quiet residential area that he called home, his brick ranch house is overflowing with artifacts of his life. Following his death, his mother allowed nothing to be removed. Opened officially in 1988 as a museum, the facility is owned and operated by the city. Everything from his credit cards to his toothbrush to the roll of $100 bills he had in his pocket when he was killed are on display. An advertisement from a mattress company rests on his bed. "Big Buford Bedding, designed to honor a man who walked tall in Tennessee."

The years he spent as sheriff were hard ones on this "soft-spoken country gentleman." He was shot eight times, knifed seven times, and gunned down in an ambush that killed his wife. Many residents believe the flaming auto crash that took his life was no accident.

According to the museum's hostess, Pusser was constantly on guard and often remarked that he was "on borrowed time." His home is a reflection of that attitude. He had a special entrance built on the lower level, where his underground bedroom and living quarters were. He slept with his head against the earthen wall to help protect himself against the continuous threats.

In addition to his personal belongings, numerous scrapbooks of newspaper clippings, a videotape of television interviews, and a copy of his 1956 high school yearbook are on display. Admission is charged. For extra fun, plan your visit for the last weekend in May. That's when the **Buford Pusser Festival** takes place, with live music, a carnival, and free admission to the museum. Visit www.sheriffbufordpusser.com.

Up Highway 224 near Leapwood, the **Coon Creek Science Center** reveals that this whole area was under a sea about 70 million years ago. The center, opened in 1989, is owned and operated by the Memphis Museum System, although it is more than 100 miles from that city.

When emptied, the warm, shallow ocean left behind an abundance of unusual and significant geological treasures. The marine shells found here in the bottomlands are not actually fossils but the real things, since they have not undergone the process of mineralization and have not turned to stone. The clay of the area has preserved the shells in their original form.

Known as the Coon Creek fossil formation, the entire area attracts geologists from all over the world. The center has been established to preserve the area and to provide an educational facility for the study of the earth sciences.

Various educational exhibits and programs have been established and are available for groups of 15 or more. If you're not in a specific group and want to see the place, the center sponsors several "family days" during the year when individuals can sign up for a program. Call (731) 632–4850; www.cooncreek .ontheinter.net.

The hog is king at *Pappy Johns,* located on U.S. Highway 45 South, a few miles outside Selmer. Here you've got to be hungry for pork or chicken, because that's all they have. No burgers, no fries. Open daily except Sunday, pork ribs are cooked up three nights a week—Wednesday, Friday, and Saturday—while the rest of the hog is available all the other times. A good deal of the business here is takeout, but if you enjoy eating near the hickory pits where the cooking is done, there are tables inside. Famished? Call (731) 645–4353.

Hardeman County's first courthouse, now known as the *Little Courthouse,* was built in 1824, making it one of the oldest original courthouses in western Tennessee. Located at 116 East Market Street in *Bolivar,* the restored structure now houses the county museum.

The original part of the existing building was a two-story log structure that served as the courthouse. In 1827 the building was purchased and moved to its current site, where additions were made to the log structure. It was converted into a family residence in 1849 and more additions were made, turning it into a large Federal-style home.

The building itself is worth the stop, but some of the items inside highlighting this county's past are fascinating in themselves. Open by appointment or by chance; admission is charged. Check their hours at (731) 658–6554.

Another historic structure in Bolivar is *The Pillars,* former home of John Houston Bills, one of the original settlers of West Tennessee. Built prior to 1826, the building saw the likes of James K. Polk, Davy Crockett, Gen. Ulysses S. Grant, and Sam Houston. Open by appointment or chance; admission is charged. Learn more about this historic site by calling (731) 658–6554.

The *Magnolia Manor* is this area's premier bed-and-breakfast. The 1849 structure has been completely restored to its early splendor with wooden floors throughout. Owner Elaine Cox currently run the five-guest room antebellum inn. Rates range from $110 to $135, including a choice of meals. In the hallway you'll find portraits of four famous generals who stayed here many years before you found out about the place. Commissioned by the Cox family, the portraits feature Ulysses S. Grant, William T. Sherman, John A. Logan, and James B. McPherson. Located at 418 North Main Street. Contact them at (731) 658–6700 or www.magnoliamanorbolivartn.com.

The small community of **Grand Junction,** located near the point where Highway 57 is joined by Highway 368, is known throughout the world as the home of the **National Field Trial Championships.** Held nearby at the 18,600-acre Ames Plantation since 1896, the annual February event is often called the Super Bowl of Bird Dogs.

Competition lasts eight to ten days, with the winning dog earning the title of World Champion Bird Dog. Hunting mostly for quail, the dogs and handlers are followed by a large gallery of spectators on horseback. As quail raiser Joe Jordan says about the mounted spectators: "There must be 4,000 or 5,000 of them out there at a time. They never see a dog, but they sure have a good time."

Ames Plantation, located 4.3 miles off Highway 18 just north of Highway 57, is not only synonymous with the quest for canine excellence, it also plays an integral part in the University of Tennessee's livestock and agriculture program. The facility is one of the 11 branch experimental stations in the university's system. Built in 1847, the magnificent **Ames Manor House & Plantation** is open for tours on the fourth Thursday afternoon of each month, March through October, with a $2 admission charged. Adjacent to the manor house is a small collection of original log cabins that have been moved here to create a small farmstead, which is open daily. There is no fee to walk about the cabins, but it's wise to check in with the office in the manor house first. Call (901) 878–1067 or visit online at www .amesplantation.org.

theroadsscholar

Ever wonder about the highway you're driving on? Where it starts, where it ends, how long it is, when it was built? There's a Web site that gives you all that information, plus more on the U.S. numbered highways. Sign on to www.ushigh ways.com and then click on Tennessee, or any other state, on the "individual states" link.

Across the street from Dunn's is the **Field Trial Hall of Fame and National Wildlife Heritage Center.** It was created by the Bird Dog Foundation; the dedication plaque reads: "Dedicated to preserving the past, protecting the future for sporting dog fanciers the world over."

Films, paintings of some of the most famous bird dogs of the past hundred years, artifacts, literature, photography, and other memorabilia are featured here and help tell the story of the talents of well-trained bird dogs. If you're not familiar with any of this, don't worry; the folks working here are more than eager to share their love of the sport and of the dogs with you. Closed Monday; admission is free. Just call (731) 764–2058 or visit www.birddog foundation.com.

Over at 133 Madison Avenue on the town square in Grand Junction, you'll find a real gem. The **_Tennessee Pewter Showroom_** is the only commercial producer of a full line of pewter products in the South. Pewtersmith Byron Black uses both the spin and the cast methods of production to make all kinds of things, from beer steins to sugar bowls to pitchers to dinner plates. In all, he and the other craftspeople make about 435 different items.

The showroom is open Monday through Thursday 9:00 a.m. to 4:00 p.m., but if you want to see Black in action, you'll have to show up between 9:00 a.m. and 4:00 p.m. on Tuesday or Wednesday. Those are the days he's most apt to be casting the molten pewter. Find out more at (731) 764–2064, or visit www.tnpewter.com.

Heading toward Memphis on Highway 57, you'll find **_LaGrange,_** a quaint little village that has been able to avoid the commercialization that the others have fallen to along this busy highway corridor. In addition to a couple of antiques shops, the streets are lined with a plethora of well-kept little white cottages with green shutters and trim. Settled in 1819 on the site of an Indian trading post, the town was named for General Lafayette's ancestral home in France. Translated to mean "beautiful village," it was occupied by Union forces from 1862 to 1865. It was an antebellum center of wealth, education, and culture, having had two colleges, four academies, two newspapers, and 3,000 residents in 1862.

The best way to get into Memphis from this part of the state is to continue west on Highway 57. If you do that, you'll go through **_Collierville,_** a neat little community with a historic town square and a countless number of antiques shops and unique eateries. Along the square, which serves as a gathering place for the locals, the Fair on the Square takes place the first weekend of May each year, a free Sunset Concert Series is held every Thursday evening during June and July, and a first-class juried art competition is the centerpiece of the Mulberry Festival in October. For more information on this sleepy little suburban community, call the chamber of commerce at (901) 853–1949 or go to www.colliervillechamber.com.

The Delta Region

With a population of about 650,000, **_Memphis_** rests along the Mississippi River and is one of the river's largest inland ports. Among many other things, the city is famous for its impact on the development of popular American music as well as the blues.

For a good overview of the area call (800) 8–MEMPHIS or visit www .memphistravel.com.

The history of music in the Memphis area revolves around the King of Rock and Roll, Elvis Presley. Although he died in 1977, Elvis is even more popular today than when he was alive, and his estate is worth much more now (more than $100 million) than it was when he died ($4.9 million) because of his home (Graceland Mansion), souvenir and tourist shops, and museums. Estate revenues were topping $15 million annually by the late 1980s, more than the singer made in any one year of his career.

Graceland Mansion, at 3765 Elvis Presley Boulevard, is one of the many unique places in the state where the beaten path catches up with the unbeaten path. There's nothing like this anywhere else in the world, and it shouldn't be missed. Elvis and members of his family are buried here in the Meditation Garden, and tours of the mansion are run daily year-round, except for Christmas, Thanksgiving, and New Year's Day. Closed Tuesday in November and December.

You'll get a chance to walk the grounds, see Elvis's private recording studio, and tour his bus and his private jet, the *Lisa Marie,* named for his daughter. You'll also have the opportunity to add to his estate at a variety of merchandise shops across the street from the mansion. It would be a good idea to make reservations, because the lines can get very long, especially during the summer months. Admission is charged. Contact (901) 332–3322 or www .elvis.com.

Each year in mid-August Memphis hosts the **Elvis International Tribute Week,** an action-packed week of events that include trivia contests, candlelight vigils, special tours, tournaments, and parties. Humes Junior High School, where Elvis graduated in 1953, is also open for tours and features a special exhibit room and a chance to walk across the stage where Elvis performed in a talent show.

A funky place to spend the night while in Memphis is the **Heartbreak Hotel,** based and themed on Elvis's big hit of the same name. It's a fashionable boutique hotel with 128 rooms and suites and, located at 3677 Elvis Presley Boulevard, it's convenient to everything else Elvis. Rates range from $110 for a basic room to $545 for a themed suite (and boy is it themed!). Several money-saving packages include a room, meals, and tickets to Elvis attractions. Phone them at (877) 777–0606. Their Web site is really cool—plenty of music, fun dialogue, and unexpected diversions; go to www.elvis.com.

Sun Studio, where Elvis recorded a song for his mother for $4, is open to the public. Founded by disc jockey Sam Phillips, Sun was the first studio to record such musicians as Presley, Jerry Lee Lewis, Carl Perkins, and Johnny Cash. The studio is located at 706 Union Avenue, just a few blocks from Baptist Hospital, where Elvis was pronounced dead on August 16, 1977. Open seven days a week from 10:00 a.m. to 6:00 p.m., with tours scheduled every hour on the half hour; longer hours during the summer. Admission is charged. Reach them at (901) 521–0664; their Web site is www.sunstudio.com.

Beale Street, in downtown Memphis, is considered the spiritual home of the other type of music the city is famous for, the blues. During its heyday in the twenties and thirties, there wasn't a tougher, more swinging street in America. The zoot suit originated here, and Machine Gun Kelly peddled bootleg on the streets. Always a mecca for musicians, the street's nightclubs were frequented by the country's best blues artists, including the man known as the Father of the Blues, the legendary William Christopher (W. C.) Handy.

Today the street is once again a hot nightspot with numerous clubs, restaurants, and shops. And the best part is that the sound of the blues has not been forgotten. Several clubs now offer traditional blues and jazz, including the *Rum Boogie Cafe* at 182 Beale, (901) 528–0150; www.rumboogie.com; and *B. B. King's Blues Club,* at 143 Beale, (901) 524–5464 or www.memphis bbkingclubs.com.

Virtually unchanged through the years is *Schwab's* dry goods store, where a sign still hangs in the window proclaiming IF YOU CAN'T FIND IT HERE, YOU'RE BETTER OFF WITHOUT IT. The clerks still offer old-time service with a written receipt for each item purchased.

The Schwab family has created a museum, and having been on Beale Street since 1876, they have been able to collect quite a few memories of the "good ole days" to display. Upstairs, the store sells all sorts of items, from dream books to straw sailors to crystal balls to size 74 men's pants. Forty-four kinds of suspenders are kept in stock. Call (901) 523–9782.

Less than a block south of Beale Street, at 145 Lt. George W. Lee Avenue, is the new Gibson Guitar Factory. Upstairs over the factory is the *Memphis Rock 'n' Soul Museum,* an intimate salute to the early soul music that permeated Memphis culture. The museum features the Smithsonian Institution's Rock 'n' Soul: Social Crossroads exhibit. Six different galleries within the museum present a chronology of the hearts and souls that created the Memphis sound.

The exhibits feature artifacts, pictures, and of course music. With each admission purchased, you get an audio gallery guide with more than 300 minutes of information, music, and interviews of dozens of soul music pioneers.

Those who helped create the *Memphis Sound* include Elvis, Otis Redding, B. B. King, and Jerry Lee Lewis. The city's recording studios produced more than 120 top 20 hits. Many musicologists call Memphis the Holy Ground of American Music. In fact, when the Smithsonian began putting this exhibit together, an official of the National Museum of American History was quoted as saying: "In our quest to identify an American popular music, all roads led to Memphis."

Open daily, 10:00 a.m. to 6:00 p.m. Call (901) 543–0800 or visit www .memphisrocknsoul.org.

Two white marble lions guard the entrance. A large bronze bell gongs every 90 seconds. With its 50-foot pagoda, tinkling waterfall, goldfish pond, bamboo stands, and strutting pheasants, the home of the giant pandas at the **Memphis Zoo** seems like China's Forbidden City. The three-acre, $16-million China exhibit immerses visitors in the history, culture, and wildlife of China.

The Memphis Zoo has come a long way from its simple beginnings with a bear named Natch. The black bear was a mascot for the Memphis baseball season. After the baseball season ended, Natch was chained to a tree in Overton Park. Col. Robert Galloway took pity on him and began lobbying for funds in 1904 to build Natch a real home. In 1906, the Memphis Zoo opened with 23 simple cages and a row of concrete bear dens. In the 1990s zoo officials and local folks organized a tremendous fund-raising drive to turn the facility into a world-class zoo. Open all year, the zoo is home to over 3,500 animals representing more than 500 species. Call the zoo at (901) 276–9453 or visit the Web site at www.memphiszoo.org.

A new taste treat awaits you a few doors down from the police museum. **Dyers Burgers** features deep-fried hamburgers, and the grease they are cooked in has not been changed since 1912! It has been strained, but the same basic grease has been used all these years, and officials say it has never been allowed to cool and has never been solidified. When the restaurant was moved here from another part of town, the truck with the hot grease was given a police escort to make sure they could make it before the grease got cold. Open daily and located at 205 Beale Street, its phone number is (901) 527–DYER.

For a listing of all the clubs, restaurants, and shops on Beale Street, as well as a listing of concerts and events, visit www.bealestreet.com.

If it's history you came to Memphis for, take the short trip out to **Mud Island,** out in the Mississippi River across from downtown. The city has developed this area to display its rich river heritage. The **River Walk** is a 5-block-long scale model of the entire Lower Mississippi's 1,000 miles from Cairo, Illinois, to the Gulf of Mexico. Every twist, turn, and split that the river makes is shown on the model. Each step equals 1 mile along the miniriver, where each bridge and town is also depicted. Markers along the way point out interesting facts and figures. Water flows down the model into a one-acre Gulf of Mexico.

The 18-gallery **Mississippi River Museum** is also located on the island and is a showcase for the people and the history of the river, with exhibits ranging from Indian arrowheads to a replica of the pilothouse of a modern diesel towboat.

One of the galleries traces the 1865 wreck of the steamboat *Sultana,* which burned and sank nearby, killing 1,547 people. It is considered the worst maritime disaster in United States history. Call (901) 576–7241 or visit www .mudisland.com.

A visit to the ***Peabody Hotel,*** at 149 Union Street in downtown, is a must. Built in 1925, the grand hotel has been restored and carries on a tradition started back in the mid-thirties. Each morning at 11 o'clock, five ducks are transported by elevator from their penthouse facilities to the lobby of the hotel.

As the doors slowly open, a red carpet is unrolled from the big fountain to the elevator as the "King Cotton March" is played over the sound system. With official Duck Master Jason Sensat in control, the ducks waddle to the fountain, where they will spend the day. At 5:00 p.m. the action is reversed, and the ducks go back to their duck palace on the roof. During the day, if you visit the roof home of the ducks, you'll find a sign on their door proclaiming: GONE TO WORK IN THE LOBBY. BE BACK AT 5:00 P.M.

To get a prestigious gig like this, a duck first has to be lucky enough to be recruited from a duck farm in Arkansas. Mostly three-year-olds get the job. The lucky duck gets sent to Memphis, where he spends two weeks in training, learning from the veterans already working there. Once he becomes a part of the first team, he'll work for about three months before being returned to the farm.

The penthouse is open to visitors, but that's not all you'll find up there. You'll also find a very impressive view of the river and downtown Memphis. Lots to see! Call (901) 529–4000 for more information or go to www.peabody memphis.com.

I hope the irony isn't lost that Peabody's famous ducks live just across town from the ***Ducks Unlimited National Headquarters.*** Founded in 1937, the international organization's mission statement reads: "To fulfill the annual life cycle needs of North America's waterfowl by protecting, enhancing, restoring, and managing important wetlands and associated uplands." The headquarters is open for tours Monday through Friday 8:00 a.m. to 4:00 p.m., with no tours during lunch. Along the way you'll see exhibits of DU memorabilia and displays of wetland ecosystems. Located on One Waterfowl Way, DU can be reached at (901) 758–3825 or visit www.ducks.org.

Metalsmithing, everything from delicate gold jewelry to massive wrought-iron fencing, is the subject of one of the area's most unusual museums. Located in downtown Memphis on a bluff overlooking the Mississippi River, the *National Ornamental Metal Museum* was opened to the public in 1979 as a memorial to metalsmithing.

Changing exhibits is the basis of the museum, but its permanent collection contains a variety of items from jewelry to handmade nails to large outdoor sculptures to ancient iron locks. In the museum's smithy (anyplace where metal is worked) work is done daily by resident artists and members of museum classes. On the third weekend of October each year, Repair Days

A SAMPLING OF AFRICAN-AMERICAN SITES AND ATTRACTIONS

Meharry Medical College
1005 D. B. Todd Boulevard
Nashville
First medical education program in
United States for African Americans
(615) 327–6111
www.mmc.edu

Fisk University Historic District
1000 17th Avenue North
Nashville
Founded in 1887 as "free school"
for blacks; area consists of vintage
buildings, theaters, galleries
(615) 329–8720

Bethlehem Cemetery
U.S. Highway 51 North, Henning
Alex Haley's family burial plot; where
Chicken George is buried
(731) 738–2240

National Civil Rights Museum
450 Mulberry Street, Memphis
Housed in Lorraine Motel, where Martin
Luther King Jr. was assassinated
(901) 521–9699
www.civilrightsmuseum.org

W. C. Handy Home & Gallery
352 Beale Street, Memphis
Where W. C. Handy penned his many
famous songs; memorabilia and artifacts
(901) 527–3427
www.heritagetours.com

WDIA Radio Station
47 Union Avenue, Memphis
Founded in 1948 as first African-
American formatted radio station in the
United States
(901) 529–4300
www.am1070wdia.com

Beck Cultural Exchange Center
1927 Dandridge Avenue, Knoxville
Archives, research, and museum for the
city's African-American citizens
(865) 524–8461

Highlander Research Foundation
1959 Highlander Way, New Market
An important training center for the
modern civil rights movement; graduates
include Dr. Martin Luther King Jr. and
Rosa Parks
(865) 933–3443

**Afro-American Museum & Research
Center**
200 East Martin Luther King
Boulevard, Chattanooga
Portrays history and culture of the
city's African Americans and their
contributions to society
(423) 266–8658
www.caamhistory.com

are held. People from all over the South bring in their broken metal items to be fixed. On average, 60 craftspeople are available during that time to repair "broken, bent, or otherwise mutilated metalwork."

Make sure you pay attention to the front gates as you enter. Known as the Anniversary Gates, the tall metal gates contain nearly 200 specially designed rosettes, each made by a different metal craftsman. Each was submitted as part of the museum's tenth anniversary project and placed in an S scroll on the gate. Designs range from the traditional to contemporary, abstract, and whimsical. This is a great piece of unique art, and in no way should you visit Memphis without seeing it.

The grounds immediately surrounding the museum are also unique. Talk about artistic yard art! Wonderful metal sculptures and doodads are placed throughout. In the gazebo, you can see the Mississippi River from high above.

The museum grounds, at 374 Metal Museum Drive (formerly known as West California), are a part of what was once known as the Marine Hospital, with the oldest of the three large brick buildings dating from 1870. That building was used in the extensive Memphis research that led to a cure for the yellow fever epidemics that once swept the area. The museum's main exhibit building was built as a Works Progress Administration (WPA) project in 1932 and once served as a nurses' dormitory for the hospital complex. Admission is charged. Get more information by calling (901) 774–6380 or visit www .metalmuseum.org.

At **Huey's** restaurant and bar you are encouraged to use your straw to shoot toothpicks into the ceiling! Name another eatery that permits that. The menu consists mostly of burgers, salads, pitas, and other sandwiches. Make sure you bring your Sharpie—you're allowed to write on the walls. Open daily at 11:00 a.m. or noon and closes well after midnight. Located at 77 South Second Street, across from the Peabody Hotel. Phone this unique eatery at (901) 527–2700 or go to www.hueyburger.com.

Tad Pierson owns **American Dream Safari** tours. Tad also owns a pink 1955 Cadillac. "Well, it really isn't pink," Tad said. "Cadillac calls it Pecos Beige, but I call it pink, and the power of suggestion makes everyone think it's pink!"

This guy knows his Memphis and environs. Book a tour with him and he'll load you into his classic auto and take you on a fun and informative journey. He has several different tours to choose from. His Greatest Hits tour takes three hours and includes what he calls "lots of Elvis, Beale Street, Mississippi River lore and legend, the Lorraine Motel, and Southern mansions on tree-lined boulevards." It's $50 per person. His Juke Joint tour starts at 9:00 p.m. and lasts until it's over. The tour takes you deep into the Memphis juke joint culture, and it's a real hoot!

Tad says there are only two reasons to go to a juke joint full of blues. Either you feel good or you feel bad. He said that most of his tours are booked before the people get to Memphis, so calling ahead is a good idea. He'll pick you up at your hotel. Call him at (901) 527–8870, or visit www.americandream safari.com.

Soul music was practically invented in Memphis, mostly in a small neighborhood just south of downtown known today as *Soulsville, USA.* Stax Records and Hi Records were both located in this area in the late 1950s, and this is where the greatest soul singers of all time were born, lived, or recorded. Aretha Franklin was born in the neighborhood, and the likes of Al Green, Ann Peebles, Rufus Thomas, Maurice White, Isaac Hayes, and Booker T. and the MGs spent countless hours here.

The center of attraction was the Stax Records studio, where the hottest soul records of all time were recorded between 1959 and 1975. During that 15-year period, Stax released 300 LPs and more than 800 singles. An incredible 167 singles made it to the top 100 Pop Chart, and 243 made it to the Top 100 on the R&B charts.

The *Stax Museum of American Soul Music* is now located on the same corner where Stax Records once stood. Now run by a nonprofit group for inner-city youth, the museum showcases an amazing collection of more than 2,000 artifacts, photos, and exhibits. Along with a running historical commentary and the legendary Stax Sound, the museum also spotlights the music of Muscle Shoals, Motown, Hi, and Atlantic Records.

The "real-cool" exhibits include Isaac Hayes's 1972 gold-trimmed, peacock blue "Superfly" Cadillac, Phalon Jones's saxophone recovered from the lake where the airplane of Otis Redding and the Bar-Kays crashed, and Albert King's famous purple "Flying V" guitar.

It's open daily year-round Tuesday through Saturday from 10:00 a.m. to 5:00 p.m., Sunday from 1:00 to 5:00 p.m. Closed Mondays. Admission is $12 for adults, $11 for seniors; and $9 for children nine through 12. Children eight and under and museum members get in free. The gift shop has a super selection

you'llfretover thistour!

One of the factories making famous Gibson Guitars is located in downtown Memphis. Knowledgeable tour guides lead you through 16 of the workstations, creating a unique factory tour. Located below the Memphis Rock 'n' Soul Museum, near Beale Street, at 145 Lt. George W. Lee Avenue. Your contacts: (901) 543–0800 and www.gibsonmemphis.com.

of music to buy! Located at 926 East McLemore, at the corner of College Avenue, less than 3 miles from Beale Street. If you need more information, call (901) 942–SOUL, or visit www.staxmuseum.com.

A good Web site to surf for additional Memphis music attractions and links is www.memphislocal.com.

The *National Civil Rights Museum* is the nation's first museum dedicated to documenting the complete history of the American civil rights movement. Constructed around the Lorraine Motel, where Dr. Martin Luther King Jr. was assassinated on April 4, 1968, the center features an interpretive education center, audiovisual displays, interactive exhibits, and civil rights memorabilia. Large exhibits portray several memorable moments in the movement, including the arrest of Rosa Parks for not moving to the back of the bus when requested, the sanitation workers' strike in Memphis, and the assassination of Dr. King.

King used to stay in Room 307 at the motel when he came to Memphis, and it was outside that room on the balcony that he was shot. Visitors can now walk into that room and be immersed in the assassination story. It's quite moving, and if you see nothing else, this is the one exhibit you shouldn't miss. Located at 450 Mulberry Street, the museum is open daily year-round. Admission charged; call (901) 521–9699 or visit www.civilrightsmuseum.org.

The *Commercial Appeal,* the daily newspaper of Memphis, has prepared an extensive archive of articles written through the years about the civil rights movement, Dr. Martin Luther King Jr., and the city's favorite son, Elvis. It's all free and a good way to get some background on what made Memphis the city it is before you get here. The Web site is www.gomemphis.com.

Danny Thomas, entertainer, humanitarian, and founder of St. Jude Children's Hospital, is buried in a memorial garden in front of the hospital, next to a beautiful pavilion that features his life, his career, and his love for his fellow man. There are videos of his *Make Room for Daddy* television series and a wall full of photos of Thomas posed with other legendary stars. In addition, there are hundreds of personal items and most of the trophies and awards he won during his illustrious career. Located in downtown Memphis at 332 North Lauderdale, the pavilion and gardens are open seven days a week during summer, Monday through Friday during winter. Admission is free. Call (901) 495–3508 or visit their Web site at www.stjude.org.

There's nothing off the beaten path about the *Sleep Inn at Court Square,* in downtown Memphis. In fact, it's on the path as well as on the trolley line. It's the best place for your dollars if you want to stay within a 5-block walk of most of the downtown attractions listed in this chapter, including Beale Street and Mud Island. On one side of the hotel is the riverfront Confederate Park; the other side is the trolley line and the historic Court Square. A great continental breakfast is included. Located at 40 North Front Street. Call (901) 522–9700 or www.sleepinn.com/hotel-memphis-tennessee-TN451.

The **Crystal Shrine Grotto,** inside the Memorial Park Cemetery, is a must stop if you're looking for the unusual in unusual locations. A unique cave was constructed by cemetery founder Clovis Hinds and Mexican artist Dionicio Rodriquez during the period of 1935-38. The cave and exterior environs were built of concrete in imitation of rocks, boulders, and trees. The entranceway appears to be through a tree trunk.

Natural rock and quartz crystal collected from the Ozarks form the background for nine different scenes from the life of Christ. Because of those scenes, the local kids often call the cavern the Jesus Cave. It's beautiful and quite an unusual work of naturalistic art. The shrine is open daily 8:00 a.m. to 4:00 p.m. Located at 5668 Poplar Avenue, just off Interstate 240 east of downtown. It can be reached at (901) 767–8930.

In **Mason,** just across the Tipton County line at 342 Highway 70, is **Bozo's Restaurant.** Look for one of those tiled cafe buildings that dotted America's landscape in the 1950s, and you'll find Bozo's.

Founded in 1923 by Bozo Williams, the restaurant stayed in the family until 2001, when Hayne Ozier purchased it from Bozo's great-grandson. Famous for its pork shoulder barbecue sandwiches and plates, Bozo's has a full menu that has not changed since shortly after World War II.

Having never advertised, the restaurant's 100 seats are filled by longtime customers and newcomers who have heard about the place from a friend. On weekends about 50 percent of the business comes from Memphis, 35 miles away. Bozo's is open Tuesday through Saturday from 10:30 a.m. to 9:00 p.m. and offers the same menu items all day. Call (901) 294–3400.

Farther north on U.S. Highway 51 in Tipton County is **Covington,** where you'll find an eclectic architectural area known as the **South Main Historic District.** In all, there are more than 50 different structures reflecting "architectural styles that were sought by the emerging, affluent members of

andthebelltolls

The bell on top of the gingerbread-enhanced Carpenter Gothic Cottage, inside the Elmwood Cemetery, tolls for each interment today, just as it has since 1870. The 80-acre, circa 1852 cemetery is now the eternal home to two governors, four U.S. senators, 22 mayors, soldiers from all U.S. wars, including 19 Confederate generals, and an array of jazz singers, madams, suffragists, and beer drinkers. Purchase a map or rent an audio car-tour tape at the cottage and take a tour of this beautiful parklike facility. It's located at 824 South Dudley Street. Call (901) 774–3212, or visit www.elmwoodcemetery.org.

onthebeatenpath

Interstate highways—you know, those concrete ribbons that cross the state and all look the same? Well, there are 1,074 miles of them in Tennessee, and although they can save time, they certainly aren't the way to go if you want to see more than cows and billboards. Want to avoid truck traffic? Stay off the interstates! In 2008, more than 12 million semi trucks and commercial vehicles stopped at the state's five interstate weigh stations.

society in the late 19th and early 20th century," reads the historic marker. Among the styles represented: American Four-Square, Prairie Bungalow, Colonial Revival, and Queen Anne. Call (901) 476–9727.

The restored **Ruffin Theater** on East Pleasant is part of the historic district. Built in the Art Deco style in 1937, it now serves as a performing arts center for the community. For details call (901) 476–9727.

Over in **Brownsville,** West Tennessee's most unusual outdoor sculpture is located 3 blocks from the courthouse on West Main Street. Reaching heights of 75 feet, **Mindfield** is a work in progress by local artist and welder Billy Tripp, who lives in his welding shop behind the sculpture. The huge, eclectic steel structure symbolizes life and the process of growing up, and it's up to all who see it to interpret it for themselves. He adds to it constantly and says he will do so for as long as he physically can.

Nestled among the old structures in Brownsville College Hill historic district is the College Hill Community Center. Situated at the top of the hill at 129 North Grand Avenue, the center houses the Morton Felsenthal Lincoln Collection. Now the property of the city, the large collection of books and memorabilia concerning the 16th U.S. president is an all-encompassing exhibit.

The **Haywood County Museum** is also located at College Hill and features a good view into this part of the Mississippi Delta region. Adjacent to the museum is the Haywood County Sports Museum, featuring high school sports in the county dating back to the early 1900s. The three College Hill facilities are open Monday through Friday 10:00 a.m. to 4:00 p.m. and on Sunday afternoon. Call them at (731) 772–4883.

A walking tour of the historic homes in this historic area is available; brochures can be obtained at the chamber of commerce at 121 West Main Street.

The blues music heritage is alive and well and in good hands around here. The annual **Brownsville Blues Fall Fest** is held in late September or early October and features live blues music all day, a barbecue contest, a scarecrow contest, and various children's activities. Get in touch with them by calling (731) 772–2193 or visit www.brownsville-haywoodtn.com.

The **West Tennessee Delta Heritage Center,** located at exit 56 off I–40, is the state's newest and probably coolest visitor center. Not only can you obtain information for the entire Western Plains area of Tennessee, but there's also a museum here with four major exhibit areas, a gift shop offering the work of regional artisans, an ATM machine, the Sleepy John Estes house, and an outside amphitheater, where concerts are held to promote the arts and musical heritage of the area.

The four exhibit areas are the Tennessee Room, which showcases West Tennessee towns and attractions; the West Tennessee Music Museum, highlighting such area talent as Tina Turner, Eddie Arnold, T. J. Shepherd, and Carl Perkins; the Scenic Hatchie River Museum, explaining the entire river watershed and ecosystem; and the Cotton Museum, which shows how cotton has affected the lives of West Tennesseans and its economic impact upon the area.

The house where **Sleepy John Estes** last strummed his guitar is part of the center. This is where the blues legend was living when he died in 1977. There are photos and memorabilia, and blues music fills the house. Open Tuesday through Saturday. Call (731) 779–9000.

Up Highway 19 from Brownsville, in the small community of **Nutbush,** Anna Mae Bullock was born on November 26, 1939, to sharecropper parents. She was a young girl surrounded by cotton fields and plenty of dreams. With a few lucky breaks and an immense amount of talent, this young lady moved away, got married, and became Tina Turner, Queen of Rock and Roll.

She immortalized her hometown in her 1973 hit, "Nutbush City Limits," and she was inducted into the Rock and Roll Hall of Fame in 1991. The sharecropper's shack in which she was born has long since disappeared, but the farm where that shack stood is still there. A sign now marks the farm, located on Highway 19 adjacent to the cotton gin. The high school she attended in Brownsville and the elementary school she attended in Ripley are both still in service.

The Brownsville/Haywood County Chamber of Commerce can be contacted for more information on the area. Call them at (731) 772–2193, or go to www.brownsville-haywoodtn.com.

Henning, the boyhood home of the late author Alex Haley, is a picturesque town of Victorian homes and turn-of-the-20th-century storefronts. The town probably would have progressed quietly like many small towns had it not been for native son Haley.

His 1976 Pulitzer prize–winning novel, *Roots,* and the subsequent TV miniseries, based on the family stories his grandmother and aunt told him, brought international fame to Henning, where Haley's family home is now the **Alex Haley House Museum.**

Those stories inspired Haley to research his family members who were brought to America as slaves, and the book came as a result. He recalls sitting on the front porch of his boyhood home and listening for hours to the stories.

Haley's museum by description is a "tribute to Kunta Kinte's worldwide family." Built in 1918 by a Kunta Kinte descendant, the house has been restored and serves not only as a tribute to Haley but also as a good example of rural small-town life in West Tennessee. It is also the first African-American state historic site and the only writer's home open to the public in Tennessee.

Following his death on February 10, 1992, Haley was buried in the front yard of the house, and his grave site is available for viewing at any time. Located at 200 South Church Street at Haley Avenue, the museum is open Tuesday through Sunday. Admission charged. Call (731) 738–2240.

In a bright red caboose in downtown Henning, the area's historical society has its records and artifacts on display in its heritage museum. Located on Main Street, adjacent to the city hall. If you'd like to visit, go into city hall and someone will come out and unlock the doors for you. Open hours are scarce and sporadic. To be sure not to miss it, call first at (731) 738–5055.

believeitornot!

Remember the 1986 **Hands Across America** effort to help raise awareness and money for the homeless? Americans joined hands from New York to Los Angeles, and the halfway point was at the intersection of Cleveland Street and U.S. Highway 51 in Ripley, Tennessee.

North of Henning, just off US 51 is **Ripley,** the seat of Lauderdale County. Believe it or not, this place has a wonderful array of interesting buildings, including two magnificent structures created by the Works Progress Administration in the 1930s. On Court Square is the Lauderdale County Courthouse, which is listed on the National Register of Historic Places. The center of the lobby has a colorful map, made of tile, of the county. Phone (731) 635–3500.

At 117 Jackson Street is the Ripley post office. In the lobby of this WPA structure, which is listed on the National Historical Register of Post Offices, is a beautiful oil mural, worth a stop by even if you don't need stamps. Phone them at (731) 635–9691. The Sugar Hill Library, at 123 Jefferson Street, is housed in the first wood-frame house built in town. Their phone number is (731) 635–1872. The bell in use when the First Presbyterian Church opened in 1892 is still in use today and is made of the silver dollars donated to the bell fund. Hear it at 130 North Jefferson Street. Call (731) 635–9751.

Farther north on US 51 is Halls. Among its interesting structures is its public library, housed in an original 1930s-era Art Deco building, formerly a Sinclair service station. Call for hours open: (731) 836–5302. More than 20,000 bales of what the locals call White Gold are processed each fall at the Halls (cotton) Gin Company. Located at 1279 Industrial Road, this modern, computerized gin is adjacent to the Halls Dyersburg Army Airbase, where an exceptional air show takes place each year.

While in Halls, stop by and meet Murray Hudson, who owns and operates **Hudson's Antiquarian Books & Maps.** It's a collector's paradise where you'll find maps, globes, and books. It's kinda cool to see all those globes when you first walk in, and Murray, a former English teacher, certainly looks the part of a map and globe collector! It's located at 109 South Church Street; call (731) 836–9057 or go online at www.murrayhudson.com.

Here's one for the "engineers" who are looking for off-the-beaten-path mechanical wonders. Outside Dyersburg is the world's only surviving "swing span, pony Pratt through truss bridge." Known for the town from which it came, the **Lenox Bridge,** as it is now known, was built in 1917 and moved and restored in 1985. The bridge was positioned for land travel. When a ship would need to go through, it would blow its whistle to alert the bridge tender, who would come down, walk out to the center pier, and crank the bridge open by hand. The bridge would turn away from both riverbanks and line up out of the way of the ship in the middle of the river, parallel with the shores, supported only in the center.

The bridge is 150 feet in length and 14 feet wide, and the pier is 18 feet in diameter. Jere Kirk, whose grandfather helped with the construction of the original bridge, bought and refurbished the bridge. It is now on display over a body of water in the Lakewood subdivision. Take Highway 78 north out of Dyersburg. From Interstate 155, go 2.7 miles and turn left on Highway 182 South. Go 1 mile and turn left into Lakewood. Stay right; the bridge is on your right, just past the lake.

Delta Flyway

The **Obion County Museum,** in **Union City,** is the only regional history museum in this part of the state. All the other museums are specialized, so this is the place to go to get a good overview of what northwest Tennessee is all about.

County historian Rebel C. Forrester is the perfect guide as he walks you through the displays and explains little tidbits of history that only a county historian would know. An amazing collection of "documentary" photos from

1919 to 1924 gives a good visual feeling to the other exhibits. Among the items on permanent display are a Model T Ford, Native American artifacts, and a horse-drawn hearse.

Adjacent to the museum is a two-room log cabin with exhibits. The museum is open Saturday and Sunday afternoon and is located at 1004 Edwards Street, directly behind the high school. Admission is free; call (731) 885–6774.

About a block from the museum at the end of Edwards Street is the first monument erected in honor of the unknown Confederate soldier. It was dedicated on October 21, 1869.

Gun collectors worldwide probably already know about this city's **Dixie Gun Works,** while noncollectors across town may have never heard of it. Founded by the late Turner Kirkland in the early 1950s, the business is now considered the world's largest supplier of antique guns and parts. The firm sells about 80,000 guns a year, including antique reproductions.

At any given time a walk through the Dixie Gun Works' showroom is like walking through an antique firearms museum, except that you can buy most of the guns you see here. Usually, more than 1,500 guns are on display. Kirkland's other passion, antique automobiles, is also in evidence. Adjacent to the gun showroom is an auto museum with more than 30 cars, including a 1908 Maxwell.

A small log cabin gunshop is a part of this attraction. Originally built in this area around 1850, the shop contains two rifling machines and more than 1,000 gun-making tools. The complex is located on the Highway 51S Union City Bypass. Admission is charged for this interesting museum; their phone number is (731) 885–0561 or visit www.dixiegunworks.com.

Adjacent to the county courthouse, in the center of Union City, is the **Flame of Freedom,** an eternal flame dedicated to "all veterans of Obion County in all wars and conflicts, past, present, and future." It was dedicated in 1971. Along the railroad tracks on South Depot Street next to the municipal building, Kiwanis Park offers a nice place to rest for a spell. Make note of the Confederate monument in the park. It's one of the few in the South that looks north. There's a bandshell, fountains, playground equipment, and plenty of huge shade trees.

If it's architecture you like, don't overlook the **First Christian Church** at West Lee and South Second Streets. The circa 1912 domed church is the third to be built on the site. The bell that is on display on the church lawn was the first bell of the brick church built on this site after the 1862 destruction of the 1857 frame church by Union forces. Check out the beautiful stained-glass windows of the church.

The Masquerade Theatre Company, a community theater group in Union City, raised the money to buy and has now restored the beautiful circa 1927 *Capitol Theater,* at 118 South First Street. Through the years, it was used as a film house, a stage for traveling legitimate theater, and a vaudeville stage. The theater group will produce several shows a year in the 364-seat venue and will host a bevy of local entertainment events such as recitals. Make sure you check out the ticket box out front. Inside is a life-size cutout likeness of Louise Harper, who sold most of the tickets used at the Capitol from 1930 to 1962.

If you're hungry for what a lot of people around here consider the best cheeseburger in the world, stop by *P.V.'s Hut.* It's open Tuesday through Saturday 11:00 a.m. to 7:00 p.m. and is located at East Florida and South Perkins Streets. Call the hut at (731) 885–5737.

Following World War II, housing was in demand throughout the United States, and as a result many all-steel pre-fabricated homes were built. They were quick to put up and reasonably inexpensive for the returning servicemen. Only one re-mains in Obion County. It's at 1020 Church Street and has been maintained quite nicely through the years.

A couple streets over in the oldest residential neighborhood in town, the home of Lexie Parks still stands at 822 East Main. The house contains the first elevator in town—and the ghost of the wealthy Mr. Parks. He was killed in the house by his butler, who was never convicted of the crime. Residents who have lived here since have documented Parks and his congenial hauntings as he walks through the house. It seems he is upset that the butler got away with the murder.

Additional information about Union City and Obion County can be had by contacting the chamber of commerce at (731) 885–0211 or www.obion county.org.

Reelfoot Lake is the result of a true quirk of nature. The *worst earthquake ever measured* in American history took place in this area in 1812. On February 7 the quake hit, and the lands of northwest Tennessee near the Mississippi River dropped as much as 20 feet.

little-knownfood factsabout tennessee

Every Pringle potato chip ever eaten anywhere in the world was made in Jackson.

Like Christie Cookies? All the cookie dough and all of its wholesale cookies are made in Nashville.

Coors Brewing Company is in Colorado, but all its nonalcoholic and malt drinks are brewed in Memphis.

The "Real Legend" of Reelfoot

Once upon a time in the early 1800s, there ruled a mighty Chickasaw chieftain whose only son had a deformed foot. The son ran with a rolling motion, so the tribe nicknamed him *Kaolin,* meaning "Reelfoot." When the son became chief and was to be married, he found he had no feelings for any maidens in his tribe.

He went searching for a wondrous beauty and found her among the Choctaws. She was the daughter of the chief. Reelfoot immediately fell under the spell of the princess and asked her father to allow a marriage.

The old chief replied: "It is true that my daughter is enchanting, and she will only be given in wedlock to a Choctaw chieftain. I will not ever permit her to join a tribe which is so unfortunate as to have a clubfooted chieftain." Reelfoot was more determined than ever, but the Great Spirit had a few words for him. "An Indian must not take his wife from a neighboring tribe, and if you disobey and take the princess, I will cause the earth to rock and the waters to swallow up your village and bury your people in a watery grave."

Reelfoot chose not to believe the Great Spirit, and within months he had captured the princess and brought her back to West Tennessee. As the marriage rites took place, the earth began to roll, and Reelfoot cried out for mercy on his people. The Great Spirit answered, "I will show you and your people mercy, but you will have to pay for your disobedience. I will form a lake where I stamp my foot, and you and your people will forever watch over the lake, for I will rest your souls in the cypress."

The 1812 earthquake continued, the lands dropped, and the Mississippi River filled the new basin. Cypress trees became abundant and Reelfoot Lake was formed.

For 15 minutes the river's water flowed backward to fill this major void, which had been a swampy forestland. Now the area is a 13,000-acre shallow lake, an average of 5.2 feet deep, with the remains of the forest just under the surface, which makes boating quite an adventure. The water is a dark green color, with visibility never more than a few inches. The area surrounding the lake is now a state park, and a journey through here is truly a trek into unspoiled nature. The combination of shaggy cypress trees, some of them centuries old, and water lilies is most unusual for this state.

Reelfoot Lake is the winter home to more than 100 American bald eagles. The birds, with wingspans of 6 to 8 feet, come here from their northern summer homes to spend the winter in a warmer, ice-free environment. The park provides numerous eagle programs, including bus tours of the area, during winter.

The park's museum offers the chance to experience an earthquake firsthand. The 1812 quake has been reproduced, to a lesser degree, and allows guests to feel and hear what took place during those 15 minutes. You can also sit in a stump jumper; learn about its creators, the Calhoun family; see Native American artifacts; and read firsthand accounts of the creation of the lake. The museum is also the loading site for the lake's sightseeing cruises.

Each morning at 9, a three-hour pontoon boat cruise leaves for a trek around the southernmost part of the lake. The guide is usually David Pike, a naturalist with the park. He grew up in these parts and really knows the lake, the animals, and the history of the area.

The park has camping sites, a camp store, and hiking trails. Guided "swamp tromps" are offered during the year. The entrance to the park is located off Highway 21.

An annual calendar lists the best times, month by month, to see the various wildlife around the lake. A copy can be obtained by calling the ranger's office at (731) 253–7756. A three-day arts and crafts festival is held each October at the park.

A fantastic place to stay while you're in this area is the **_Bluebank Resort,_** on Highway 21 a few miles east of Tipton-

wildlifegalore

Reelfoot Lake is an oasis for wild-life because of its shallow, pristine waters, marshlands, and dense stands of bald cypress trees. In addition to the 100-plus American bald eagles that winter there each year, more than 60,000 geese and a quarter million ducks visit the area annually. There are also 54 species of fish in the lake, and there have been 53 mammal species spotted in the area. Who counts these things anyway? What a job!

ville. Located on the water's edge, the rooms are rustic in style but are new, are clean, and offer great views of the lake. The water practically comes up to your door! Rates are about $90 per night, per room. Special hunting and fishing packages, which include lodging, boat, motor, bait, and ice, are available and can save you quite a bit of money. Call this unusual site at (731) 253–6878.

The **_Bluebank Fish House & Grill_** is located closer to Tiptonville, at the Bluebank Motel, and is owned by the same people. The restaurant opens early each morning with a hearty breakfast and has steaks, quail, frog legs, crappie, country ham, ribs, and chicken for dinner. Phone them at (731) 253–6878 or go online at www.bluebankresort.com.

Places to Stay in the Western Plains

BOLIVAR

Magnolia Manor
418 North Main Street
Antebellum bed-and-breakfast
(731) 658–6700
www.magnoliamanor
bolivartn.com

CAMDEN

Birdsong Marina
RV Campground and rental cottages on
Tennessee River/Kentucky Lake
(731) 584–7880
www.birdsongresort.com

COUNCE

Hampton Inn—Pickwick
90 Old South Road and Highway 57
Three stories, outdoor pool, meeting rooms
(731) 689–3031

Little Andy's Sportsman's Lodge
Highway 57
1950s-era motel with knotty-pine rooms
(731) 689–3750

DYERSBURG

Hampton Inn
2750 Mall Loop Road
Close to all northwest Tennessee attractions
(731) 285–4778

JACKSON

Highland Place Bed-and-Breakfast
519 Highland Avenue
Circa 1911 mansion
(731) 427–1472
www.highlandplace.com

MEMPHIS

Heartbreak Hotel
3677 Elvis Presley Boulevard
Boutique hotel convenient to everything Elvis
(877) 777–0606
www.elvis.com

Memphis Graceland RV Park & Campground
3691 Elvis Presley Boulevard
Laundry, showers, pool, store
(901) 396–7125
www.elvis.com

Peabody Hotel Memphis
149 Union Avenue
World-famous historic landmark
(901) 529–4000
www.peabodymemphis
.com

**Sleep Inn at Court Square
40 North Front Street**
Close to downtown attractions
(901) 522–9700
www.sleepinn.com/hotel-memphis-tennessee-TN451

PARIS

Econolodge
1297 East Wood Street
Pool
(731) 642–8881

PICKWICK DAM

Pickwick Landing State Park Inn
Highway 57
Pool, tennis, restaurant
(731) 689–3135

TIPTONVILLE

Bluebank Resort
Highway 21
Rustic rooms with lake views
(731) 253–6878
www.bluebankresort.com

Blue Basin Cove
Air Park Road
On shore of Reelfoot Lake in old fishing lodge
(731) 253–9064

WILDERSVILLE

Pin Oak Lodge and Restaurant
In Natchez Trace State Resort Park
Cabins, swimming, hiking, fishing, camping
Open year-round
(731) 968–3742

Places to Eat in the Western Plains

DECATURVILLE

Broadway Farms
Old Perryville Road
Country cooking in rustic setting
Open Friday and Saturday 5:00 p.m., Sunday at noon
(731) 852–4559

HORNBEAK

P.V.'s Hut
At East Florida
and South Perkins Streets
Best cheeseburgers
in the world
Tuesday through Saturday,
11:00 a.m. to 7:00 p.m.
(731) 885–5737

JACKSON

Brooks Shaw & Son's
Old Country Store
Casey Jones Village
I-40 at US 45 Bypass
Bountiful, all-you-can-eat
breakfast, lunch, and
dinner buffets every day
(731) 668–1223
www.caseyjones.com

Redbones Grill & Bar
584 Carriage House Drive
Steaks, chicken, seafood
(731) 660–3838

MASON

Bozo's Restaurant
342 Highway 70
Pork shoulder barbecue
sandwiches
Tuesday through Saturday
10:30 a.m. to 9:00 p.m.
(901) 294–3400

MEMPHIS

Arcade Restaurant
540 South Main Street
Breakfast all day; plate
lunch specials; since 1919,
neon signs, vinyl booths
7:00 a.m. to 3:00 p.m.
(901) 526–5757
www.arcaderestaurant.com

Automatic Slims Tonga Club
83 South Second
Southwestern and Carib-
bean cuisine and decor;
coconut mango shrimp,
Caribbean voodoo stew
Lunch Monday through
Friday 11:00 a.m. to 2:30
p.m.; dinner Monday
through Sunday 5:00 to
11:00 p.m.
(901) 525–7948
www.automaticslims.com

Dyers Burgers
205 Beale Street
Delicious deep-fried ham-
burgers cooked in grease
not changed since 1912
Open daily at 11:00 a.m.;
closes when everyone
leaves
(901) 527–3937
www.dyersonbeale.com

Huey's
77 South Second Street
Allowed to write on walls
and shoot toothpicks into
ceiling
Open daily at 11:00 a.m. or
noon until after midnight
(901) 527–2700
www.hueyburger.com

Rendezvous
52 South Second
World-famous barbecued
ribs; a Memphis tradition
since 1948
Tuesday through Thursday
4:30 to 11:00 p.m.; Friday
and Saturday 11:30 a.m. to
11:30 p.m.
(901) 523–2746
www.hogsfly.com

SAVANNAH

The Worleybird Cafe
641 Pickwick Road
Black Angus beef, home-
made chicken salad, fried
green tomatoes
(731) 926–4882

SELMER

Pappy Johns
On US 45 South
All pork and chicken menu
Open daily except Sunday
(731) 645–4353

TIPTONVILLE

Bluebank Fish House & Grill
Highway 21
Steak, quail, frog legs,
crappie, country ham
Open for breakfast, lunch,
and dinner
(731) 253–6878
www.bluebankresort.com

Boyette's Dining Room
Highway 21
Famous for catfish, country
ham, and family-style meals
since 1921; adjacent to
Reelfoot Lake
Open daily 11:00 a.m. to
9:00 p.m.
(731) 253–7307

Index

About the Author

An award-winning journalist, Jackie Sheckler Finch has covered a wide array of topics—from birth to death, with all the joy and sorrow in between. She has written for numerous publications and has been named the Mark Twain Travel Writer of the Year by the Midwest Travel Writers Association a record four times, in 1998, 2001, 2003, and 2007. She also has won many photography awards. Jackie shares her home with resident guard and entertainer, a black dog named Pepper. One of her greatest joys is taking to the road to find the fascinating people and places that wait over the hill and around the next bend.